i

COVER PHOTO IDENTIFICATION

<u>Top left:</u> *Gigi,* Ch Amor Non Ami Gucci Girl.
Owned by Mary Lopez and Gina Klang. Bred by Mary Lopez and Gina Klang.
Sire: Ch Los Companero's V Havaluv. Dam: Tapscott's Isadorable.

<u>Top center:</u> *Mars,* Cuban HU Champion Pricipe Dorado de Lariomar.
Owned by Maria Paterne and Zsuzsanna Gazso-Podel. Bred by Maria Larianova.

<u>Top right:</u> *Punxsy,* Ch Meme Zee's Spirit O Roughrider CD.
Owned by Kathryn Braund. Bred by Martha and Michael Burns.
Sire: Ch Meme Zee's Bob A Loo E CDX. Dam: Ch Seta Cane Lamb Zee Divy CD.

<u>Center right:</u> *Striker,* Am/Can Ch Tapscott's Lightning Strike.
Owned by Laurie Parrett (Canada). Bred by Pamm and Jeanne Tapscott.
Sire: BIS Ch Westcreek Hot Shot Tapscott ROM. Dam: Beautiful Carleta vom Salzetal.

<u>Bottom right:</u> *Silly,* Silly Miss Sally Sweet Honesty.
Owned by Meta von Hout. Bred by Meta von Hout, Sweet Honesty Havanese
(Netherlands).

<u>Bottom center:</u> *Rudy,* Ch Overlook Root Beer Float.
Owner/breeder: Russell and Natalie Armitage and Lynn Nieto.
Sire: Ch Alderons Overlook Cola Float. Dam: Ch Soapstars Mirra Mirra of LP.

<u>Bottom left:</u> *Gabby,* Ch Overlook Talk of the Town.
Owned by Cindy Lisai. Bred by Russell and Natalie Armitage.
Sire: Ch Braveheart of Los Perritos. Dam: Ch Los Perritos Overlook Salsa.

<u>Center left:</u> *Naughty,* Ch Feliz NiceN Naughty Roughrider CD.
Owned by Kathryn Braund and Mr. David W. Haddock. Bred by Lizbeth and Robert
Johnson.
Sire: Ch Recuento Dante by Lejerdell. Dam: Cirrus La Reina Abigail.

<u>Center:</u> *Alan,* American Dutch French Luxembourg Belgium Ch Alan V.'T. Leurse
Hoefpad.
Owned by Sheryl Roach. Bred by Marinus Hoefnagel (Netherlands).
Sire: Macho's Atractivo. Dam: Macho's Lady.

The Joyous Havanese

by

Kathryn Braund

A dog book to remember!

KB - Kathryn Braund Publications

ISBN: 0-9720585-2-4

First Edition -June 2005
Second Printing -November 2005
Third Printing -September 2007

Printed by

PrintingCenterUSA

117 9th Street North

Great Falls, Montana 59401

406-761-1555

1-800-995-1555

Fax: 406-771-7777

Visit our web site: www.printingcenterusa.com

Publisher:
Kathryn Braund Publications
178 Highwood Drive
Great Falls, MT 59404
406-454-0537
kathrynbraund@3riversdbs.net
www.joyoushavanese.com

Dedication

To my dear friends . . .

Jane and Bill Larson

Tanya McDonald

Carol Oakes

Jean and Stan Webster

Contents

Illustrations

Note: The illustrations only list name of owner and dog's call name and/or event shown in the photo.

Illustrations on Color Spreads

Foreword

The title of this latest work by Kathryn Braund sets the tone for her whole book. By using the title *The Joyous Havanese,* she captures what appears to be the very essence of this breed, verified in the introductory page, where she aptly describes their "exuberance of life and joy." As you read this book you will also come to realize that this unique little dog can bring tremendous joy to anyone who lives with, or even comes in contact with him.

Those of you familiar with Mrs. Braund's previous writings will be aware that she is more than well qualified to undertake this endeavor, as her writings are a reflection of her life story.

The remarkable detail in dealing with the history of the Toy breeds is indicative of her meticulous research into the origins of canine breeds, and reflects her Librarian background. It is probably the only convenient source of comparison of the FCI standards with those of the AKC standards for the Havanese, giving a description of how this breed has evolved, and will undoubtedly continue to evolve as a work in progress.

Her editorial skills are once again evident in the inimitable and entertaining style for which she is well known. Her books and articles are a delight to read, as her many years of experience as an author and editor have honed her skills to combine factual information with a charming and irresistible quality. This remarkable ability is prevalent throughout.

After reading her lively descriptions of the physical and temperamental aspects of the Havanese, those of us who have not had personal contact with the breed certainly have an extraordinary insight into the breed's essential qualities and character. The novice as well as the seasoned dog person will appreciate her simple and unpretentious way of presenting what would elsewhere be too scientifically described to be enjoyed.

Those chapters devoted to breeding, through the care, mannering and grooming of the Havanese puppy reflect her many years of experience as a conscientious breeder of several breeds, as do those chapters devoted to training and showing reflect her many years as a successful Obedience instructor.

I was both pleased and flattered to be asked to read her manuscript, and allowed herein to express my conclusions with regard to it. The book is both informative and enjoyable for any dog lover to read, and certainly should be a must for those who are seriously involved with the Joyous Havanese.

Betty Trainor
Oxford, Massachusetts

About the Author

As I sit here, delighted that "Joyous" is going to print, I am 84 years young. I am blessed.

Looking back at my words in this book, I realize I've left out some of the things I wanted to say. That is the way it is with books. An author can hold on to a manuscript for years and add words here and there. It's time I said adieu! I hope you enjoy the words I wrote.

I have been writing about dogs these past 33 years and have won over 30 wonderful writing and publishing awards from my peers. As well as being an author of six dog books (The Complete Portuguese Water Dog" was Best Dog Book of 1986) and one historical novel, I also have thoroughly embraced life as an actress, wife, mother and dog breeder.

Dogdom credits range from serving as Secretary-Treasurer of the Dog Writers Association of America, Inc. for five years and as its newsletter editor for 16 years. I was Obedience Editor for "The Spotter," the Dalmatian Club of America quarterly for 10 years; and editor of "The Courier," the Portuguese Water Dog Club of America bi-monthly for 10 years, winning, as editor of the latter, three prestigious Maxwell Best awards.

In my spare time for the last 30 years I have enjoyed teaching dog obedience classes. I personally have bred, trained and shown Dalmatians, Portuguese Water Dogs and Havanese. Eleven of my Dalmatians and nine of my Portuguese Water Dogs earned their Obedience titles. This included three to CDX and two to Utility Dog. My first Portuguese Water Dog champion, Diver, a five-time Group winner in conformation, was the first male UD in that breed.

Living with me now are my retired champions, Lucky and Seabee, two Portuguese Water Dogs; Katie, a Dalmatian; and five Havanese.

I'm about to embark on training several of my Havanese in Obedience. Trust you'll join me.

Love, *Kitty*

Saying goodbye.

Acknowledgments

It is with pleasure and gratitude that I thank Suzanne McKay of Winnipeg, Manitoba, Canada for her wonderful input to "Joyous." Suzanne has contributed two chapters, "Rainbow Colors of the Havanese" (Chapter 9) and "The Havanese in Canada" (Chapter 14). Extraordinarily well-versed in all things Havanese, Suzanne writes the monthly column about Havanese in the Canadian National Dog magazine "Dogs in Canada." She has also written numerous short articles under the by-lines of "Fuzzy Tales And Faux-Paws" and "Prairie Pawprints" for other Canadian magazines.

Suzanne McKay with a Havanese friend.

Suzanne grew up dogless in an allergic household. She looked forward to being grown up so she could add a dog to her life. She writes, "I started looking into my first purebred after a few years and a few dogs. My idealistic choice was a dog who embodied all the best traits of all the dogs I had ever known, preferably also wrapped up in a smaller package. One day I found it, tucked in the corner of a magazine, a tiny two-inch picture of a black and tan Havanese. The accompanying write-up was a perfect match for my wish list." Two years passed before Suzanne met her first real-life Havanese. She was hooked forever when she acquired her first. She soon added a second and then a third.

"I've now evolved 15 years later to being involved in a bit of everything, including being the current President of the Havanese Fanciers of Canada. I am an Obedience instructor for a local Canine Education Center and teach a specialty class exclusively for toy dogs. I train and compete in Conformation, Agility and Obedience and all my Havanese are certified Therapy Dogs. My Havanese are my life's delight and an endless source of inspiration."

I double this pleasure and gratitude with the contributions submitted by Susan Nelson of California. You'll find her engrossing writing tidbits, "Why I Feed Raw" in Chapter Ten and "Why I Love My Havanese" in Chapter Thirteen. You'll also find photos of Susan and several of her dogs that will set you thinking about you and your Havanese joining one or more of the exciting canine performance events the HCA and AKC offers.

Susan Nelson has been a member of the HCA since 1993. She served as an HCA Regional Director for two terms, served on its Health committee, its Membership committee and helped coordinate the 2000 HCA National Specialty. She has also presented a Judges

Educational Program and for 14 years has chaired a Havanese Breed Booth at Southern California's "America's Family Pet Expo." Importantly, her beloved Havanese enjoy career life to the fullest with their great owner/trainer guiding them in their fun performances.

I thank Dr. Rick Scherr of the Big Sky Animal Medical Clinic of Great Falls, Montana. Dr. Scherr has guided me successfully through a breeder's worries regarding artificial breedings, both AIs and Surgical Implants. Dr. Scherr's fine canine reproduction services are in high demand throughout the northwestern United States and Canada.

I am also thankful for the absolutely wonderful pictures sent to me via e-mail from a group of Havanese fanciers I correspond with on the Internet's e-mail. All photos were offered via e-mail attachments. Sizes vary. I regret not being able to use all I received. Although computer advances of this technological age are fabulous, I have personally found computers have faults (or is it the operator?). There are big black holes in my computer which swallow up pictures as fast as they arrive via e-mail. Unable to retrieve them from goodness knows where they still hide, they missed the "Joyous" deadline.

I thank my two dog-show handlers, Martin Cabral and Beverly Wilson of Escondido, California, who have shown each of my wonderful Havanese to their championships. Their care and affection for the dogs in their keeping is outstanding.

Craig Barber, CEO of The Printing Center USA, has my deep gratitude for his friendship and professional help in getting this book ready for printing. Tim Paul of the Great Falls College of Technology has my thanks for his review of sections of this book. I thank my dear friend, Billie Cotton, for her work in the final round of editing. She has deepfelt thanks for always being right there when I ran into problems and needed a shoulder to lean on; and, of course, I wish to thank my superb "socialization engineers," Stephanie and Annie Cotton, for their great assistance in puppy socialization.

Last but not at all least, I hug each of my run-like-hell furballs, Punxsy, Tawney, Naughty, Viva, Sassy and now Billie for letting me write about them and for introducing me to all the joyous Havanese who lighten our hearts and brighten our lives.

The first Havanese to win an All Breed Best in Show anywhere in the world
BIS Champion Westcreek Hot Shot Tapscott ROM
Hotshot *(his photo also appears opposite on page 1)* is owned by
Pamela and Jeanne Tapscott.
He was bred by Westcreek Havanese.
His sire was Seta Cane Silver Sparkler and his dam Silverdales' Pomona Peach.
Hotshot was Number 1 Havanese in the U.S. two years running and still holds the
record for Havanese owner/handler wins.

Welcoming you to *The Joyous Havanese* are two absolutely marvelous Havanese owned
and trained by Susan Nelson. These two are also the first and only Havanese Best in
Show Brace in the world. Although from different litters bred by Susan Nelson, they are
brother and sister.
Buster: **AKC/UKC/INT Champion Shaggyluv's Blockbuster NA NAJ CGC**
Sandy: **AKC Champion Shaggluv's Precious Moment CGC**
Sire: *Sparky,* AKC/ARBA Ch Shaggluv's Energizer ROM, OA OAJ RN
Dam: *Tippy,* AKC/ARBA/HCA Champion Shaggyluv's Golden Girl ROM OA OAJ RN
CGC TDI

Chapter One

Introduction to the Havanese

This is a book about the toy dog called the Havanese (a Cuban dog). It is a breed I call the "sturdy sunshine toy." A few theorists insist the toy Havanese, in its homeland, was renown as a herding dog (herding family chickens). That may be true for a limited number. In essence, the Havanese was and is a family dog, an exceptional small companion dog.

This beautiful breed is to me a reflection of God's love and joy. Both males and females are sweet, adoring, willing, merry and mischievous. I have never met a quarrelsome Havanese. Put two or a "pack" together and they bubble over with friendliness and zest for life. Let them romp in an area where they have a little space and they become "run-like-hell" dogs. That's the delightful appellation breed fanciers have for them. They move over the ground as swiftly as a herd of deer, almost flying in their exuberance of life and joy, chasing each other at a full gallop, hair in the air, tails awry, mouths grinning, eyes alight.

It certainly is a "run-like-hell" funfest every evening as my five little "furheads" race together down the hallway to the big bedroom, three of them dashing into their little sleep time kennel cabins, the other two leaping high onto my bed. One has to laugh delightedly. They are simply adorable dogs to watch, in everything they do.

Hotshot, the first Best In Show Havanese. Ch Westcreek Hot Shot Tapscott ROM. Breeders: Kay and Gary Dyke. Owners: Pamela and Jeanne Tapscott.

In town, walking can be done on two legs as well as four, particularly if an onlooker stops to admire its happy face, lovely coat and perky manner. Sneaking kisses from strangers with a tail waving brightly cannot be denied. A Havanese in the dog show ring is just as charismatic. The breed's characteristic happy bounce, alert head carriage and gorgeous large almond eyes make you want to pick it up and hug it tightly.

A Havanese in the show ring cannot be denied as Harley demonstrates here. Ch Amor's Easy Rider is owned by Claudie and Phil Parrish.

They are instant friends of small children. They fawn, wag their tails and dance about, leaping up into the air in hopes of licking the tiny cheeks and arms of small fry. We are careful to try to teach the Havanese in our household not to jump up on children (a useless endeavor). It has to be remembered that as lightweight as they are, they spring with such eagerness, they can knock a small child down.

Their instinctive love of children does not mean one should purchase a Havanese and allow it to romp with children without supervision. No! Some wee children are very rambunctious in their cause-and-effect learning episodes. Small children react in play; they cannot yet reason why they should or should not do something. Small children toss balls *at* dogs rather than *to* or *by* them, since they cannot yet discriminate between "at" or "by." They really do not understand that the effect of this may be pain. It is a common sense rule never to allow a small child to be alone, unguarded, with a Havanese or any domestic animal, small or large.

A Havanese has an instinctive love for children. Sassy is owned by Bonnie Keeney.

The Havanese have insatiable curiosity and are extraordinarily willing to please. Thus, they are easy to train. This is a breed which likes to show off their talents. They delightfully develop into loving, mischievous opportunists (dogs are the most celebrated opportunists in the animal world)!

As an owner, exhibitor, breeder, dog obedience trainer and instructor, I believe the Havanese are without doubt the most joyous, happy and responsive breed I have ever trained.

They do have one cosmetic problem. They are a "drop coat" breed. This means the dense inner coat of this double coated breed drops its hairs onto the outer coat. These dropped hairs form tangles with the outer coat. The consequences? This results in tangles and mats. Unless the coat is maintained in a short Companion Dog cut, most Havanese require daily grooming. Show coats are difficult to maintain, even when brushed and combed daily.

Weather variables - rain, snow, humidity, dryness - do not agree with coat dropping dogs. Mats form when you turn your back, particularly during the nine to 15 month (puppy to adult coat change) growth period. Thankfully, many coats do stabilize at about two years of age and maintenance becomes a great deal easier.

I personally will not allow anyone to adopt one of my Havanese puppies who will not allow a Havanese to be a dog - and that means allowing it to run through weeds and bushes, dig holes (Havanese can be diggers) and enjoy the beautiful, wonderful outdoor world we are blessed with. In order to thrive as a great family companion, these sturdy little dogs with their high activity level require exercise in this marvelous green, white, rainy, hot, dusty, humid, and magnificent world of ours.

Let's learn to understand the Havanese by looking at the whole canine species and finding out together what makes the dog tick. You'll want to know how genes and experiences make up the intelligence and instinct potential of the Havanese. Understanding what makes a dog act and behave as he does, helps you become a good dog owner. You are able to care for him correctly, outwit him when he attempts to outwit you, and train him as he needs to be trained. That is one reason you

The Havanese needs to enjoy the wonderful world of outside. Alan does. American Dutch French Luxembourg Belgium Champion Alan V. 'T Leurse Hoefpad is owned by Sheryl Roach. Marinus Hoefnagels was his breeder.

are reading this book. You are, or want to be, an owner of the very beautiful and joyful toy dog called the Havanese.

Let's find out together.

We know what the canine species looks like. We also know what many individual breeds in the species look like. We are aware dogs have five senses as we do - smell, touch, hearing, sight and taste. We're going to add temperature and pain as sense-ations because of the canine's acute perception and sensitivity to environments which are interpreted through memory stimuli. And for those who believe dogs do not think, bah! They certainly do. Along with the thought process which enables them to function as dogs, they possess an excellent memory. The species' memory retention depends on their needs as well as the individual desire to retain environmental stimuli. In many, attention span appears short, the reason being they do not retain what they are not interested in.

What are the canine needs? We could also call their "needs" "wants."

They need (want) to be comfortable. Dogs avoid stimuli which produce uncomfortableness or pain.

They need (want) to be loved. It is the essence of their nature.

They need to be a member of the family. Annie Cotton, a "socialization engineer," is cuddling this puppy, Roughrider Potomac Ms. Kitti, owned by Carol Oakes.

They need (want) to be touched. This is a physical as well as a mental requirement.

They need (want) to be a member of a family (pack), either as leader or follower.

They need (want) to express talents ancestors bequeathed to them and which man has enhanced by genetic intensity isolation - digging, chasing, guarding, protecting, hunting or as a companion. There are nuances here, of course, depending on the breed or combination of breeds.

Depending upon which genes have been singled out by breeders as desirable in a particular breed, some excel in herding, some in chasing, some in tracking, some in guarding. All excel, when socialized properly by man, in companionable attitudes.

And because they have only legs and no arms, everything they investigate or eat must go directly into their mouths. This causes great trouble with some owners, who often do not relate mouthiness (chewing, biting) with investigation, but only as a behavior problem. These individuals believe these are characteristics to be punished.

Dogs must also clean themselves by licking themselves clean. Not an awful thing to do for a scavenger, which is what the dog is. Dogs were scavengers when they took up with man. They kept his campsites clean of garbage. Garbage was part of their diet.

It is doubtful that scientists will ever unravel the history of the canine's beginning. We certainly will never find out if their essence eons and eons ago was like it is today. We don't know if it was gradually formed in the centuries of development and by the influences they received. It is doubtful dog possessed the genes of the wolf and mutated into hundreds of forms. While he may be cousin, it is far more likely he was a separate species from the very beginning. His genes are capable of assuming a wide variety of forms within the canine structure.

Neither will we know how long humans have intervened in the breeding of dogs. We have learned from archeological findings and early historical records that many of the breeds in ancient times looked and acted as they do today.

All creatures are born with certain instinctive traits befitting their species. Yet the burden of personality proof is not all genetics. In dogs, it is divided (albeit unequally) between genetics, and what they learn from the dam, the breeder, and the environments in which the puppy is initially and then permanently reared.

As stated earlier, in order to be a good dog owner you need to understand your dog so you can help him if and when behavior problems show up. We always have to remember, first and foremost, that canine companion dogs are not human. They are animals who live in a foreign world. They do not understand many of the things we do, although they are amazingly quick to catch on to how to manage us and have us do things they want us to do.

Most of our conversations with the dog are lost on him. He responds better to body movement, touch and sounds. And the more we can explain ourselves in terms the dog understands, using body language, sounds and touch - the better we can reach down to him, the closer the bond will be and the better his behavior. That is why we are looking at canine temperament in terms of the species. Because all dogs do certain things; all are aroused by certain stimuli and ninety-nine percent learn in an identical manner.

Let's look at canine temperament in the following analogy - soup.

Soup? It's easy to understand that way. You can trace how the temperament of the dog is put together.

Soup's basic stock is water. All water contains minerals. In this case the minerals are the genes the dog obtains from his ancestors, 50 percent from his dam's side and 50 percent from his sire's side. However, both dam and sire's genes reach back into their pedigrees, so each dog is the product of generations of genes - not just his dam and sire.

Let's add a very flavorful ingredient to the soup pot stock - the dam's imprinting. Each canine mother imprints her puppies with habits she has and with the way she responds to their and her human guardian's every action. The flavor of this ingredient does not dissipate with time.

Now the pot has the first makings of a soup.

Two more ingredients:

1) Interaction with siblings (brothers and sisters), including all body movements, touch and sounds; sharing of bed and food; play and play-fights. It includes many actions within the litter until each leaves for its permanent home.

2) Interaction and/or socialization with the breeder, who oversees birth, litter activity, diet, and socialization through placement with permanent homes.

These two important ingredients make the soup taste good or bad. The stock bubbles as these ingredients are added.

Our next ingredient: permanent home socialization from eight or 12 weeks to 20 weeks during the teething period. Now the soup is simmering (we hope). If we forget about it, let it boil over, or allow the stock to evaporate and the soup begins to burn, we ruin the meal.

The fifth ingredient: the final touches, adolescent to 12 or 15 months: socialization during this period cements all past genetic and environmental happenings in the not-quite-closed brain.

Socialization! is ongoing.
Roughrider's Emma is owned by Jane Larson.

Note that many genes do not come into play unless they are utilized. Take the gene for retrieving, for example. All puppies rush to grab something and either return it to where they were playing or to an owner until they are about 10 weeks of age. If this retrieving play is not cemented (used) or encouraged by the owner, the retrieve gene loses its place in the brain; it atrophies and is often difficult to recover when the puppy becomes an adult.

Today it is recognized that a puppy's relationships with humans begins in the whelping box. These relationships are most malleable from the age of four weeks to 16 weeks with the height of malleability at ages of seven and eight weeks of age. When a puppy comes to live in your house, you help him develop multilayer behaviors.

It is in the litter box (whelping box) that the personality of dogs is developed. Thus, as stated earlier, the burden of proof is not all genetics. It is divided between the dam, the breeder, the environments in which the puppy is initially reared, and then with the permanent owner.

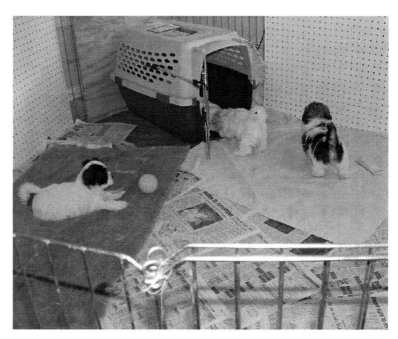

It is in the litter box that the initial personality of dogs is developed. This is a Roughrider living room x-pen.

Let's now see exactly what makes the Havanese tick. We already know the Havanese has genes honed into him through centuries of rearing, which make him extremely loving, exceptionally happy and bouncy. His stereotype is of a sensitive, willing, attention-seeking, charming, athletic little dog.

The Havanese Standard says this about the temperament of the Havanese: *"Playful and alert. The Havanese is both trainable and intelligent with a sweet, non-quarrelsome disposition."*

The above is a short, sweet statement about the Havanese temperament which is absolutely true. However, each Havanese is an individual and each has been gifted or denied by nature and environment with certain talents above and beyond the breed's basic characteristics. Each Havanese will develop different emotional responses to experiences he meets in life. There is no doubt that many are possessed of high intelligence.

It's good to remember that the Havanese you own (or will) completes his personality development and his uniqueness through interaction with you and your family.

Playtime is learning time. "Socialization engineer" Stephanie Cotton is checking soft bites on these Roughrider puppies.

Love is essential. Brandon Fleisher is in love with his Percy, a Heavenly puppy whose registered name is HeavenlyHavs Perseus. Mary Williams is Percy's breeder.

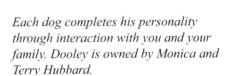

Each dog completes his personality through interaction with you and your family. Dooley is owned by Monica and Terry Hubbard.

Chapter Two
History of the Present Day Havanese and Its Ancestors

The Havanese history of pleasing mankind with its charming personality began with the appearance of the first toy dog in the world, long before history as we know it began.

We could sum up the history of this joyful little toy canine furball (once mistakenly called the White Cuban or Silky Poodle) very quickly. Settlers, traders and merchants carried toy spaniel types to Spain's "New Spain" - Cuba - in the 16th and 17th centuries. There, toy dogs were developed by canine breeders until one became famous in Cuba as the Blanquito de la Habana and in Europe as the White Cuban. Then in the 18th century, in Cuba, the Blanquito de la Habana was claimed to be mated with the toy Poodle to increase size, leg and type of coat. The Bichon Havanese was born. But during the mid-20th century revolutions, breeders had to forego furthering the Bichon Havanese breed. In 1959 high-bred dogs fell in disfavor, as did many of their wealthy landowners. The Havanese as it was known then moved to humbler surroundings. Some, once pampered lap dogs, became street dogs. It was not until the 1970s when Dorothy Goodale of Colorado rescued 11 Havanese from enforced obscurity that the breed was rejuvenated. She, the first American Lady of the Bichon Havanese, is the one who introduced it to American dog lovers. It became AKC registrable in January 1999. In these young years of our 21st century it has climbed up America's purebred canine popularity polls to a dangerous high.

But why would we want to sum up this delightful toy's history so quickly? Its toy ancestral history is fascinating. The short synopsis above does not tell us when, where and from what the breed was developed.

So let's enjoy a bit of reflection. Come with me while we go back in time and discover how toy dogs developed. It's always been a question if they evolved from the same stem.

The Englishman, E. Topsell, described toy dogs in the year 1607 thusly: "Nowadays they have found another breede of little dogs to all nations. . . either made so by art as enclosing their bodies in the earth when they are whelped so as they cannot grow great by reason on the place, or else lessening and impayring their growth by some kind of meat or nourishment. They are not above a foote or halfe a foote long and always the lesser the more delicate and precious. Their head like the head of a mouse, but greater, their snowt sharpe, short legs, little feete, long taile, and white colour, and the haires about the shoulder longer than ordinary is most recommended. They are of pleasant disposition, and will leape and bite without pinching, and barke prettily, and some of them are taught to stand upright, holding up their aforelegs like hands to fetch and carry in their mouths that which is cast onto them."

Topsell's remarks of genetics and/or the breeding of small dogs show you how little the Englishmen at that time in history knew about the subject.

All that has been definitely established about the history of dogs, says Richard Lewinsohn in "Animals, Men and Myths," is that by "the Middle Stone age there were dogs hardly distinguishable from those of today."

A bold statement, backed up by fact.

Some knowledge of the canine species comes from archaeologists and goes as far back as 14,000 B.C. A fossil of a dog (called the Petagaura Dog) was found with human remains in Iraq. Maxwell Riddle, one of the great dog men of the 20th century, in his story of the Sumarians (who had a written language) wrote, "We can be sure many races of dogs were well known to all three (all three meaning Mohenjo Doo, Bahrain and Egypt)."

It was necessary for the early peoples to breed dogs for utilitarian reasons in those "kill and eat or be killed and eaten" times. Most were fierce dogs. They could attack, kill and eat the enemy in war. They hunted down meat with their masters. The clashes, the fights, the killing, the blood, the eating of torn, raw flesh was horrendous.

We know that the dog is a cousin to the wolf. The dog, *canis familiaris,* has the same number of chromosomes as the wolf, 78. And we know that the wolf, *canis lupus*, can take many forms. Archeologists have found bones of one, now extinct, called the Japanese wolf. It was only 14 inches at the shoulder. This small eastern breed was probably one of the first domesticated wolves. Like the wolf, the dog, as Maxwell Riddle pointed out, has great "plasticity of the germ plasm" which allows immense variation in size and shape.

"The most tractable dogs were bred from, the least tractable eaten," states Dr. Fogle

("The Dog's Mind"), "and then over the ages, local admixtures of genes from other breeds gave us the great genetic variation of today."

In these early years of the 21st century, scientists and theorists are now beginning to theorize the dog was of a completely different species than the wolf. This is quite plausible. I agree with this thinking; however, only time will bear out its truth.

We do know tiny dogs have always played a part in history, regardless of where its germ plasm originated. But we do not know this from what ancient scribes wrote on clay tablets, which served as text books. They only wrote about large and medium sized hunting and war dogs.

They did not write about women's pet dogs. Why not? Well, women were second class citizens, their wisdom given behind the scenes, seldom in the scene. Their pet dogs consequently bore the same label. Although the sanctity of marriage was born in the early days of the world, the seeds of disdain and contempt along with violence towards and against women had also been sewn. Until the mid-twentieth century, women were always called the second class gender, held to be inferior to men. When they dared speak out against difficult family conditions, they could be (and still are in some civilizations) killed or maimed for any infractions of personal "place."

Why do I bring this up in this history section of the Havanese? Because women's toy dogs were their comfort and sweetness in work-worn, strife-filled lives. So breeding of toy dogs went on behind the public and scribes' eyes in the early world.

Toy dogs of Chihuahua type were certainly well known in the Egypt of 3000 years ago. A mummified remains of one tiny dog was described by zoologist K. Hadden in 1910.

I found a picture in an art catalog of a "Colimia Pottery Redware Barking Dog," standing with plump body, tail pointed and curved upwards, perky ears, almond eyes; it was a likeness of a dog living in 200 B.C. to 300 A.D. He was definitely a Chihuahua type.

An amulet, dated 2900 B.C., is of a dog with a ring tail. Greek, Roman and Egyptian children played with toy models of dogs. They were tiny dogs, all with tails curled over their backs, resembling both Maltese and Pomeranian types. Another was a toy spaniel, looking very much like the present-day Havanese, except for prick ears. In the museum of Regio de Calabri in Greece, there is a small dog, in bronze, from the fifth century B.C.

"In ancient China tiny dogs were regarded as treasures belonging to the Emperor" ("Dogs Through History"). Ancient Chinese dog breeders (men) could gain high positions breeding dogs pleasing to the Emperor. And because the Emperor could not keep all offered, traders

obtained some of those toy rejects. They carried them over the two trade routes from the Orient to the Mediterranean, the hub of the ancient world. There they were grabbed up by those who enjoyed wealth.

The Pekingese had its birth in ancient China. Rejects were carried to the Mediterranean where some of their genes mingled with dogs all across that area. The Shih Zsu which traveled in ancient times from its homeland in Tibet to China crossed with the Pekingese. There is little dispute that the modern Havanese carries genes from the Shih Zsu.

In 25 A.D. Strabo wrote: "There is a town in Sicily called Melita whence are exported many beautiful dogs with long, glossy silky hair called canis Melitei." This had to be the Maltese. It was also called "Melitea Caletta, meaning one nourished for pleasure; Canis Digne Throno because princes held them in their hands sitting upon their estates;" and nicknamed "shock" dog because of its white hair.

"Besides the Maltese dogs, others were often kept in private houses as pets and do not belong to any species," said Aldrovandiese. Homer gave the latter the name "table dogs," because they could stand under the tables eating crumbs.

In Rome, lap dogs became so popular that Julius Caesar asked if Roman ladies had ceased to have children and had dogs instead." ("Man's Best Friend," National Geographic Book of Dogs.)

Rome fell. In the chaos that swept over Europe after its demise, most dogs, unless owned or bred by nobles for hunting or to guard estates, were feared. Good reason. Packs of displaced fierce war and hunting dogs roamed vast territories of the earth, digging up graves for food and savagely attacking and eating unfortunate humans who ran across them.

Lap dogs survived!

"In the unwashed middle ages small ladyees poppees bere awaye the fleas" (National Geographic). Small dogs, commonly called "curs," were also kept as scavengers. They cleaned up man's wastes and garbage. Others lived in land owners' palaces while some served as "fair" entertainment, working with bands of gypsies jumping through hoops, turning somersaults and dancing on hind legs.

In the 14th and 15th centuries small dogs were used everywhere when the presence of rodents was a danger to public health. Many small dogs roamed decks of ships, hunting and killing rats.

Culture returned in the Renaissance. Dogs were once again treasured. "It is really with

Romanticism that the dog makes its triumphal entrance into literature," wrote Calvert and Cruppi.

Dwarf spaniels, in particular, became beloved pets of nobility. Their canine images flourished in all arts. Toy dogs were in such high favor in England that in 1576, the annual budget for royal dogs was 100,000 gold crowns. There were so many dogs wandering about Henry VIII's palace, that the king finally ordered all dogs to be contained outside "except some small spanyells for ladies or others." Many not belonging to the elite were used by profiteers for cruel amusements.

The leading breeders of the Renaissance were the French. They created many varieties because French ladies adored all sorts of lap dogs, either smooth or heavy coated. All had their hair cropped or crimped and they were petted and perfumed constantly.

Of interest to Havanese fanciers, the Maltese was bred with the small Barbet. Authorities tell us the Barbet was developed from the rough water dog, Canis Aquaticus, which had been carried from Russia to many European countries. Named the Poodle in France, when sequestered in Portugal it became familiarly known as the Portuguese Water Dog.

The French developed the Barbet and called it, "Caniche," "Chien Canne" or "le petit barbet." It was a small dog with long, curly hair and weighed from 15 to 20 lbs. In 1845, W.C.I. Martin wrote that he grouped the little Barbet with "spaniel and fancy varieties," saying of them, "hair, long and fine; muzzle, moderate; forehead, developed; scent, acute; intelligence at a high rate."

One resulting cross was called the Silky Toy Poodle. Breeders then added Spanish miniatures to the breeding pool and formed the toys of the Bichon family. Today these are called Bichon Frise, Bolognese, Havanese, Silky Poodle Bouffety, Burgos, Lowchen and the Maltese - to name some of the most popular.

Dr. Erich Schneider Leyer ("Dogs of the World") writes, "The Havanese is part of many French toy breeds, part of the Bichon family. Bichon was the common name of the four types of Bichons - the Bichon Maltais, the Bichon Bolognais, the Bichon Havenais and the Bichon Teneriffe." The Teneriffe, which was carried to the Canary Island of Teneriffe, made its appearance in France under Francis I, the patron of the Renaissance (1515-1547). The Teneriffe later became famous as the Bichon Frise.

Some claim the Skye Terrier of Scotland, which became a fashionable pet of English nobility in the 16th, 17th and 18th centuries, also played a part in the makeup of the modern Havanese. It has a celebrated coat over 5-1/2 inches in length.

Who knows?

Then came the magnificent voyages of discovery beginning in 1492 with that of Christopher Columbus. These voyages were in part abetted and systematized by governments and merchant companies.

Merchant companies had for centuries voyaged independently, supplying precious metals and spices to all on their trade routes. In the late 15th century, the need was desperate. More spices were needed to make food edible. More metals were needed to make coin. Marco Polo's accounts of his adventures became the impetus for many exploratory voyages. Cathay, the fabled rich country he had traveled to where spices and metals were plentiful, was supposed to be directly across the ocean from western Europe. Also, all exploring voyages were made with the belief that voyages to heathen lands would be called "divinely inspired" when infidels were converted to Christianity.

Christopher Columbus opened up a whole new world when he crossed the Atlantic in search of China. As we all know, instead of finding China, he made the discovery of the Americas. He thought he was close to Cathay when he landed on Cuba on his first voyage. He called Cuba, in a letter written by him to the King of Spain, "the loveliest land that human eyes have beheld."

He also wrote from Jamaica in 1503 that when he landed on Cuba he found turkeys and dogs the only domesticated animals. "A small kind of dogs," he said, "which were mute and did not bark as usual." (The Complete Dog Book, Chihuahuas, official publication of the American Kennel Club). This was the Techichi, a heavy boned small dog, regarded as indigenous to Central and South America. In the book, "Animals, Men and Myths," it is written that the Techichi, was "used by natives only for food. All other dogs were a 'present' from abroad."

However, legends abound that the Havanese is descended from the Bolognese dogs which were carried by Italian peasants to Argentina. There, these small white and black dogs (the original colors of the Bolognese) were crossbred with several small poodle types. Carried then to Cuba, this dog became a favorite of the wealthy plantation owners.

Cuba became "New Spain," and settlers with slaves and merchants and workers hurried to settle there. Most brought domesticated animals and cats and dogs. Those dogs and cats that survived the gruesome voyages arrived on land either in the arms of merchants to be sold to the wealthy, or escaped overboard as soon as dry land was reached.

Small dogs were always welcomed on board. They chased and ate rats. Rats and roaches always vied for space and food, and the long voyages on roily seas with rotted food and insect-filled vats caused many deaths. Merchant companies hired musicians to calm the miserable and frightened humans. The musicians often carried small dogs with them to help entertain the voyagers.

Consequently, Cuba was settled with a variety of small as well as large dogs. Among the large were Greyhounds, Mastiffs and hounds. The medley of toy spaniels and mongrels came from all countries. The best began living on plantations; the wealthy landowners keeping their favorites inside plantation walls.

All dogs carried by migrating people were changed by climate, terrain and crossings. With close breedings during the 17th and 18th centuries one toy became smaller and smaller. Traders, knowing "sleeve dogs" were popular in Europe, traded for them, carrying them back to Europe. The English nobility fell in love with this tiny dog from Cuba and it soon became famous as the White Cuban sleeve dog. Soon English dog brokers began recklessly breeding them - father to daughter, mother to son - without any regard for structure and temperament. They were in a hurry to make them even smaller, the sizes elite ladies wanted. Soon the dogs became unhealthy, and with nasty temperaments.

They were frequently brought to the English shores for sale and held up to passengers by brokers touting royal backgrounds. But they were long-haired little wretches, washed, starched and combed with clipped feet and muzzles. Popularity waned quickly, and although some found places in circuses, the tiny White Cuban declined.

Unfortunately, many writers thought the White Cuban was the Cuban Havanese, which it was not. Even as late as 1971, the noteworthy dog authorities Stanley Dangerfield, Elsworth Howell, and Maxwell Riddle, wrote in their "International Encyclopedia of Dogs" that "The Havanese, now rarely seen, weighs two to four pounds, and is pure white. It may have been called the Lion Dog because of its fighting habits."

Nothing could be further from the truth.

Today's Bichon Havanese was developed in Cuba in the 18th century. It was more likely the result of matings of toy Poodles, the Italian Tenereffe (now the Bichon Frise), and the Banquito de la Habana, the latter bred by breeders "who preferred a miniature white dog with long silky hair and an extremely loving and lively character" (Bichon Havanese).

Careful breedings of the cross gave strength and vigor to the dog they now call Bichon Havanese. The resulting dog was not cobby like a Maltese or the Chihuahua (used in some crossings). It was rectangular like its ancestor, the Barbet. It was not as small as a Maltese or

Chihuahua. And unlike the Maltese and Toy Poodle, it has a double coat. Other differences: the ears are slightly raised, moderately pointed, and the Havanese has a slight rise over the croup.

In the 1863 Paris Dog Show, with 850 to 900 dogs exhibited, in the Class XXIX called "Pet Poodles," there were Havana lap dogs, Peruvian, Maltese, Balearic, Austrian and Lion Dogs. There were, it was claimed by onlookers, beautiful specimens of the Bichon Havanese. It was said they had come into their own.

But change came. During the mid-twentieth century political upheavals in Cuba, revolutions disrupted Cuban lives. Due to political pressures after 1959, dogs fell in disfavor. The lovely little Havanese, the favorite dog of the Cuban upper class, went to the streets. In humbler surroundings some earned their keep by herding family chickens. Others were hugged for comfort in the uncertain times. Still others, owned by Cuban sugar plantation owners who were unable to adapt to the political changes, were carried away from Cuba.

Three families that we know of who took Havanese with them when they left Cuba were the Perez, Fantasio and Barba families. The first two migrated to the United States. Senor Barba went to Costa Rica. Little is known what happened to the others. They probably disappeared into family back yards, wherever the families migrated. "What is known," writes Schalene J. Dagulis, "is...there might not have been very many of these dogs kept by anyone."

In 1974 eleven dogs, representing three different bloodlines, were sold to a United States breeder from Colorado. And it is this breeder, Dorothy Goodale, who developed the present day Havanese from the stock she received. We owe much to her for its present day looks. Most of the dogs the Goodales purchased averaged around 10 pounds, stood about nine to 10 inches at the shoulders, and were friendly and gentle. They were also of different sizes.

The Goodales, who had raised purebreds for many years, in particular Irish Wolfhounds and Soft Coated Wheaten Terriers, were well versed in breeding quality pure-breds to AKC breed standards. They sought a breed standard for the Havanese. They learned the 1963 FCI breed standard was the only one in existence. Following that standard, they began to create the Havanese we know today.

They also gathered a group of people interested in furthering these gentle toys to recognition in America. In fact, the first registry for Havanese was initiated by Dorothy Goodale in 1979.

Two years earlier, in 1977, it was reported that the first Havanese went to the Netherlands from Cuba. But it was not until 1991 that the breed was listed in the Cuban Registry. The

FCI published its "Valid Original Standard" on October 12, 1996.

The Havanese entered AKC registry on June 30, 1995. It was then allowed to be shown in its Miscellaneous Class in February 1, 1996. It received full registration privileges on January 1, 1999, being allowed to compete in AKC's Toy Group. (It was the AKC's 142nd breed.)

Unfortunately, Dorothy Goodale no longer played any part in furthering the breed she remolded to AKC recognition. She and a group of her followers, in disagreement with those who founded the Havanese Club of America, registered their stock with the United Kennel Club (the second largest canine registry in the world).

So this is the history, as we have researched it. As with all dog breed histories, our research brought us face to face with many inconsistencies. And of course the breed is presently undergoing growing pains, not just in its history but in its structure and cosmetic points. The types we presently see in the conformation ring are varied: some tall, some tiny; coats of different textures and structures deviate from the present AKC standard.

Inside this living dog there is no inconsistency. The present day Havanese is a most magnificent toy dog, beloved of its owners.

Let's hope its way forward in the 21st century is fostered with integrity and quality that it does not become a favorite of unscrupulous "modern brokers."

It is such a wonderful little dog, the present day Havanese.

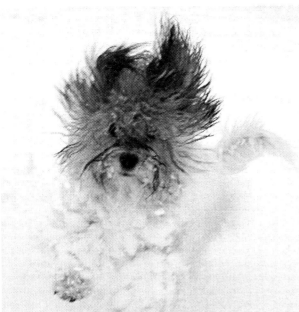

Cathy Wiley is the owner of this wintertime Havanese snow enthusiast. Tapscott's It's Da Bomb likes to be called Shug.

Smudge, Ch Tapscott's I'm a Hottie, is a winter sports enthusiast.
Owned by Gloria S. Dittmann, Smudge is a willing model when the photo is taken by Gloria.

"Let it snow, let it snow, let it snow," say these run-like-hell Havanese who belong to Rita Thomas of Canada. Sonrisas Havanese is the name of Rita's kennel.

Chapter Three

The Havanese Breed Standards

The emergence of a dog breed on the landscape of the world is the result of a group of people getting together and breeding animals to look like and perform the way the group desires. In other words, they create a dog with a certain structure and certain instincts which enables it to perform particular functions.

These initial creators set down in writing the animal's particular characteristics in what is called the "standard" of the breed.

Without the dreams, visions and physical creation of these people, no particular breed could ever have been created.

Modern fanciers who follow the lead of the original organizers will always owe a debt to the creators.

The original standard for the Havanese breed was the one approved by the Federation Cynologique Internationale (FCI) in 1963. At that time this prestigious European canine club recognized the Bichon Havanese as having been developed in Cuba. As stated earlier, it is the standard the Goodales and a group of fanciers followed when they founded The Havanese Fanciers Club of America (1974). In 1979, Mrs. Goodale began the first Registry for Havanese. Unfortunately, as the club grew, dissension arose. In 1979 several fanciers tore away from the original group and formed a new club called the Havanese Club of America.

As they did, the original Havanese Fanciers Club of America sought recognition from the United Kennel Club (UKC) (the world's second largest kennel club). The UKC registered the Bichon Havanese belonging to members of the Havanese Fanciers Club of America in 1991.

The group who had formed the Havanese Club of America (HCA) pursued recognition from the American Kennel Club (AKC). To satisfy requirements, members of the HCA drew up a new standard, receiving approval of it by the AKC in June 1995. The breed was then allowed to be exhibited in AKC's Miscellaneous Class as of February 1, 1996. Three years later the AKC gave full registration privileges to the Havanese breed. HCA members began competing their dogs in AKC's Toy Group on January 1, 1999. The standard was again revised and approved by the AKC May 7, 2001, effective June 27, 2001.

We reprint all four of these standards here for your perusal: 1) the FCI standard dated September 24, 1963, 2) the FCI standard published in 1997, 3) the standard developed in 1995 for the AKC, and 4) the revision accepted by the AKC on June 27, 2001.

Be mindful of the differences in the standards. It has changed. Included with the texts are comments by this author. This author's opinion is purely personal, in no manner official.

Study the standards. There are important characteristics which differentiate the Havanese from other breeds in both structure and temperament.

The English translation of the FCI 1963 standard was commissioned by Dorothy L. Goodale.

FCI Standard for the Havanese Bichon (Bichone Havanais)
dated September 24, 1963

The Havanese dog is of small size.

BODY: The body is a little longer than tall, ribs rounded, flanks well-raised; the line of the back ends with a well-dropped croupe.

LEGS: The legs are straight, rather lean, the feet a little elongated, the toes thin.

TAIL: The tail is carried crooked over the back and is trimmed with long silky hairs.

HEAD: The head across the skull is broad, the front a little raised.

EYES: The eyes are rather large, deep-set, preferably black. Almond-shaped eyelids.

MUZZLE: The muzzle is rather sharp, the cheeks very flat, not jutting out. The jaws adapt well, the nose black.

COAT: The coat is rather flat, rather soft, forming locks, the end of which curl in rings.

COLOR: Rarely completely pure white, natural more or less dark, from a tobacco brown, gray, or white largely marked with specified colors.

The hair on the muzzle can be trimmed, but it is better to leave it natural.

WEIGHT: Not to exceed 6 kilos (lk = 2.2 pounds; 6k - 13.2 lbs).

The FCI 1997 English translation was accomplished by Mrs. Peggy Davis. This standard is also used as the Canadian Kennel Club (CKC) standard.

FCI Standard No. 250, March 3, 1997 - GB

The origin of the Havanese was in the Western Mediterranean basin, development Cuba.

Patronage: FCI.

Date of Publication of the Valid Original Standard: October 12, 1996.

Utilization: Companion and toy dog.

FCI Classification: Group 9 – Companion and toy dogs

Section 1 Bichons and related breeds without working trial.

HAVANESE BICHON (BICHON HAVANAIS)

Brief Historical Summary:

The breed comes from the Western Mediterranean region and has developed along the Spanish and Italian coastal region. It would seem that these dogs were imported early in Cuba by ocean navigating Italian captains. Erroneously, the most frequent brown colour of these dogs (tobacco) gave birth to the legend which would mean it to be a breed originating from Havana, capital of Cuba. The political events however, have led to the total disappearance of the old blood lines of the Havanese in Cuba; apparently a few dogs could be successfully smuggled out from Cuba; their descendants have survived in the U.S.A.

General Appearance:

The Havanese is a sturdy little dog, low on his legs, lively and quick, with long abundant hair, soft and preferably wavy.

Important Proportions:

The length of the muzzle (tip of nose to stop) is equal to the distance between the stop and the occipital protuberance. The relation between the length of the trunk (measured from the point of the shoulder to the point of the buttock), and the height at the withers is of 4/3.

Behaviour/Temperament: Exceptionally lively and talented, he is easy to train as an alarm dog. Affectionate, of a happy nature is attractive; he is amiable, a charmer, playful and even a bit of a clown. He loves children and plays endlessly with them.

Size: Height at the withers from 23 – 26 cm. Tolerance from 21 – 29 cm.

Coat and Colour: Hair: undercoat wooly and not very developed, it is often totally absent. The topcoat is very long (12 – 18cm in adult dog), soft flat or wavy, and may form curly strands. The usage of scissors to cut the length of the coat and all trimming is forbidden.

Exception: tidying up the hair on the feet is permitted, the hair on the forehead may be slightly shortened so that it does not cover the eyes and the hair on the muzzle may be slightly tidied up, but it is preferable to leave it in natural length. Colour: there are two varieties of colour. Rarely completely pure white, fawn in different shades of light fawn to Havana brown (tobacco colour, reddish brown); patches of those colours in the coat; slight blackened overlay admitted. Permissible colours and patches (white, light fawn to Havana Brown) with black markings. Black coat.

Head: Of medium length, the relation between the length of the head and that of the body (measured from the withers to the base of the tail) is of 3/7.

Cranial Region:

Skull: Flat to very slightly rounded, broad; forehead hardly rising; seen from above it is rounded at the back and almost straight and square on the other three sides.

Stop: Moderately marked.

Nose: Black.

Muzzle: Narrowing progressively and slightly towards the nose but neither snipey nor truncated.

Lips: Fine, lean, tight.

Jaws/Teeth: Scissors bite. A complete dentition is desirable. The absence of premolars (PM1) and molars (M3) is tolerated.

Cheeks: Very flat, not prominent.

Eyes: Quite big, almond shaped, of brown colour as dark as possible. Kind expression. The eye rims must be dark brown to black.

Ears: Set relatively high; they fall along the cheeks forming a discreet fold which raises them slightly. Their extremity is in a lightly rounded point. They are covered in hair in long fringes. Neither propeller ears (sticking sideways) not stuck to the cheeks.

Neck: Of medium length.

Limbs

Forequarters: Forelegs straight and parallel, lean, good bone structure. The distance from the ground to the elbow must not be greater than between the elbow and the withers.

Hindquarters: Good bone structure; moderate angulations.

Body: The length of the body is slightly superior to that of the height at the withers. Topline is straight, slightly arched over the loin.

Croup: noticeably inclined.

Ribs: Well sprung.

Belly: Well tucked up.

Gait: According to his happy nature, the Havanese has a strikingly light footed and elastic gait; forelegs with free stride and pointing straight forward, the hindlegs giving them the impulsion and moving in a straight line.

Faults: Any departure from the foregoing points should be considered a fault and the seriousness with which the fault should be regarded should be in exact proportion to its degree.

General appearance lacking in type

Truncated or snipey muzzle, length not identical to that of the skull

Bird of prey eyes, eyes too deep set or prominent, rims of eyelids partially pigmented

Depigmented nose

Body too long or too short

Straight tail, not carried high

French front (pasterns too close, feet turned outwards)

Deformed hind feet

Coat harsh, not abundant; hair short except on puppies, trimmed coat

Disqualifications:

Depigmented nose

Upper or lower prognathism

Ectropion, entropion; rim of eyelids of one or both eyes depigmented

Size over or under the indicated norms of the standard.

Male animals should have two apparently normal testicles fully descended into the scrotum.

I deem this a good standard. Short, sweet, to the point as well as honest in regards to the structure and temperament of the Havanese breed.

1995 AKC OFFICIAL HAVANESE STANDARD

Approved: June 1995

Effective: February 1, 1996

General Appearance:

The Havanese is a sturdy, short-legged small dog with a soft profuse, untrimmed coat. His plumed tail is carried curled over his back. He is an affectionate, happy dog with a lively, springy gait.

Size, Proportion, Substance:

The height ranges from 8-1.2 to 11-1/2 inches, the ideal being 9 to 10-1/2 inches. The weight ranges from 7 to 13 pounds, the ideal being 8 to 11 pounds. Any dog whose weight deviates greatly from the stated range is a major fault. Any dog measuring under 8-1/2 or over 11-1/2 inches is a disqualification. The body from the chest to the buttocks is longer than the height at the shoulders and should not appear to be square. Forelegs and hindlegs are relatively short, but with sufficient length to set the dog up so as not to be too close to the ground. The Havanese is a sturdy dog, and while a small breed, is neither fragile nor overdone.

Head:

Medium length proportionate to the size of the body. Eyes are large, almond shaped and very dark with a gentle expression. In the blue and silver coat shades, eyes may be a slightly lighter color; in chocolate coat shades, the eyes may be a lighter color. However, the darker eye is preferred. Eye rims are black for all colors except chocolate shaded coats, whose eye rims are self-colored. Small or round eyes, broken or insufficient pigment on the eye rims) are faults. Wild, bulging or protruding eyes a major fault. Total absence of pigment on one or both eye rims is a disqualification. Ears are set neither too high nor too low and are dropped, forming a gentle fold and covered with long feathering. They are slightly raised, moderately pointed, neither fly-away nor framing the cheeks. Skull is broad and somewhat rounded with a moderate stop. The cheeks are flat and the lips clean. The length of the muzzle is equal to the distance from the stop to the back of the occiput. The muzzle is neither snipey nor blunt. Nose and lips are solid black on all colors except the true chocolate dog, whose nose and lips are solid, self-colored brown. Dudley nose, nose and lips other than black, except the solid, self-colored brown on the true chocolate dog are disqualifications. Scissors bite preferred; a level bite is permissible. Full dentition of incisors preferred for both upper and lower jaws. Crooked or missing teeth are faults. Overshot or undershot bite, wry mouth are major faults.

Neck, Topline, Body:

Neck of moderate length, neither too long nor too short. Topline is straight with a very slight rise over the croup. Flanks are well raised. Ribs well rounded. Tail is set high, carried curled over the back and plumed with long silky hair. While standing, a dropped tail is permissible.

Forequarters:

Forelegs are well boned and straight, the length from the elbow to the withers equal to the distance from the foot to the elbow. Dewclaws may be removed. Feet are compact, well arched, well padded. Any foot turning in or out is a fault.

Hindquarters:

Legs are relatively short, well boned and muscular with moderate angulation; straight when viewed from the rear. Dewclaws may be removed. Feet are same as front feet. Fault is same as the front feet.

Coat (note-includes color):

The Havanese is a double-coated breed with soft hair, both in outer and undercoat. The hair is very long and profuse, shown completely natural. The coat type ranges from straight to curly, the wavy coat being preferred. The curly coat is allowed to cord. The adult coat reaches a length of 6 to 9 inches. No preference shall be given to a dog with an excessively profuse or long coat. Short hair on all but puppies is a fault. It is permissible to braid the hair on each side of the head above the eyes, but the coat may not be parted down the middle of the back. No scissoring of the hair on the top of the head is allowed, nor trimming or neatening of the coat of any kind permitted except for the feet, which may be neatened to avoid the appearance of "boat" or "slipper" feet. Coat trimmed in any way except for neatening at the feet is a disqualification. All colors, ranging from pure white to shades of cream, champagne, gold, black, blue, silver, chocolate or any combination of these colors including parti and tri. No preference is given to one color over another.

Gait:

The gait is unique and "springy" which accentuates the happy character of the Havanese. The forelegs reach straight and forward freely from the shoulder with the hind legs converging toward a straight line. The tail is carried up over the back when gaiting. Hackney gait, paddling, moving too close in the rear, and tail not carried over the back when gaiting are faults.

Temperament:

Affectionate, happy.

Disqualifications:

Any dog under 8-1/2 or over 11-1/2 inches.

Total absence of pigment on one or both eye rims.

Dudley nose, nose and lips other than black except for the solid, self-colored brown on the true chocolate dog.

Coat trimmed in any way except for neatening at the feet.

2001 AKC OFFICIAL HAVANESE STANDARD

Approved: May 7, 2001

Effective: June 27, 2001

The Havanese is a small sturdy dog of immense charm. He is slightly longer than tall, and covered with a profuse mantle of untrimmed, long, silky, wavy hair. His plumed tail is carried loosely curled over his rump. A native of Cuba, he has evolved over the centuries from the pampered lap-dog of the aristocracy into what he is today – the quintessential family pet of a people living on a small tropical island. His duties traditionally have been those of companion, watchdog, child's playmate and herder of the family poultry flock. His presentation in the show ring should reflect his function – always in excellent condition but never so elaborately coifed as to preclude an impromptu romp in the leaves, as his character is essentially playful rather than decorative.

While historically always a toy dog and therefore never overly large or coarse, he does not appear so fragile as to make him unsuitable as a child's pet. His unique coat reflects centuries in the tropics, and protects against heat. It is remarkably soft and light in texture, profuse without being harsh or woolly. Likewise, the furnishings of the head are believed to protect the eyes from the harsh tropical sun, and have traditionally never been gathered in a topknot for this reason.

In the present standard, the Havanese is no longer "a sturdy little dog, low on his legs" (1997 FCI standard), or "a sturdy, short-legged small dog." (1995 AKC standard). He is a "small sturdy dog." The FCI and the American standard differ in that the FCI standard classifies the Havanese as "low on his legs" because length of leg corresponds to the rectangular length of body.

In both structure and gait, the Havanese is not easily mistaken for any other breed. His characteristic topline, rising slightly from withers to rump is a result of moderate angulation both fore and aft combined with a typically short upper arm. The resulting springy gait is flashy rather than far-reaching and unique to the breed. The overall impression of the dog on the move is one of agility rather than excessive ability to cover ground. These characteristics of temperament, structure and gait contribute in large part to the character of the breed, and are essential to type.

Although not mentioned in the 2001 standard, the "characteristic" Havanese topline is due in great part to its rear legs being longer than the front legs. By the time the Havanese puppy reaches adulthood, if its rear legs are not longer than the front, its topline straightens.

Size, Proportion and Substance

The height range is from 8-1/2 to 11-1/2 inches, with the ideal being between 9 and 10-1/2 inches, measured at the withers, and is slightly less than the length from point of shoulder to point of buttocks, creating a rectangular outline rather than a square one. The Havanese is a sturdy little dog, and should never appear fragile. A coarse dog with excessive bone is likewise contrary to type and therefore equally undesirable. The minimum height ranges set forth in the description above shall not apply to dogs and bitches under twelve months of age. **Disqualification:** Height at withers under 8-1/2 inches or over 11-1/2 inches, except that the minimum height ranges set forth in the description above shall not apply to dogs or bitches under twelve months of age.

It is desirable in this breed to have this three inch height allowance. In particular, the use of larger bitches with a smaller male keeps the breed stabilized in height and bone.

Head*:*

The expression is soft and intelligent, mischievous rather than cute. The eyes are dark brown, large, almond-shaped, and set rather widely apart. Dark eyes are preferred irrespective of coat color, although the chocolate colored dog may have somewhat lighter eyes. The pigment on the eyerims is complete, solid black for all colors except for the chocolate dog which has complete solid, dark chocolate pigment. No other dilution of pigment is acceptable. Ears are of medium length; the leather, when extended, reaches halfway to the nose. They are set high on the skull, slightly above the endpoint of the zygomatic arch, and are broad at the base, showing a distinct fold. When the dog is alert, the ears lift at the base, producing an unbroken shallow arc from the outer edge of each ear across the backskull. The backskull is broad and slightly rounded. The stop is moderate. Length of muzzle is slightly less than length of back skull measured from stop to point of occiput and the planes are level. The nose is broad and squarish, fitting a full and rectangular muzzle, with no indication of snippiness. The pigment on the nose and lips is complete, solid black for all colors except for the chocolate dog which has complete solid, dark chocolate brown pigment. No other dilution of pigment is acceptable. A scissors bite is ideal. Full complement of incisors preferred. **Disqualifications:** Complete absence of black (or chocolate in the chocolate dog) pigmentation on the eyerims, nose or lips.

One important characteristic of the breed is its "smile" look due to a "full and rectangular muzzle." The change in the dog's length of muzzle from equal (as in the FCI standard) to "length of muzzle is slightly less than length of back skull" is an important change. The slightly shorter muzzle gives the dog a sweeter expression. The breed has acute hearing

and ear placement is an important facet of the breed. Small dogs are close to the ground and excellent hearing is a plus.

Neck, Topline, and Body

The neck is of moderate length, in balance with the height and length of the dog. It carries a slight arch and blends smoothly into the shoulders. The topline is straight but not level, rising slightly from withers to rump. There is no indication of a roach back. The body, measured from point of shoulder to point of buttocks, is slightly longer than the height at the withers. This length comes from the ribcage and not from the short, well-muscled loin. The chest is deep, rather broad in front, and reaches the elbow. The ribs are well sprung. There is a moderate tuck-up. The tail is high-set and plumed with long, silky hair. It arcs forward over the back, but neither lies flat on the back nor is tightly curled. On the move the tail is carried loosely curled over the rump. The long plume of the hair may fall straight forward on either side of the body. The tail may not be docked.

The statement, "slightly longer than the height at the withers," is an expression in standards used for the majority of short-backed, longer legged dog breeds. Under "Size, Proportion and Substance" the 2001 standard points out that the Havanese creates "a rectangular outline rather than a square one." The rectangularly built Havanese must never be a leggy dog. I am certain this point would be under consideration for correction in a revision.

Forequarters:

Shoulder layback is moderate, lying not more than 40 degrees off vertical. Extreme shoulder layback will negatively affect proper gait, and should be faulted. The tops of the shoulder blades lie in at the withers, allowing the neck to merge smoothly into the back. The upper arm is relatively short, but there is sufficient angle between the shoulder and upper arm to set the legs well under the body with a pronounced forechest. The elbows turn neither in nor out, and are tight to the body. Forelegs are well-boned and straight when viewed from any angle. The distance from the foot to the elbow is equal to the distance from elbow to withers. The pasterns are short, strong and flexible, very slightly sloping. Dewclaws may be removed. The feet are round, with well arched toes, and turn neither in nor out. Pads and nails may be black, white, pink, or a combination of these colors. Chocolate dogs may also have brown pads and nails.

The sentence, "Forelegs are well-boned and straight when viewed from any angle" may describe an ideal Havanese breed. Each standard, the 1963, the 1997, the 1995 and the 2001 calls for straight legs. Unfortunately, it does not describe many present Havanese. Quite a few Havanese have some degree of bow in the forelimbs. The bow asserts its characteristics in radius and ulna bones as the growth plates are being set. Nature is compensating for the "deep, rather broad in front" chest in order to "set the legs well under the body." If a Havanese is slab-sided or narrow chested, it would be abnormal for it not to have straight legs. On the other side of the coin, it would be abnormal for a achondroplastic breed as is the present Havanese to have straight legs. Nature must compensate when setting the legs well under the body as called out in the present standard.

"The crooked shape provides a firm cradle-like support for the forward chest portion" (Canine Terminology").

A well-respected judge was recently heard to remark that the Havanese has a problem with crooked fronts. "Breeders," she said, "need to do a better job of what is correct in the standard and not send any dog out as show quality. Pass the word," she continued, "that if you have a dog with a crooked front, don't bother showing it to me." This judge is absolutely correct in her evaluation of the words concerning forelegs in the current standard.

For further comment, please refer to Chapter 11, "Health, Etc."

Hindquarters:

The hind legs are well-boned and muscular through the thigh, with moderate angulation. The hocks are short and turn neither in nor out. In normal stance, the hind legs are parallel to each other from hock to heel and all the joints are in line when viewed from the rear. The rear assembly, in which the rump is slightly higher than the withers, contributes to the breed's unique, springy gait. Dewclaws should be removed. The hind feet fall slightly behind a perpendicular line from point of buttock when viewed from the side. Hind feet have well arched toes, and turn neither in nor out. Pads and nails may be black, white, pink or a combination of these colors. Chocolate dogs may also have brown pads and nails.

Coat:

The coat is double, but without the harsh standoff guard hair and woolly undercoat usually associated with double coats. Rather, it is soft and light in texture throughout, though the outer coat carries slightly more weight. The long hair is abundant and ideally, wavy. An ideal coat will not be so profuse nor overly long as to obscure the natural lines of the dog. Puppies may have a shorter coat. A single, flat coat or an excessively curly coat are equally contrary to type and should be faulted.

Many Havanese have wooly undercoats until maturity. Coats and texture will remain variable for a long time. Ideal is the "soft and light" spun-like-silk textured coat.

Disqualifications: A coarse, wiry coat. An atypical short coat on an adult dog (atypical would be a smooth, flat coat with, or without furnishings).

The standard calls out "an atypical short coat on an adult." What about atypical long but single-coat or a short coat." This wording is confusing. Although a corded coat is mentioned under presentation, a description of a corded coat in the standard is needed.

Color:

All colors are acceptable, singly or in any combination. No preference is given to one color over another. The skin may be freckled or colored.

This is an excellent change from the 1997 FCI standard. It explains colors well.

Gait:

The Havanese gait is lively, elegant, resilient, and unique, contributing greatly to the breed's overall essential typiness. The characteristic "spring" is caused by the strong rear drive combined with a "flashy" front action effected by the short upper arm. While a truly typey dog is incapable of exaggerated reach and drive, the action does not appear stilted or hackneyed. The slightly higher rear may cause a correctly built specimen to show a flash of pad coming and going. The front legs reach forward freely. There is good extension in the rear and no tendency toward sickle hocks. The topline holds under movement, neither flattening nor roaching. Head carriage is typically high, even on the move.

The description "show a flash of pad coming and going" is confusing. This section calls for reworking in order that the layman understands.

Temperament

Playful and alert. The Havanese is both trainable and intelligent with a sweet, non-quarrelsome disposition.

Temperament could be described more fully than it is in the present standard. Potential owners need to know as much as possible about a breed's temperament. The Havanese possesses an outstanding companion dog temperament and it would be appropriate to address it in the standard as in the FCI standard of 1997.

In addition, the standard should mention that the Havanese is not a yappy dog. He makes a fine guard dog, cautiously checking out a visitor and watching his master's acceptance of the visitor before he gleefully jumps into the visitor's lap.

Presentation

The dog should be shown as naturally as is consistent with good grooming. He may be shown either brushed or corded. His coat should be clean and well conditioned. In mature specimens, the length of the coat may cause it to fall to either side down the back but it should not appear to be artificially parted. The long, untrimmed head furnishings may fall forward over the eyes, naturally and gracefully to either side of the skull, or be held in two small braids beginning above the outer corner of the eyes, secured with plain elastic bands. (No ribbons or bows are permitted.) Corded coats will naturally separate into wavy sections in young dogs and will in time develop into cords. Adult corded dogs will be completely covered with a full coat of tassle-like cords. In either coat, minimal trimming of the hair at the inside corner of the eye is allowed for hygienic purposes only, not an attempt to resculpt the planes of the head. Minimal trimming around the anal and genital areas, for hygienic purposes only, is permissible but should not be noticeable on presentation. The hair on the feet and between the pads should be neatly trimmed for the express purpose of a tidy presentation. Any other trimming or sculpting of the coat is to be severely penalized as to preclude placement. Because correct gait is essential to breed type, the Havanese is presented at natural speed on a loose lead.

Faults:

The foregoing description is that of the ideal Havanese. Any deviation from the above described dog must be penalized to the extent of the deviation keeping in mind the importance of the contribution of the various features toward the 'original purpose of the breed.'

Disqualifications:

Height at withers under 8-1/2 or over 11-1/2 inches except that the minimum height range shall not apply to dogs or bitches under twelve months of age.

Complete absence of black (or chocolate in the chocolate dog) pigmentation on the eyerims, nose or lips.

Coarse, wiry coat.

An atypical short coat on an adult. (Atypical refers to a smooth, flat coat with, or without furnishings.)

Two beautiful specimens of the present-day Havanese.
The top picture is of American Dutch French Luxembourg Belgium Champion Alan V. 'T Leurse Hoefpad.
Alan is owned and handled by Sheryl Roach. His breeder is Marinus Hoefnagels.
The bottom picture is of Canadian Champion Sonrisas Tiny Thomas, owned and bred by Rita Thomas.
Tiny is handled by Drobel Rojas.

Chapter Four

What Makes a Havanese a Havanese

Now that we have perused the standard of the breed and have read what the ideal Havanese should be like in structure and read a brief glimpse of what it is like in disposition, let's go after some fine points.

First off, not only is the Havanese absolutely charming, life to the Havanese is a kaleidoscope of absolute wonder and joy. The Havanese possess an unbridled delight in playing which mirrors their happy and joyful temperament. One seldom sees a frown or hears a growl. The breed is intelligent and quick-witted; they adore children.

Seven week old Jasmine was bred by Suzanne M cKay. She is owned by Susan Bel. Jasmine's formal name is Mimosa's Champagne Princess.

One could say in a nutshell the Havanese is an active, highly motivated bundle of loving animal companionship. However, the Havanese, although willing to do what you want him to do, will, if he can get away with it, live in your house on his terms, not yours. His energy spurts need release in activites, at least part of each day. You'll also find he possesses a lively sense of humor, something all of us need in our up and down paths of life. The saddest owner has to smile in delight when observing the breed's activities. You simply have to agree with this four legged charmer, "Yes, life is a wonder. I'm happy to be alive."

Best of all, the Havanese is a family dog. It never wants to be away from its owners except when playing one of its favorite games, "Catch Me If You Can."

The Havanese are not only excellent companion dogs, they love each of any four legged

Havanese love each of any four-legged housemates they live with as Tawney and Viva demonstrate here.

housemates they live with. They toss and tumble, pull each other's hair, jump from chairs onto a comrade, but always with that incredible grin and mischevious glee in the doing.

Their noses are keen. Thank goodness, the standard calls out that the *"length of muzzle is slightly less than length of back skull."* Too shortly muzzled dogs don't have as many scent cells. The more the dog has, the better he can search out smells. The Havanese has a good share and he uses his very well. Don't get me wrong. The breed must not have a short muzzle, just "slightly less." than the length of back skull. And long muzzles in this breed erases breed type.

Along with having absolutely beautiful eyes, so beguiling in his steady gaze at his master, their largeness and almond shape makes it seem that he can see around corners. Because the Havanese is so close to the ground, his range of vision could be restricted by his height, so his large almond eyes are an advantage. He can spot movement a long way away.

I live on five acres. My Havanese' abilties to see Richardson Ground Squirrels (large rat type creatures commonly called "gophers") is amazing. Their observation of detail is extraordinary. When my grass and weeds are cut short, they are able to observe movement five acres distant. If a Richardson ground squirrel is seen moving, off they go in their "run-like-hell" mood, chasing the unwanted creature until they are stopped by the fence line. Back they return to me, delighting with their adventure, grinning the whole distance, tails flagging high. One has to stand and shake one's head in laugher and exclaim, "Aren't they simply adorable!"

The Havanese nose is keen as shown here by Mitzi raiding the pantry. Mitzi was bred by Cathy Enns and is owned by Suzanne McKay.

I prefer uncovering their beautiful eyes by cutting the hair hanging over the forehead in bangs - despite what the breed standard says - because their untrimmed head furnishings obliterate eyes from my view. I enjoy seeing their heads cock and their eyes full of question marks when they want to know what you are doing; the love their eyes display when you purse your lips and throw out a kiss; the unfailing sensibility seen in their eyes when responding to your moods. One of the hallmarks of the breed, as far as I am concerned, is their sixth sense - an intuition of what is going to happen next.

Some breeds of dogs hear better than other breeds. Even though the Havanese have medium sized ears with lots of hair covering them, which help dissipate the heat (one reason the Havanese thrive in warm climates), their hearing is excellent. Their ears are *"set high on the skull ...and broad at the base,"* well constructed to lift instantly and listen to far-away sounds. They are aware of thunder rumbles long before storm clouds are in sight. They dismiss the menacing sounds if the storm skirts the skies above, but come running for lap holding as soon as the sounds churn closer. Their hearing makes them good watch dogs. However, the breed is not a yappy breed. People walking by on the street certainly arouse them. They voice their concern. They bark when they hear the motor of your car as you approach the driveway. "Hi, you are home now," they excitedly proclaim. If you desire a silent house pet, you might want to look elsewhere.

As for children, they are kin. Carry a baby into the house, they are in their glory. They are ever so gentle with small children, not the least disturbed by a small child's quick gestures and uncoordinated yet speedy movement. Of course, supervision is always necessary! It's a necessary precaution to teach children to tread softly and never to run or jump excitedly when playing with a nine to 15 pound Havanese. Bones do break in play with boisterous children.

A kiss from Sassy, the adored Havanese of Bonnie Keeney and family.

Like all dogs, each has its very own personality. Some are laid back, some zip through the day as if every moment is precious and should be lived to the fullest, and some would rather be hugged on your lap than carouse about.

Let's not forget this sweet, adoring, picture-perfect Havanese also has a charming, if challenging, independent streak. Centuries of people manipulation has made him an expert at wrapping his owners around his precious paws and getting away with wild, sometimes unruly behavior. From his puppyhood "catch me if you can" antics to his adult "Well, tables are for dogs too" kind of games, he gets away with mischief not tolerated in a bigger dog.

Let's read what Anchorage, Alaska, owner Kay Barnum writes about her Havanese:

"If a perfect dog exists, I have it in this wonderful little Havanese, my Tango. I have had lots of other dogs of a variety of breeds in my lifetime, loved them all deeply, appreciated all their different personalities, and marveled at the ways in which they displayed their intelligence. However, Tango must have written the book on intelligence and personality, not to mention beauty.

Roughrider's Tango as a puppy. He is owned by Kay Barnum.

"I have never known such a happy dog. I mean he is happy every moment of every day and he makes me happy just watching him. He is curious about everything in the whole world, has to smell every blade of grass, every leaf and every flower, and inspect every hole and bump in the trail. Going for a walk with him is total delight, with me laughing the entire time because of his antics.

"He has never done anything destructive. I don't consider unrolling the toilet tissue and shredding it to be destructive, so I have never had to scold him. When I have to leave him at home he waits patiently on the back of the couch, looking out the window to wait for my return. I suspect that he probably does not leave his post the whole time I am gone.

I only have to tell him in a normal voice what he needs to do or not do and he immediately responds. He seems to understand everything I say, even when I am not speaking to him. When I say I am going to go sit down and relax, he beats me to my chair in the living room. If I say I am going to go take a shower, he will be in the bathroom waiting for me. When the phone rings, no matter where he is or what he is doing, he runs to the phone and waits for me to come pick it up. He truly is amazing!!

"He truly demonstrated his intelligence and ability to problem-solve with a mechanical mouse I had bought for my cats. You pull the tail of the mouse out and the mouse would run in circles until the tail returned to the original position and the mouse would stop moving. Of course, the cats would have nothing to do with it. One day while I was working, I kept hearing a *zzzzzzzzzz* sort of noise and could not figure out what that was. Upon investigating, I found Tango with this mouse, holding the body with his paws and pulling the tail out with his teeth. His paws were not far enough away from his mouth to pull the tail out the entire way, so after getting it partway out he would reposition the body with his paws while continuing to hold the tail out and then proceed to pull the tail the rest of the way. When he would get it all out he would let it go and watch the mouse run, chase it until it stopped, pick it up and begin all over again. I had never ever showed this toy to Tango, so he figured this out all by himself. He played with this so much, the tail finally broke off, so I had to replace it. I think he is on his third mouse now.

"I could go on and on and on about my amazing Tango because he does something to surprise me every day. I am thankful I have a dog of this marvelous breed."

I, and Havanese owners all over the globe, share her opinion: the Havanese is truly a delightful breed, easy to house (although at times difficult to groom), and easy to share one's life with. It's a precious example of the joys God has given us on this earth.

Ch Amor's TedE Ruxpin D 'Bella is owned by Kathy Patrick and Mary Lopez. Teddy, eight months old in this photo, is the son of Ch Los Companero V Havaluv and Ch Amor's That Girl. Breeder is Mary Lopez.

The name of this nine week old climber is Del Prado's Sol O Sombra, better known as Abby. Gene and Jody Wood are her breeders and she is owned by Sue Klover and Gene and Jody Wood.

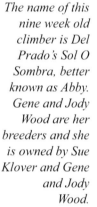

Above: Two little seven week old Roughriders, Billie and Dawson, all tuckered out.

Sharron Davis of Riverbreeze Havanese owns these tug-of-war playing puppies as well as the four enjoying a "I see you!" game.

Striker, shown above, is really AM/CAN Ch Tapscott's Lightning Strike. His sire is Ch HotShot and his dam is Beautiful Carlita vom Salzetal. Striker is owned by Laurie Parrett of Canada and bred by Pamm and Jeanne Tapscott.

Linus, shown below, is Danish Ch Little Linus VT Leurse Hoefpad Heronsbridge. His breeder is Marinus Hoefnagels. Owner is Lynda Read.

Janet Hicks owns Hero. Bred by James and Rosemary Cushman, Hero's registered name is AM/CAN Ch Janizona's Hero by Homespun.

In a run-like-hell mood is Phoebe, AKC/HCA Ch Los Perritos Overlook Salsa. Owned by Russell and Natalie Armitage, Phoebe was bred by Lynn and Jose Nieto.

On the left is Tapscott's El Bodeguero at one year and nine months of age. Bogie was bred by Pamela and Jeanne Tapscott and is owned by Arlene Etzig. The black and white Parti-colored bitch is Ch Disneyland's Viva For Tapscott's. Viva was 10 months of age in this photo. Breeder is Ursula Geipel and owner Arlene Etzig.

Ch Gingerbread Starkette, Sprite, when not winning in the show ring (she won Best of Opposite Sex at the 2004 HCA National Specialty) loves romping on the California beaches with her owner, Stan Holt. Nona Dietrich is Tinker's breeder.

Along with standing straight and proud in their beautiful coats, Havanese are good swimmers. The three photos below are of Patricia Herrick's Havanese, Lucy, formally known as Ch Gingerbred Final Answer. At left below she stands ready to be shown; at right she is diving into a wind-stroked lake and bottom, she is swimming back to shore. Nona Dietrich of Gingerbred Kennels is her breeder.

Chapter Five

Homework Before Making Breeding Decisions

So, you have fallen in love with the Havanese breed, studied the Havanese breed standards, read all you could about the breed's pluses and minuses, researched breeding do's and don'ts and have decided your wonderful little Havanese should be bred to further the quality of the breed. You are certain its minor faults will disappear in a generation and s/he (bitch or male) will deliver absolutely wonderful puppies - just like your little dog - and that the ones you cannot keep will be loved and adored all their lives by new owners.

Let me address some cold, hard facts:

First, Humane Shelters, pounds - pet animal extermination centers - all over the world presently overflow with "pets" the so called dog-loving public no longer wants. Most of these will die, long before their time to die, from extermination procedures. The workers who have to put them to death, to make room for more unwanted-about-to-be-put-to-death dogs, suffer. Snuffing out lives of dogs who give unconditional love to the humans who created them is heartbreaking. Just think how you would feel if you had to give up your precious Havanese and it would end its life like that - alone, unwanted, from home to pen to death chamber. Unbelievable? No, it is not. It happens all the time.

Secondly, if a pet you create through your lovely Havanese is no longer wanted by the people to whom you sold it, will you take that pet back? Do you have room for another? Another dog with behavior or toilet problems? Do not believe that scenario cannot happen to you. Ethics demand that responsible breeders take back rejects they sold, no matter in what condition they are returned.

Thirdly, will you be able to bounce back from the heartbreaks and money setbacks responsible breeders encounter? Pups whelped dead; pups handicapped with genetic diseases which cannot be cured; the tears and monies that must be expended when things go wrong. And go wrong they do! I have been breeding for 30 years; I've seen much sadness and heartbreak. And if you think hobby breeding is a money maker, think again. Kurt Unkelback says in his book, "The American Dog Book" (1976): "Those hobbyists who claim a profit are either amateur puppy farmers or deluded souls who keep incomplete records on overhead, such as the hourly rate on their own time." Kurt's words ring true today also. Think about it: care costs, food costs, training costs, veterinarian costs, performance events costs, materials costs, etc. Dog breeding done correctly is an expensive hobby.

Lastly, are you aware of the amount of backbreaking work raising a quality litter of puppies entails? I'm not writing about self-proclaimed breeders who raise their dogs' litters in barns, cellars, basements, etc. and often see the pups perish during the dam's rearing because of the dam's neglect, low-quality canine milk, or by being stepped on or eaten, or by getting a disease and not taking sick pups to a veterinarian because "they cost too much!" Or puppies not surviving because of lack of warmth, etc. These dog owners shrug their shoulders and say, "So be it." The surviving puppies are sold to anyone who offers money for them. "Gotta get rid of these pups, you know! What a mess they make."

In Montana recently (and it happens all over the country, in every state - every month a new "collector" or psuedo breeder of animals is charged) a puppy mill was discovered. The 100 plus dogs were mired in filth, feces, sat among dead animal bodies, were chock full of parasites, had unbelievable sores in their mouths, and spent their existence in tiny open air pens, usually two males to a female so the female could be bred each heat. When the dogs were seized, the owners exclaimed, "But these are breeding dogs." As if dogs were livestock. Cattle, at least, are given freedom to move about on pastures before their end comes. On examination by humane workers, none of the dogs had any conception of what life was all about. They were like "things" moving about. Yet dogs have identical emotions to people. They emotionally feel the same stresses as humans do, although they are much more stoic about them. Perhaps it was for the better that these dogs had lived in a vacuum.

All right. I'll change the subject. I should be writing about your "to-be" quality litter, several of which are already conversation-sold to friends who exclaim, "Oh, I'd love to have a puppy by your Mitzi. She is just so adorable."

I'll initiate you on the steps an ethical breeder takes in this avocation. If after digesting

this information, your answer is "yes, I want to be a responsible breeder of dogs," and you have the honest willingness to follow through on everything you should do to complete your homework, you have my congratulations and best wishes. The world always needs responsible breeders of pet animals. We do not want dog lovers to deal with uncrupulous psuedo dog breeders or commercial dog brokers, so prevalent today.

Let me digress for a moment. It's good to know the history of breeding. After my digression, I'll end the chapter with the necessary minuses and the optimum pluses.

Ready?

Today's dog breeders owe a great deal to early man. He was at one with the vast number of animals with which he lived in those beginning earth times. He could not survive in the tumultuous, harsh, tough early world without a relationship, good and bad, with the animals around him. Not only did he hunt, eat and utilize hides and furs, he welcomed the scavengers which kept his living sites clean. We'll probably never know how one of these scavenger animals (*canis familieres)* and man became friends. They did. Eventually, these scavengers (dogs) moved from the fringes of his campsites right to his side by the campfire. They became his warning system, shared his hunt and followed him wherever he went, not only as clean-up aides but as companions.

They helped man develop remarkable talents of observation. Consciously or unconsciously, early man nurtured form and function to the highest degree in his breeding practices. If those that bred whelped young without structural forms to withstand perilous hunts and journeys in search of food, they were eaten. If those that bred whelped young without functions of willingness, trainability and problem solving, they too were eaten.

There is no doubt the first dogs were close family mated; they were look-alikes. Different breeding opportunities arose only when early man traveled. That is how a variety of breeds were born, each developing structural and behavioral characteristics which weather, terrain and need demanded. That's why at the beginning of recorded history many of the breeds we know today were already developed.

Unlike the days when early man lived, when today's unthinking individuals breed dogs just to breed, those animals can't be eaten. Instead, they proliferate out of hand. That's why warehouses are filled, waiting for responsible individuals to adopt dogs. If no adoptees come forward, the dogs are culled by hatchet, gun, gas, electrical jolts or poisoned needles.

Today's responsible breeders are blessed with our age's technology. Technology helps shape breedings for form, function and health. Yet, now and as it was from the beginning, nature holds the trump cards. Nature continually surprises us in our breedings, imparting to some young "unwelcome genes" we thought long ago had disappeared from the breed.

Thus, breeding dogs can be a gamble. Place your hand in a bag of 50 marbles, half of them black and half white. Draw out your closed hand. Each marble you hold is black. "But there are white marbles in that bag," you exclaim. "How is it I didn't get any of those? White is what I wanted."

Breeding is like that.

Mysterious fun, hard work, a delight (ah, those precious puppies) and terrible heartbreak.

There are three types of breeding: in-breeding, line breeding and out-cross breeding.

IN-BREEDING

While I shall describe in-breeding, I do not believe today's dog breeders should practice it. Check with any veterinarian. They see the heartbreaking rejects from such practice. They'll respond with a big "NO!" In-breeding may perpetuate certain desirable structural and behavioral traits, but it certainly leaves destruction in its wake in most of the puppies ensuing from such a breeding. Sires and dams are close relatives - father to daughter, mother to son and sister to brother. The dogs selected are supposed to be superior in qualities one wants accentuated. But accentuation of the good points in the get seldom occurs, even though a thorough investigation of the good and bad traits of each of the ancestors in the pedigree has been done. Nature pops in too many faults in this doubling up of genes. Only a few inbreedings ever work out. Most pick up genetically derived health problems, bad structure or behavior problems. Because the new lives cannot be discarded (early man never threw away anything), today's breeders should, but often do not, take responsibility for such misfits.

Although in-breeding is claimed to "stamp" a strain (produces look and act-alike siblings) quickly, you can easily see it is the cause of much dissension between breeders and veterinarians. The latter observe the results from those who have purchased the rejects of the litter. Any veterinarian will affirm what I say even though I'll get a lot of flack from some breeders.

LINE-BREEDING

While line-breeding takes longer to "stamp" a strain, it is preferred by responsible breeders for common-sense reasons. Uncles, aunts and cousins are used in this popular type of breeding, with possibly the repeat of an excellent sire or dam on each side several

generations back in the joint pedigree. In other words, to line-breed, you select a dog which has much of the same blood as your dog has. Line-breeding will pick up faults of some of the ancestors as it does superior qualities. That is why it is vitally important to look at the ancestors behind yours, particularly the bitches. Bitches are often more prepotent than the male.

You want to select a mate for your dog that will complement yours; that is, have good points where your dog does not. If, for instance, you have the choice of two dogs and one has a magnificent head but a body that is not desirable and the other has a great body, and its head, though in balance with its body, is not an outstanding head like the first, go with the good body. You can bring back the head you desire in a later breeding. Structure and balance are more important points than a head.

Line breeding is capable of producing dogs which stamp the developing strain with excellence. It is a slightly slower method than in-breeding.

OUT-CROSSING

This type of breeding often involves use of a sire or dam that fits the breed type without regard to pedigree analysis or analysis into faults and pluses ancestors possess. It's a "There's a male of this breed down the street that looks pretty good. I'll breed my bitch to him" type of breeding. It's a head in the sand breeding. Offspring of these breedings often litter our humane shelters because of innate health, structural and behavioral problems. Responsible breeders do use an outcross to bring into their line a desired structural or cosmetic feature (such as fronts or coats or sweetness of temperament), knowing they might bring in a bad fault. They are willing to do so in order to correct a particular fault in their line. They are extremely judicious in their choosing and return to line breeding after this one use.

It is interesting to note that as we are becoming inundated with technological advances our animal breedings are becoming more refined and less a game of chance. Each pure breed has a parent club which asks member breeders to list health faults prevalent in the dogs they own. This is called an Open Registry. Dogs suffering from diseases, or with immediate ancestors who exhibited them, are taken out of the ethical breeding pool. No responsible breeder wants to deliver a defective puppy to a new owner.

Now let's return to what the pluses and minuses of responsible breeding of Havanese. Here is homework that should be done before you commit yourself to breeding.

1. Puppies purchased and/or chosen to be future brood bitches or stud dogs should show potential in both structure and temperament.

2. Quality diet should be a standard requirement for a potential breeding dog, beginning with the puppy.

3. Socialization of the puppy to people and environment must be an on-going, everyday endeavor.

4. Good mannering obedience classes are essential for the future brood bitch or stud dog; also classes for learning how to present your dog in dog shows are desirable.

5. You should join a local or national breed club.

6. You must complete genetic testing (CERF, BAER, OFA for hips, patellas, front legs).

7. You need to exhibit the dog at dog shows under judges to ascertain quality and obtain the dog's championship before entering the dog in a breeding program.

8. Peruse books on genetics, canine structure and temperament; acquaint yourself with the various performance events. NOTE: Havanese excel in obedience, agility and tracking.

9. Conduct research into the pedigrees of your puppy's background and conduct a thorough investigation of the pedigree of the stud dog you intend to have your bitch mate with. The stud you choose should help you breed away from your bitch's faults. If you own a male, the same studies should be conducted on bitches you choose to have him mate with.

10. Follow through with necesary veterinarian care.

11. Be able to travel with your bitch to the stud's residence and/or work with a reproduction veterinarian if chilled or frozen semen is going to be used for mating. If you own a stud dog, be sure you have the ability to house and care for the bitch for the length of her estrus and be able to supervise the mating.

NOTE: Step 11 requires knowledgeable assistance by a mentor or veterinarian for the first several breedings.

If you are willing to abide by hard work in this hobby, expend all the monies necessary, and obey the ethics, you will encounter deep joy as a responsible breeder of Havanese. You will also find yourself immersed in dog world activities. You must however, be able to face the heartbreaks of breeding, and there are many, I assure you. You need to bounce back smiling.

In this hobby, and it is an expensive one, you will meet many people who seek personal power via their involvement with dogs. Their attitudes and jealousies will be disconcerting. On the plus side, you will meet many people who will become lifelong friends. They are that wonderful.

Nevertheless, breeding excellent dogs is not for the faint-hearted. Recognition in the dog world is seldom accomplished overnight. You have to pay your dues.

Anybody contemplating the breeding of Havanese should definitely avail themselves of the fine books pertaining to dog genetics. It is vitally important to learn the principles of genetics if you want to produce Havanese of quality mental and physical attributes as well as free of inherited defects as is possible.

A common statement by first-time breeders is, "Why all the puppies in this litter look like show quality pups." By the third breeding, the common statement becomes, "I hope I get more than one show quality puppy out of this litter."

And if you become a breeder, you're going to hear the following statement repeated many times. "Oh, the Havanese breed has such a small gene pool."

Every breed in the world has a small gene pool. The gene pool never widens. As more and more dogs are used in breeding, however, more genes from the ancestors emerge. Consider this fact: There are over 25,000 genes on each pair of chromosomes and both sire and dam have 39 paired chromosomes, making a total of 78 chromosomes. With such an infinite variety, a fantastic pattern from nature, you can understand there can never be a dog look and act-alike.

I quote an excerpt from my book, *The New Complete Portuguese Water Dog:* "The joys of being a breeder outweigh the work and the possible agony of potential tragedy."

And whoever coined the axiom, "Never mix business with pleasure," certainly was not very successful at breeding dogs or rearing puppies. This hobby requires lots of love and attention as well as adherence to sound practices.

Chapter Six

Breeding

In the old days, and that includes all the centuries before the 20th, understanding of the breeding of animals was handed down by those well versed in the act of animal breeding. No tests were done to determine the correct day or days of breeding. And breeders of dogs felt no need to document the natural sequence of events which enabled dog and bitch to mate. The dogs were together or were put together. The male chased the female. The female stood for the dog until they were tied. The dogs mated naturally, or didn't.

Today, we manipulate many breedings. Because of technological advances, domestic animal breeding is becoming more refined and less a game of chance.

Regardless of the wealth of wonderful mind-boggling technological know-how, nature remains in control. She has given animals cycles in which breeding is possible as well as cycles in which breeding is not possible.

We're going to examine the dog breeding cycles (in layman's language). If you have made up your mind to breed your Havanese, you'll come away with a good understanding of nature's trump cards.

Most toy breed bitches enter their first estrus (commonly called "heat" or "season") after six months of age. Normal Havanese bitches usually begin their first estrus about nine to 12 months. Why so late? Havanese are slower maturing toy dogs.

Novice breeders often ask: "Since nature allows bitches to come into heat before they are a year of age, why shouldn't they be bred at their first heat?" You might say first heats are developmental heats. Nature gives puppies a trial estrus period while preparing the reproductive system for maturity. Seldom are first heats as long or full as those of mature bitches. Dogs under a year of age are still developing both physically and mentally, and puppies born of early unions are usually more susceptible to stresses, their immune systems weaker. Vero

Shaw, who wrote "The Classic Encyclopedia of the Dog" in 1879, wrote, "Young bitches often exhibit symptoms of an inclination to breed at the age of eight or nine months, but it is undesirable to place them at the stud until they have reached the age of at least eighteen months. Stunted and puny puppies are almost sure to be produced from a young mother; and the injury they are likely to do to her constitution is incalculable." As this 19th century dog man stated, bitches do not reach maturity until they are about 18 months old.

A few show puppies may be produced from early litters; however, they are usually fine-boned and display more structural faults. I have a good example in one of my Havanese. Both her parents were less than a year of age when they were mated. I was not informed of this by the breeder; however, when I received this female at eight weeks of age, she was so frail I took her immediately to my veterinarian. He suggested I return her to the breeder. But I did not have the heart to place this tiny dog on another flight. She was mine once she landed in my arms. However, she never developed side teeth, her coat took over a year to even look "Havanese'ish" and at a year and a half I learned she had luxating patellas (knee joints that slip in and out). Because they were causing her severe pain she had to have them operated on. She still limps slightly (so I cannot even show her in my favorite dog sport of obedience). I had purchased her as a potential show dog. These afflictions could have been caused by faults in the genetic background of the sire and dam but also by breeding immature dogs together. It is a dangerous practice.

Another sound reason for not breeding dogs younger than 18 months is that many pure breeds in the developed countries of the world have parent clubs with "open" registries. As mentioned earlier, these registries are for member breeders to list health faults prevalent in the dogs they breed. Dogs suffering from certain diseases or with immediate ancestors who suffered from them are pulled from the breeding pool. Many of the health tests given (these vary with each breed because of predisposition to a specific disease) are not valid unless the dog is well past a year of age. Hip dysplasia, a debilitating disease which attacks pure breeds and mixed breeds alike, can develop under environmental stresses if a dog is genetically predisposed to it. Many are. The Orthopedic Foundation of America (OFA) does not grant an OFA certificate to qualifiers until a dog is two years of age. Unfortunately, we have many Havanese who, although they qualify for an OFA number, have only fair hips, others have bowed front legs, which do not always show up until a dog is about nine months to a year in age. The Havanese Club of America health recommendations at this writing (2004) are for a yearly CERF (eye examination) with numbers, a BAER (hearing test), an OFA Patella test, an OFA x-ray of hips, the last (unfortunately) without numbers; that is, without stipulating if the hips are Fair, Good or Excellent). These numbers are important to know, since a standard requirement is for the dog to have a *"strong rear drive."* There is no requirement for listing of dogs with achondroplasia of the forelimbs, which is a condition of dwarfism characterized by the shorten-ing of limbs; "Normal," say veterinarians, in certain breeds, such as the Havanese. Achondroplasia is not achondrodysplasia, dysplasia meaning abnormality. "A hereditary interference with cartilage production at the growth plate is seen as a rare dwarfisn," writes Robert L. Leighton V.M.D in "UC Davis Book of Dogs."

This toy dog, a Shih Zsu, does have achondrodysplasia of the forelimbs, an abnormality.

A question frequently asked is this: "How often does a healthy bitch come into heat?" Estrus normally occurs every six to seven months. A small number of bitches enter estrus every three to four months (these bitches often have breeding problems or have an estrus cycle without ovulation). Another and smaller group enter estrus only every ten to 12 months. (In the wild, estrus appears every 12 months.) A few bitches have split heats, entering proestrus for a week after which the reproduction hormones seemingly cease to perform, then suddenly return, with the bitch entering true estrus after a week or more of silence. Stephen J. Ettinger in "Textbook of Veterinary Internal Medicine" (W.B. Saunders Col., 1989), explains split heat this way: "Bitches with split estrus periods exhibit signs of target tissue stimulation by estrogens (vulvar swelling, seroanguineous discharge) for a few days as follicles develop. The bitch may or may not be receptive to mating. This is followed by a regression of vulvar size and cessation of the discharge for a few weeks until the bitch enters a "true" season and ovulates. If the bitch is mated appropriately during the second part of a split estrus, fertility should be normal."

Other exceptions occur when there are several bitches in one household. The first bitch to come into estrus usually drags the others into estrus. In some of these instances, the bitch dragged in may not have a fertile estrus - she does not ovulate - particularly if the length of time from her last estrus is short.

Pronounced weather changes such as lengthening of daylight in Spring and shortening of daylight in Fall also affects hormonal changes. Spring and Fall are usual estrus cycles.

A BITCH'S ESTRUS SEASON WALK THROUGH

First we'll look at the season of estrus (commonly called "heat") in canine bitches. Note: all dates are normal approximate. The 21 day cycle usually, not always, follows this three-part pattern:

1) proestrus (nine to 12 days)

2) true estrus (six to nine days)

3) metestrus (three days). Metestrus occurs at the beginning of the 60 day Diestrus.

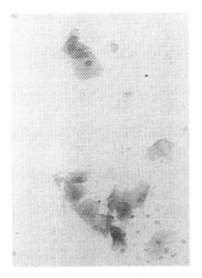

Pro-estrus smear - shown on a slide taken May 21, 2003.

Stellar players in the fascinating reproduction life of a bitch are hormones. Hormones are chemical substances produced by cells which, when released into the bloodstream, take action on target cells in some other part of the body.

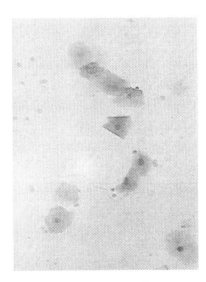

Late pro-estrus smear - shown on a slide taken May 23, 2003.

Hormones, which play important functions in all phases of life, play an incredible role in reproduction. Firstly, they prepare (proestrus) the reproduction organs for true estrus; secondly, they introduce true estrus by sending leuteinizing hormones (known as LH) from the pituitary gland down to the ovaries; and thirdly, they return the reproduction system to a state (metestrus/diestrus) in which progesterone is the leading hormone. Diestrus lasts 60 days. Progesterone secretions then stop and the bitch's reproduction system rests in anestrus for approximately 120 days.

In summary, after hormones set the stage, the pituitary gland releases LH (called the LH surge). This hormonal surge is a result of the drop in estrogen (female sex hormones which emanate from the ovaries). Progesterone (the hormone which maintains the reproductive organs during pregnancy) rises.

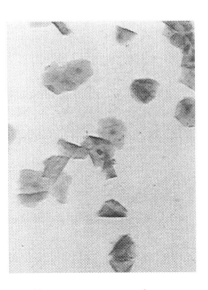

True estrus smear - shown on a slide taken May 30, 2003.

50

Put even more simply, the LH surge signals the chemical estrogen to fall and the chemical progesterone to rise. True estrus is standing heat and complete vaginal cornification.

Given this profound LH stimulus, eggs form in the ovaries. At this initial stage they are immature and are called primary oocytes (immature eggs). Nature gives these primary oocytes up to three days to develop into mature eggs. They are then called secondary oocytes. In essence, the LH surge stimulates the growth and subsequent release of eggs (called ovulation) which occurs two days after the LH surge, or on the third day of true estrus.

How and where are the eggs developed and released? Leading from the ovaries where the primary oocytes (immature eggs) form, are two long thin tubes, called oviducts. These tubes (oviducts) connect the ovaries to the uterus. The tiny immature eggs (primary oocytes) must travel down these tubes to the uterus. On the way down they develop into secondary oocytes (mature eggs). It takes two days for the eggs to complete the journey from the ovaries to the uterine end of the tubes. Once there, snug and safe, they are ready to be fertilized by sperm from the male. And nature never wastes time. She gives three days of life (approximately) to the ova inside the uterus. If sperm are present, they are fertilized. If no sperm are waiting or if none arrive in time to fertilize the eggs, the ova die.

As stated, nature gives the ova three days to mature, three days for the ova to accept sperm and two to three days to die. If you add up the days, you'll see true estrus (standing heat) lasts six to nine days: 1) three for the LH surge and consequential forming and maturing of eggs, 2) three for fertilization of the eggs, and 3) three for the ova to live or die. Whether the eggs are fertilized or not, progesterone levels remain high for 60 days. After that period, progesterone ceases to be released. The reproduction system returns to preestrus status. It rests.

If the bitch has been bred, eggs form into zygotes. At approximately 21 days, these little forming bodies (embryos) can be felt by an expert palpator. It is never wise for an amateur to attempt to palpate the bitch since inexperienced probing can injure or kill the tiny forms emerging from eggs. Some veterinarians like to palpate for signs of pregnancy at 24 days, others at 28, 30 or 32 days. At 24 days, forms encased inside the uterus of the Havanese bitch can be as large as small peas; at 30 and 32 days as large as grapes. After that time, the protective uterine locules (placenta) closes in on each form. It is useless to palpate.

Cat scans given at 35 to 38 days do show encased forms in both uterine horns; however, there are many number misjudgments. It's easy to understand why. Some bitches carry their young high in their abdomen, a few seemingly right under the breast bone and they are well nigh impossible to see or feel for. Other bitches carry their puppies low in their abdomen. The manner in which the bitch carries her young (high or low) affects the amount of food she can consume at a meal. Most bitches become queasy in early pregnancy as her infants begin to push against her stomach. So morning sickness is common around the 20 to 30 day mark. Other bitches sail right through pregnancy with nary a thought as to what is happening inside them.

Here is the author's bitch, Naughty, cut down for her first pregnancy. You can just discern a slight bulge in her tummy. Naughty carried her puppies low. Her appetite was excellent throughout her pregnancy.

Some breeders have an X-ray taken of their bitch when she is about 45 days into pregnancy. They desire or deem it necessary to know how many and what position the unborn puppies are in. But X-rays, even at 45 days after breeding, have risks. Although many veterinarians and breeders poo-poo such concerns, others (my opinion included) believe it is better to have this procedure (if necessary) done when pups are getting ready to come into the world - say at 55 to 57 days. X-rays do radiate!

Depending on the size of the litter, an enlarged abdomen is seen by the fifth week of pregnancy. Puppies do the most growing between the sixth and eighth weeks. Cosmetic growth (nails and hair) is pronounced during the last week of life inside the mother. Movement is felt and seen the last 15 days of pregnancy. The soft, even tick-tick pulsing of heart beats can also be felt the last 15 or so days. At that time also the bitch begins to shed hair on her abdomen and hair on her flanks stick out instead of down. Her vulva, small when not pregnant, becomes looser in texture and wider in form. Natures prepares her for whelping by stretching this tissue. An enlarging soft vulva is not supposed to be a reliable pregnancy sign, however, it is a sign I expect to see if one of my bitches is pregnant. A slight discharge lubricates the vulva during pregnancy keeping the passageways soft and pliable, more than likely to make travel smoother for her babies' entrance into the world.

During the last five days of pregnancy, the babies start moving towards the exit. The abdomen sags with their weight as they drop down, although with a birth of one or two babies, little change is noted.

A STUD DOG WALK THROUGH

The male's reproduction system is comprised of the testes (testicles), a duct system, a prostate and the penis. Hormones again are the star players in his breeding life, particularly testosterone. Nature has bequeathed male dogs with an extraordinarily powerful dose of this potent hormone. One of its many duties is to impart sexual performance.

Sperm (spermatozoa) develops in the two testicles (called testes) and is manufactured continually during a dog's life. It matures in the dog's duct system (epididymis) and is transported through the epididymis and urethra (both are tubular male reproductive organs), gaining fluids on this journey. These fluids sweep the sperm onto the prostate (where more fluids smooth the passage of the sperm). The sperm's last stop (it doesn't tarry, it rushes) is through the dog's penis into the bitch's vagina during the dog's ejaculation after the penis has entered the vagina. A clear glandular fluid from the urethra precedes the sperm. Following it, flooding the uterus, is prostate fluid. However, on successful so-called "outside ties" and in AI procedures where the penis is not inserted into the vagina, only a scant amount of prostate fluid enters the vagina. So it is not yet known how essential the prostate fluid is for successful insemination.

It takes approximately ten weeks for sperm to mature. And a male dog can breed anytime. Developing and mature sperm are always available in the dog's reproductive system. Except!

Nature, as always, has the last hurrah. A dog can only mate when the bitch's hormones come into play during late proestrus and when she is in standing heat. The hormones give out an odor so enticing the male loses all sense of decorum. He becomes an obsessed animal. The odor of the female is so deliciously powerful, so potent, that the male goes berserk. He is totally intoxicated. His reactions are so strong he can remate in as short a period as five minutes after a previous mating. The cleanest house dog will begin urinating on furniture in the house if the female resides in the same house. Forgive him. He really is not cognizant of what he is doing. He is establishing territory! Nature's elaborate propagation strategy makes the dog vulnerable to this exquisite hormonal attack upon all his senses. His drive for sexual ecstasy is absolute. It's as if those billions of mature sperm inside his testes are clamouring to swim to make a new life.

When the dog ties with the bitch, his sperm shoot out from his penis and swim upwards to the bitch's oviducts where eggs are being formed or where eggs are mature enough to be inseminated (dogs do mate before the LH surge, as well as during and after). Sperm, bil-

lions of them, are swept along by contractions of the bitch, who herself is completely sense driven by sexual anticipation.

If no eggs are present, sperm lie in wait for them. Experiments have shown they are able to live as long as seven days for eggs and still be fertile. Scientists suspect they are able to live that long with the energy supplied by the prostate fluid. Some theorize there is fluid in the uterus that sustain them. These theories are conjecture only. And a seven-day life for sperm is unusual.

As soon as the eggs arrive, sperm crowd around them. A sperm's head contains enzymes which allow it to penetrate the egg. But only one can gain entrance to an egg. Once one sperm penetrates, fertilization occurs almost immediately; the walls of the egg tighten up. Other sperm are repelled. Those that do not connect with an egg languish and die.

BEHAVIOR OF THE BITCH IN ESTRUS

Several weeks prior to proestrus, the hormones in the bitch's body awaken from their anestrus rest. They begin to stimulate reproductive activity. The stimulation produces behavioral changes in the normal bitch since hormonal activity affects brain functions as well as functions in the reproductive system. She becomes more loving to her owners. "Hug me," she pleads with her eyes as she leaps upon your lap. Her tongue reaches out to lick you on the face and hands. She may mount her female housemates in play or in an attempt to dominate them. Some males she'll mount, others she shuns. Bitches have definite likes and dislikes. If she is in the mood to play with a male, she'll chase him, then "run-like-hell" when he goes after her and sometimes growl and snap at him as he comes close. She's aware of her power to make him cringe while he is batting his eyes in newfound love for her. Reactions in bitches vary. A few become aggressive with housemates. Others are quiet; they lie about as if they do not feel well; they pick at their food.

During proestrus, which begins with an enlarging vulva and a discharge that she scrupulously endeavors to wipe away with her tongue - most bitches are fastidious in this regard - she will begin to urinate more frequently. Many bitches will slightly lift one of their rear legs as they do.

Owners don't always notice the first bloody discharge of proestrus. Knowledgeable breeders do watch for a slight swelling of the vulva. Even before there is swelling, in anticipation, if they have kept a record of the bitch's past heat cycles, they'll place a tissue against the opening of the vulva daily. As the bitch enters proestrus her vulva will show a trace or two of blood. These are cast-off cells from the walls of her uterus. Some bitches flow heavily, others have only slightly colored and thin discharges. Maiden bitches may look in disgust and even fear at their discharge. As proestrus progresses, her behavior can begin a radical change. She will become more interested in a male. She'll tease him by rushing up to him, perhaps touching him with her nose and then coyly sitting, still not allowing him to sniff her "privates" or try to mount her. She is quite in command as her sexual urges mount.

Teasing comes to an abrupt halt when true estrus begins. As it does and when the LH surge takes over her body, shy or dominant, her tail flags, she flirts; runs with him, plays with him, presents her rear to him, and even mounts him to show him how if he is hesitant. Unless she has been taken away from her dam at at too young an age or has had little contact with other dogs, unless she has been spoiled by her owner, the normal bitch in true estrus has no inhibitions. Those few who do, who prefer to run away, sit and growl and even bite when the male dog tries to mount her, can be difficult to breed naturally. The normal bitch's instincts tell her what to do. It's a heady sexual period for her. Tease, flirt, play, stand for the dog, and allow his penis to enter her vulva. Once inside, the bulb of the penis swells, resulting in what is called a tie. Neither dog can be freed from the other until the swelling of the bulb of the penis subsides (five minutes to one hour), and the penis slides out of the vulva.

When the tie ends, the bitch will immediately sit down to clean herself; then rest. She'll be ready again within hours. Sexual drive in the normal bitch is dramatic until major hormonal stimulations from the LH surge subside. Many bitches enjoy being bred even after the eggs inside her uterus have died.

The season of estrus and behavior of bitches can vary. I offer four stories describing variances.

I owned two bitches that entered true estrus at day 15. One accepted a male from day five until day 20; the other accepted a male from day three to day 25. We had no puppies the first breeding with the first bitch (a Dalmatian) although the male and my bitch tied twice, once on day 11 and once on day 13. "Two breedings are enough," I said. When day 14 came around, I was on my way home 800 miles away. I was wiser the second time around. I stayed in a hotel for two and a half weeks while she and the stud enjoyed their almost daily breeding experiences.

The second bitch (a Portuguese Water Dog) had a terrible whelping with her second set of puppies (her story appears in my book "Devoted to Dogs"). It resulted in a caesarean and the loss of two puppies out of 12. I did not want her bred again but kept putting off

spaying her. Lo and behold she came into heat before I had made an appointment to have this done. I kept her isolated from my young stud from day seven until day 22 (just to be sure). To my surprise, my young stud climbed the fence of her yard (the fence was six feet high) and mated with her on what would be day 24. Although it is never good for a bitch to be spayed during or close to estrus (organs do become inflamed), I wanted her spayed for health reasons. My veterinarian checked to see if she was still breedable when she had been mated. "No," he said, "she was clean."

A third story: A PWD bitch was flown to me to be bred. "She's in standing heat," her veterinarian had told her owner. And she appeared to be. My stud dog mated her four days in succession. She was flown home. No puppies arrived. "Send her to me the first day of her next heat," I told her owner. She did. The two mated the third day after she arrived (day four of her proestrus). They mated four times. She went out of estrus on what would have been day 12 (bitches successfully bred go out of heat within four days of the mating). She delivered nine puppies 62 days later.

The last story: One of my Havanese bitches came into standing heat on a Friday afternoon. She surprised me because she was only eight days into proestrus. However, I believed my male's instincts about what was going on. He was trying desperately to mate her but was not getting the job done. I called my reproduction veterinarian. He had gone away for the weekend. I called another reproduction veterinarian. She was not available. I was able to obtain an appointment with my regular reproduction veterinarian for the Monday following. At that appointment my bitch's smear showed her completely cornified. She was also willing to stand for my male. We performed three AIs (artificial inseminations), one each on Monday, Tuesday and Thursday. Unfortunately, the breeding did not take. Her eggs had evidently died before I could get the two to the veterinarian.

Always remember: the breeding window can be very short, usually only two to three days. (More about AIs later.)

BEHAVIOR OF THE STUD DOG

Nature endows a good stud dog, even before he is a stud, with a marvelous nose. He can smell the sex hormones as they begin their job of preparing the bitch for proestrus. I own a male Havanese who alerts me several weeks ahead of time that one of my bitches will soon be in proestrus. And thank goodness, until she is in advanced proestrus, he will not become so obnoxious with unrequited love I can't stand him around. Yes, he does attempt to mount her before she comes into proestrus, but, because the sex stimulations are not strong enough he'll soon stop. He'll shrug his shoulders (dogs do) and wait. When she does enter late proestrus, you can count on the following preliminary behavior tactics.

One of the first things a stud dog will do is rush around the yard she is in or has been in, looking for her urine. The hormonal influences in her urine tell him exactly where she is in her estrus cycle. He'll race from one urine deposit to another, as if hoping the next one will explain more fully. He will also sample traces of her urine and finally urinate on them, marking them as his property. Only after a thorough ground ritual will he return to her. If he considers her ready, he'll then sniff her nose and ears and neck, lick her ears and neck, lick her vulva and play bow. If she accepts his advances, he'll stand close by her, place one or both feet on her back, mount her and by hit and miss with his now erect penis, find her vulva and thrust excitedly, thrusting faster and faster. If the tip of his penis misses her vulva, he sometimes will ejaculate outside the vulva. The bitch may look back at him in disgust when this happens. However, within seconds, he's back trying again. Each time the tip of his penis strikes the lips of the vulva in his instinctive thrusting, nature introduces another trump card. Nature sends him into an absolute frenzy so that his involuntary thrusting can bring him success. Sexual desire and the consummate need to bring it to the highest point have taken over his whole being. His sperm can reach the bitch's oviduct within 25 seconds of ejaculation. It can be carried there that fast by contractions of the uterus.

If the bitch is taller than the male or too small, insertion may not happen. It is important for novice breeders to realize that the penis enters the vagina lips purely by instinctive touch. Most males will continue thrusting until they ejaculate. If he is successful with insertion, his thrustings become faster and faster until the bulb of his penis enlarges and it is locked inside the bitch's vulva. He will then slowly undo his front legs from her flanks by lifting them and turning around so he is facing away from her. Since the penis is flexible, able to twist 180 degrees without injury, the change of position is not harmful. It is, in fact, beneficial while the penis remains swollen inside the vagina for from several minutes to over an hour. An average tie lasts from 10 to 20 minutes. Many breeders believe the "riper" the eggs are, the longer the tie. I am one of those.

Owners will find most males go absolutely crazy when they reside with a bitch in true estrus. If the bitch is isolated or taken away from them, they howl, they bark and they attempt to prove their territory by marking chairs and tables. They can be almost impossible to control or live with. I learned a lesson early on in my breeding experiences: train your stud dog in obedience. By doing so, he learns good manners. He will be able to listen to you,

even if halfheartedly. My Punxsy, whose 11-month daughter was in flaming true estrus (she had evidently ovulated) the day before he was to make his first appearance in the Novice B obedience ring, was completely unenthusiastic about heeling in practice that evening. However, he did listen to my commands about behaving himself. Since she was taken away from his scenting presence the next morning, he performed as he was supposed to do in the ring and earned his first leg in Novice obedience.

Speaking of "scenting presence," it is not true that the scent of a bitch in true estrus will attract dogs to her home from a mile away. That only happens when she is walked away from her home and thereby leaves a trail of scent. Bitches that are confined to their house and yard confine their scent to their immediate proximity. It is a rarity when a dog, living a distance away, can smell her estrus scent.

It is also not necessary that one has to allow a stud dog, when meeting a bitch on a walk, to become obnoxious trying to examine her private parts. Obedience manner training helps dogs control inappropriate advances. Manners training will not deter them from mating when opportunity comes their way; it only makes them pay attention to your commands so life is easy to be around them.

It has to be noted that many inexperienced dogs mount the bitch at her head until helped by either owner or bitch where to mount. A few males faint upon completion of the tie. In one instance (I was breeding two Portuguese Water Dogs), the tie (his first) was only for three minutes. As the male fell, I thought he was suffering a seizure. Upon discussing the happening with his breeder and several veterinarians, I learned dogs can faint after this act. That is what he did.

DIFFICULTIES

When one attempts to breed a maiden bitch to an inexperienced stud dog, problems can arise. The male may need help in learning how to mount her and the bitch may resent his attentions. She may plunk herself down into a sit whenever he approaches her. While some of her insistence on sitting may be because she is not yet in true estrus, fear and timidity can also overwhelm her. So can aggressiveness. Maiden bitches often recoil when a male penetrates her vagina. Her reproduction organs may be very narrow and insertion is painful. This is one reason it is advisable for your bitch to have a complete examination by your veterinarian before she enters the estrus cycle.

Sophisticated breeders sometimes place a promising male puppy with a mellow and experienced brood bitch for some months and allow her to teach him the intricacies of sexual encounters so that when he becomes old enough he can follow through instinctively, without any help. When he reaches adulthood, he is kept apart from bitches unless they are in a breeding cycle.

However, most of today's breeders enjoy the house companionship of their males and do not keep them separated for future stud purposes. These are the individuals this book is directed to. In consequence many dogs enter stud work without initial direction. As house pets, they have been scolded for attempted mountings, etc. And that is okay. A male of sound temperament and in good health should have no problems albeit he stumble (figuratively speaking) in his introduction to mating. With a little help and direction from knowledgeable breeders, he won't have any problems.

Mating should always be conducted in a quiet and relaxed setting. There are males, however, who are embarrassed when onlookers are around during his foreplay or in initial thrusting at a mating session. If there is no problem with height, sensitivity or temper explosions on part of the bitch, it is best to leave this sensitive type of stud alone until the tie is made. Other inexperienced dogs suffer from "performance anxiety." This is one reason I insist on a visiting bitch to be brought to my premises at the beginning of her heat. I want the two dogs to get to know one another, to play with one another and eat together, so that when the mating days arrive, there is no forced attention from a strange dog. I don't believe in the "Put the bitch on the table here, bring the dog over here, help him insert his penis into her vagina" sort of breeding.

However, because most of our today's dogs are pets first (thank goodness), breeding problems do arise. So it should never be, "Throw two dogs together and they'll do what comes naturally."

Today, few of us want to ship our bitch by plane or car to another area of the country where the stud dog we want to use, lives. And in case you are not aware, stud dogs often do not perform well on strange territory. That is why it is customary to transport the bitch to the male.

Enter artificial insemination.

ARTIFICIAL INSEMINATION

Artificial insemination has been used for mating of cattle throughout the world since the early twentieth century; however, phenomenal growth of AI procedures began in the 1940's. The benefits of AIs in dairy cattle were so enormous, veterinarians began to use AI for dogs around 1950. Interestingly, the first *recorded* insemination on an animal was performed in 1784 and it was on a dog! She whelped three puppies 62 days later.

There are five insemination techniques in use today: they are put into play when the diagnostic aids show the hormone estrogen is falling and the hormone progesterone is rising. 1) Simple artificial insemination called AI (both dog and bitch are present with the semen inseminated into the bitch immediately); 2) Chilled, fresh extended semen (chilled semen is shipped express from the stud's veterinarian to the bitch's veterinarian); 3) Frozen semen (semen which has been taken from a male at some date earlier and the "sperm straws" stored in especial containers); 4) surgical implantation with either fresh, chilled or frozen semen) into the uterine horns; and 5) trans-cervical semen deposits.

The percentage of success for the first three procedures is in the 65 to 75 percent range. The reason is simple. There is diagnostic assistance in pinpointing ovulation such as smears and progesterone assays. Two important diagnostic aids for vaginal cyology are smears (slides of bitch's proestrus discharge) taken every other day usually beginning with day four of proestrus. Smears enable the veterinarian to gauge the stages of cornification before breeding. The progesterone blood assay measures nanograms. Aids and tests depend upon the skilled reproduction veterinarian's readings. And veterinarians are not magicians! A very reliable source is a good stud dog. His nose never fails! This is one reason his searching the ground for the bitch's urine and his intense examinations of each deposit are so important. Yet, too often, breeders fail to allow a visiting bitch and the stud dog to go through this important ritual. Surgical implants and trans-cervical semen deposits came into being to increase artificial insemination success. And they do.

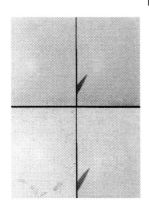

This small sperm sample is not a great collection. Usually billions of sperm can be seen swimming. However, these sperm are swimming straight and fast and no bad sperm are seen.

Before AIs are accomplished, stud dogs need to have sperm collected with a "teaser" bitch (one in either proestrus or standing estrus). The reproductive veterinarian ejaculates the male and places a sperm sample on a slide using a special stain to evaluate sperm. Under the microscope, sperm can be seen swimming in the prostate fluid which protects them. Billions can be seen in a healthy dog's sperm count. Bad sperm are also seen. The percentage of bad sperm is usually

A sperm sample is placed on a slide and immediately placed in a sperm incubator.

about two to five percent. It is important to know the volume and sperm concentration of a stud dog. Believe it or not, many dogs are found to be sterile, to have a low sperm count, or to be infected with some viral or bacterial disease, or prostatitis - findings which go unnoticed in daily living. A waste of time to inseminate or to breed this male! Corrective work can be done with antibiotics or drugs when the cause is found.

All potential breeders should know how to locate a reproductive veterinarian. If you have difficulty locating one in your area, the American Kennel Club is a good reference point, as is the web site for the Society for Theriogenology, http://www.therio.org.

AN INTERESTING ARTIFICIAL INSEMINATION STORY

Before we leave this chapter I wish to present you with this unusual breeding experience. Enjoy! (I did not at the time.)

My male Havanese, Punxsy, had returned from the dog show circuit, a champion. He was a beautiful and valuable young breeding male with a sparkling personality. He was soon asked to be used as a stud dog. Unfortunately, while Punxsy mounted and showed a high rate of excitement when the bitch came into true estrus, he was unable to perform. He could not ejaculate. Two veterinarians could not find a reason for his lack of performance. He appeared to be in excellent health.

Dr. Rick Scherr of the Big Sky Animal Medical Center in Great Falls, who specializes in both cattle and canine artificial insemination matings examined Punxsy thoroughly. Like the first two veterinarians, he could not find any clinical signs of infection or abnormalities.

Punxsy,
Ch Meme Zee's Spirit O Roughrider CD
owned by Kathryn Braund and bred by
Martha and Michael Burns.

"As soon as I find a teaser bitch available," he finally told me, "we will test Punxsy to get a sperm evaluation." When he did, Punxsy produced no sperm.

Dr. Scherr then began questioning me: "Does Punxsy have difficulty urinating or emptying his bladder? Does he seem in pain sometimes? Do you ever see blood in his urine? Does he have constipation? Any difficulty in defecating?" My answer to each question was " no."

"But," I said, "he does seem lethargic at times. Nothing really specific. I have had him checked out several times for that very reason. However, his examinations have not turned up anything. On the surface he appears in fine health. He is such a happy dog."

Dr. Scherr was quiet for a long moment. Then he said, "I'm going to assume Punxsy has a deep-seated bacterial infection of his prostate gland. It can go unnoticed. It's called prostatitis. We will place him on the antibiotic Clavamox for three weeks. When the three weeks are up, we'll recheck him for sperm with another teaser bitch. We'll see if treating him for inflammation of the prostate makes any difference."

It did. In three weeks, Punxsy produced three sperm.

"Good," said Dr. Scherr. "We're on the right track. I'm going to keep treating him with antibiotics for another three weeks. Hopefully, we can resolve this infection. He's picked it up someplace."

I told Dr. Scherr at that time that I had placed Punxsy on a daily calcium vitamin (250 mg) as a part of my herbal and nutritional therapy. Calcium is used to bolster the immune system health and that includes increasing sperm counts. Punxsy was also feasting on a high protein diet. His daily kibble was well supplemented with simmered ground beef mixed with green vegetables.

Three weeks later, in a third test with a teaser bitch, Punxsy's sperm count on the slide showed a fair amount of sperm, all swimming energetically.

"It is possible," Dr. Scherr told me, "that Punxsy, because of prostatitis, and it could be chronic with him, cannot maintain high levels of arousal or achieve penetration with a bitch. His sperm count should now increase since we have located his problem. Prostatitis is difficult to cure. It is often a deep-seated infection which antibiotics do not reach. Continue the high protein diet you have placed him on. When your bitch, Naughty, comes into estrus again, he should be able to breed her via a surgical implantation."

I did not like that idea. "I know this type of artificial insemination is becoming quite popular," I said. "I am against any invasive procedure."

Dr. Scherr explained gently that any type of artifical insemination is invasive. "Fresh inseminations are still only 60 to 65 percent viable. We have a great percentage of success with a surgical implantation."

I acquiesced.

When Naughty came into proestrus two months later, we tested Punxsy again. His sperm count had increased. He did not produce the millions or billions of sperm a good stud dog is able to produce, but the count we looked at under the slide was adequate and the sperm cells were all fast moving and lively. It was a wonderful moment.

Dr. Scherr ran a progesterone test when Naughty was five days into proestrus in order to determine her "baseline progesterone level." Smears were also taken, alternating with the progesterone assays in order to determine the day of the LH surge. Four days after the LH surge, Punxsy was brought into the office, his "teaser bitch" being Naughty. His sperm was checked on a slide.

"Oh, look at them," I exclaimed excitedly.

"A good amount for the surgical implant!" agreed Dr. Scherr. "Not a Roman army, for sure, but all swimming fast and no broken sperm nor twisted tails."

Naughty was given a light sedative and the surgical implantation was made.

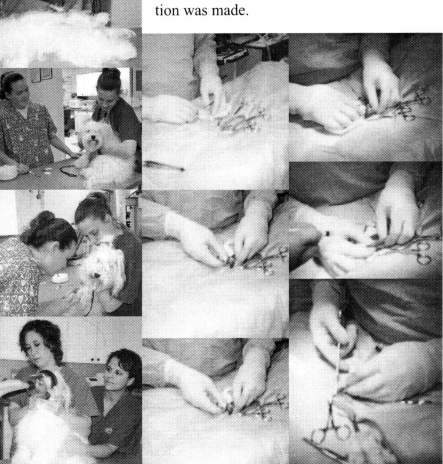

Surgical implantation

First column: Clipping down and gasing.

Second column: Initial cut, first horn, both horns.

Third column: Sperm inside and closing incision.

Naughty was given antibiotics for three days.

No incision marks could be seen by the naked eye.

Sixty two days later, six beautiful puppies were born. They were healthy, happy and blessed with the wonderful temperaments of their mother and father. (I used to believe healthier puppies came from natural breedings. The results of this artificial breeding certainly disproved my belief.)

Shortly after the puppies were placed in their permanent homes, I was told about a supplement used by several canine reproduction organizations to improve reproductive capacity in male dogs and cats where lowered fertility has been diagnosed. It is also used to aid in stabilizing cyclicity in female dogs. Called CF-Plus Fertility Formula, in chewable tablet form, it contains Perna mussel, Brewers yeast and Alfalfa. I placed Punxsy on it, giving him one tablet daily.

In 2004 when Naughty began her second estrus after the birth of her first litter, I immediately called Dr. Scherr. He prescribed a pain killer and an antibiotic for Punxsy. "If his prostatitis is still active," he said, "this should quiet down the infection." We also tested his sperm, using Naughty as his teaser bitch. The slide showed an excellent concentration of quick moving sperm.

Combination smears and progesterone assays were conducted on Naughty. Each progesterone assay was sent away overnight to a laboratory skilled in the evaluation of these blood samples. Results were returned by telephone or fax each morning.

"She should be ready to breed next Tuesday, July 6," said Dr. Scherr on Friday morning, July 2. "Her progesterone assay showed her LH peak occurred yesterday. We'll send out another test Monday morning. Meet me at the clinic again on Sunday morning, the 4th.

Unfortunately, the laboratory was closed Sunday and Monday due to holidays (July 4 and 5). Dr. Scherr tested the progesterone assay done on Sunday in house. (In house assays are not as reliable as those in laboratories which have special equipment.) I appeared with Naughty and Punxsy at Dr. Scherr's clinic on Tuesday morning, July 6.

"Her progesterone is not rising," he told me. "I do not dare perform a surgical implant. If progesterone does not rise, eggs do not mature. The breeding would be for naught. We will send out another assay and I will call you tomorrow with the results. She may have slid into a split heat."

The next morning, Wednesday, July 7, I waited by the telephone. Anxious, I prodded Naughty constantly for flaccidity of her vulva; I also kept checking to see if she would flag her tail. She did not seem ready for breeding to me. But Punxsy, although separated from her, was quite excited. Each time I brought her inside and took him outside, he told me by voice and actions she was ready.

I rushed to the telephone each time it rang. No call came from Dr. Scherr. By one p.m. in the afternoon, I could stand it no longer. I placed Naughty in the car in the front passenger seat and the other Havanese, including Punxsy, of course, in the two large wire crates in the back of my Explorer. I drove the 11 miles to the other side of Great Falls to Dr. Scherr's clinic.

He told me her last progesterone assay still showed only a 2 reading which he felt too low for eggs to mature. But after a brief discussion, an examination of Naughty, a plea from me and hearing about Punxsy's excitement, he decided to AI her with fresh semen. Punxsy was glad to be brought into the examining room. If he could have leapt upon the high table he would have. He was as pleased to be with Dr. Scherr as he was to be with Naughty.

As soon as Punxsy was collected, Dr. Scherr placed a drop on a slide. He returned within a few minutes, grinning. "Come and look," he said.

The slide showed a heavy concentration of sperm, all swimming fast and practically all straight and strong. "How wonderful!" I exclaimed.

"We did it," Dr. Scherr exclaimed. "We brought him back from no sperm to this beautiful example in one year. And he had an exceptional litter last year. He's going to do it again."

He AI'd Naughty with Punxsy's sperm.

The next morning, Thursday, July 8, Naughty was again AI'd with Punxsy's sperm. The concentration of his sperm was not as high as on Wednesday, yet it was good.

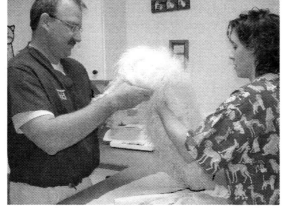

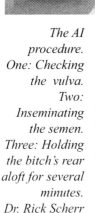

The AI procedure. One: Checking the vulva. Two: Inseminating the semen. Three: Holding the bitch's rear aloft for several minutes. Dr. Rick Scherr and his subject, the author's Naughty.

On Friday, July 9, it became obvious to me by the decrease in her vulva's flaccidity and her lack of flagging that Naughty was going out of estrus. Punxsy was still excited, but that's Punxsy.

Now we would have to wait until nature told us if Naughty was or was not impregnated when her breeding window was open.

Naughty delivered six puppies on September 5, 2004, three boys and three girls, all healthy, all very beautiful.

Long ago I had reservations about artificial inseminations. I believed puppies were healthier puppies with natural breedings. Did the fact that two fresh extended semen breedings, one frozen sperm breeding and three simple AI breedings did not work out influence my thinking?

I have since learned how influential artifical insemination has been in the world's agricultural community. The proof is in the production of superior animals. Dog breeders have a valuable tool in producing quality pure-breds through AI breedings.

SUMMARY

1. Both male and female Havanese should be at least 18 months before being bred, preferably two years of age. OFA hip x-ray preliminary evaluations can be done earlier than two years of age; however, formal OFA evaluation certificates are not given until two years of age. Be sure to have all current HCA health tests performed.

2. Do not place dogs with physical or mental problems in the breeding pool. Breed to the Havanese standard to maintain and increase breed quality. Do your homework. Evaluate pedigrees of ancestors of both bitch and male as well as the siblings of the ancestors. Only select dogs who have had ancestors with the qualities you seek to improve on in the Havanese standard.

3. Have both bitch and dog given a complete physical examination before breeding. Update all their vaccinations; have blood work performed, check for parasitic infection and abnormalities.

4. Isolate the bitch beginning on day four of her proestrus until day 21 of her cycle.

5. Have the reproductive veterinarian conduct a sperm count on the male before you decide to use him as a stud. You need to know his fertility status. Have the reproductive veterinarian check for vaginal obstructions in the bitch.

6. Feed your potential breeding animals from puppyhood on a premium diet, rich in protein.

Chapter Seven
The Bitch in Pregnancy and Lactation

Note: Although some of the material below has been stated earlier, restatement of important facts should not disturb; it is hoped they impress.

It's impossible to tell if a breeding "took" immediately after the dogs have been mated. Nature insists everyone wait. She has made the progesterone levels of a non-pregnant bitch identical to those of a pregnant bitch. The normal wait is 24 days. While it is possible to locate the uterine locules earlier, they would be difficult for a veterinarian to feel externally. Uterine locules are the protective enlargements which protect the growing puppies from conception to whelping. Even 24 days is deemed early to detect the tiny blobs inside the locules that are Havanese puppies. The puppies are only as large as small peas. Skilled hand palpation is accomplished, of course, by veterinarians (don't try it yourself, you could damage the locules). But an accurate count can seldom be made.

My reproductive veterinarian gave my Naughty a cat-scan at 28 days. We saw three little blumps on the screen. "There might be four," he said. "They hide well." She gave birth to six. Another veterinarian several years back told me when he palpated my bitch (another breed) at 32 days with a cat-scan that he thought his count of five was fairly accurate. That bitch gave birth to 13 puppies. We breeders like to have our veterinarians palpate our mated bitches, whether the count is accurate or not. It tells us if our bitches are or are not pregnant.

At about 24 days a bitch is aware something different is going on inside her. However, a first time (maiden) pregnant bitch does not know what pregnancy is. She only feels a necessity to become very close to her owners and engage in a lot of lap hugging in the early weeks of her pregnancy.

Most bitches exhibit morning sickness between day 25 and 30. The locules are moving up from the lower abdomen towards the breastbone by that time and the bitches' stomachs are rebelling. They refuse breakfast or upchuck the morning meal. This lasts only a day or two. Appetite then increases and they begin to look for a bigger and better ration in their dishes. Because it is important to have healthy and robust puppies, at 28 to 35 days into the "hopefully she is pregnant" stage, begin feeding the bitch high quality protein. I do not mean just dog kibble. Give puppy kibble, yes, but I suggest topping it with diced chicken or beef at lunch and dinner time, with a raw egg yolk mixed in with the kibble at breakfast. (See the end of this chapter for suggested diet improvements for pregnant and lactating bitches.)

If a bitch has had a pregnancy before, she'll be leaving most of her kibble in her dish at about 35 days. "Give me food I can digest easier and give me lots of protein," she is telling you as she lifts her beautiful eyes to yours. Listen to her. My suggestion is to bake or simmer chicken and beef roasts, grind up the meat in a food processor, add a few diced green vegetables, and pile these on top of a sprinkle of kibble and vitamin, assuring her a diet that will give her puppies a great nutritional start in life. I am also assured my bitch is enjoying her pregnancy. Eating, after all, is one of the dog's prime drives and being fed meat, fowl and eggs as a daily ration instead of as treats, gives her great pleasure. Some breeders add a pinch of raspberry leaves in the pregnant bitch's food starting at day 35. They claim it makes for easier whelping.

I kept a record of Naughty's diet and how she ate in her first pregnancy. Her second was almost identical. She was off her feed on day 30 and 31 and became ravenous beginning with day 32. That's when I started giving her three meals a day, knowing as the puppies grew, room inside her stomach decreased. She needed smaller and more frequent portions.

On day 40 she pushed away the dish of puppy kibble with its tablespoonful topping of meat and refused to eat it. When I opened the refrigerator and offered her a small piece of chicken, she gulped it down. From that day forward she ate chicken and beef with a sprinkle of kibble each meal. Her appetite was excellent until day 51, when she ate very little the next two days. However, she came begging for meat on day 54 and ate well even in her first stages of labor. That surprised me. Most bitches begin to refuse food eight or more hours before they go into labor. Not Naughty.

Havanese bitches hide their growing puppies very well. However, if a bitch is carrying a large litter, you will notice her sides swelling and her belly tuck-up disappearing at about 35 days. Her hair begins to stick outwards instead of down. I swore, by swelling guestimation, my Naughty had only three or possibly four (yes, I believed what the cat-scan showed) even as she was whelping. Naughty had continued to jump up on laps and chairs and sofas and visitors' laps until only an hour or so before going into labor. And until the eighth week of pregnancy (full term is nine weeks or 63 days), there was no noticeable swelling of her sides and she continued to have a fair amount of tuck-up. Bitches that will have a large litter usually develop what I call "side-cars," which get wider and wider as labor draws near; tuck-up completely disappears.

During the last 10 to 15 days of pregnancy, you can feel the puppies moving inside your bitch. Place your hand on one of her sides as she is relaxed and lying stretched out, as she must do in the last weeks for comfort. Movements of different puppies can be felt. Don't press down hard against her sides; touch her gently. You can also detect heart beats by feel or ear. But don't think you can count accurately. If your bitch is eating smaller and smaller portions of food after 48 days, you can be assured some of her pups are pressing against her breastbone and pushing hard against her stomach. Give her four small meals.

Puppy growth inside the mother is most pronounced five and one half to eight weeks. Cosmetic things, like hair, eyelashes and toenails are perfected the last week before whelping. And about five days before whelping, the tummy drops. The pups are slowly making their way towards the exit.

Some breeders have an x-ray taken of their bitch when she is about 45 days into pregnancy. They desire or feel it is necessary to know how many and in what positions the unborn puppies are in. I believe X-rays are only necessary in an emergency situation. There is radiation from them.

As the bitch nears the end of her term, she will desire to make a nest for her coming brood. Inside the house, bed sheets and blankets are moved about, your clothes pulled down from closet hangers and wadded into a nest on the closet floor, with shoes and other paraphernalia pushed aside. Outside, any small opening under the house

Outside, any small opening under the house is investigated.

or walls or decks are thoroughly investigated, and when the right one is found, she digs a deep hole. This is the time the breeder needs to keep a close eye on her pregnant bitch. It is not easy to pull up newborn puppies weighing 5 ounces from a deep hole under a wall or deck. I am aware many Havanese breeders maintain a tight watch on their bitches and some are never allowed outside on grass (artificial turf is laid down for them so as not to damage coats!). The above paragraph is for those who, like me, allow their Havanese to play in natural yards.

The best thing to do at around day 55 is to put up a whelping box and show the bitch where it is. She will probably look at it askance. Few bitches want to step foot in a whelping box until they go into labor. A bitch much prefers to sleep where she has always slept or to dig her own nest. Do you blame her? It's perfectly okay if she feels that way since when she goes into labor you are going to have that nest all set up for her and you will remain by her side throughout labor and whelping.

On day 53 of her pregnancy, take her temperature with a rectal thermometer. If you have a choice, choose a digital thermometer. It does the job fairly quickly (depending on how much money you want to spend). You are taking her temperature at this time to give you her norm. Some temperatures are at their norm at 101.5, others at 101.3, etc. Jot it down on a piece of paper. You want to remember it. In my early days of breeding, I was told to take my pregnant bitch's temperature twice a day from day 55 on. I did for several years. It was

Tearing at and scratching papers is common and usually announces the first stage of labor.

not necessary and the bitches certainly weren't happy to be poked by the thermometer twice a day for five or eight days. Now I take my bitch's temperature on day 56 and then once a day after that until her whelping.

Why, you ask, is it important to take the bitch's temperature? When she is ready to go into labor her temperature drops. It can go from her norm of 101.5 down to as low as 98 degrees. Be patient. As the end of her term nears, her temperature will probably have a tendency to seasaw, like from 101 down to 100 or 99.9 and back again up above 100. These temperature jumps tell you she is not quite ready but is getting very close to birthing. The puppies are dropping lower and lower in her body. You can almost see them drop down. They want to come out to our world. When her temperature

goes down below 100 and remains there, births are imminent. Well, within 24 hours. Be patient. Difficult to do, I know.

Jasmine, Moorea's Jolie Jasmine Blossom, in labor with helpers Angel, Dahlia and Sue. Jasmine is owned and was bred by Mary Cane.

There are three stages of labor. During labor one the bitch lies on her side; at intervals she shifts her position, panting, scratching papers for a few seconds and then settling back down again and napping. What is happening inside her? Her uterus is contracting as the puppies are getting into position to be born. Settle yourself close beside her – yes, bring her into the whelping room and box. As long as you remain with her she'll settle in – be calm, it might be a long wait. Fill your teacup with tea from the thermos, be sure you have plenty of newspapers (black and white newspapers are not toxic- colors are), towels for drying, washcloths for helping with the birth process, scissors and thread (in case you need to cut and tie off umbilical cords), plus a comfortable chair and pillow and blanket for yourself (a sleeping bag if not a chair, so you can keep close by her). A book you have been meaning to read and didn't have time for earlier is also a necessity. You have time now. I also make sure I have alcohol, peroxide, and a thermometer with a jar of vaseline. Close by the whelping box should be a cardboard box with a hot water bottle or heating pad at the bottom, with towels covering the bottle or pad. You want to place puppies in its warm environment as she is in the throes of whelping another so they don't get caught under her and get covered with goop that goes with whelping. It's best to have a nice garbage bag or two close by in which to stash soiled papers; it's also good to have a warm water sink nearby so you can sponge bathe her as is necessary even though all bitches

Jasmine lies in the whelping box with a huge smile, proud of her puppies.

clean themselves well during birthing. It is immediately afterwards that you want to complete the job for her so she is comfortable. I give mine a "back" bath in a small sink. It only takes a few minutes; she is clean and feels ever so much better.

Bitches deliver their puppies in their own manner. Each pregnancy has different connotations. One never knows what to expect, except! The first born is usually the biggest in the litter, and therefore the most difficult for the mother to expel. As the birth of the first one nears, most bitches will begin tearing or scratching every bit of paper they can find into a huge pile. A few never tear up anything.

At stage one, Naughty jumped out of the whelping box and made her way to the nice warm puppy box, lifted herself into it and sat looking at me as if to say, "Well, when I delivered puppies in my first litter, you placed them in here." I allowed her to sit in the box

Naughty said to me in eloquent body and place language, "You put the puppies in here my last litter. If you put them in here now I won't have to go through labor again."

long enough to take her picture. (A PWD bitch of mine years ago had done the same thing.) When I lifted her out, she put her nose back inside the box and rummaged in it as if looking for puppies. "Sorry, Naughty," I said, "you have to go through all the pain of whelping before I put any in this box." She raised those beautiful Havanese eyes to mine, sighed, went back to the whelping box and began panting.

Steady panting heralds the second stage of labor. At first her panting will come in dribbles and drabs, then in a steady rhythm, her breath becoming louder and louder as birthing is about to happen. Watch her closely. For a brief instant, she will push against the side of the whelping box or against the wall (whatever is handy). Her body is contracting, pushing the puppy to the exit. Write down the time. You will see a contraction every five minutes or every minute and then every few seconds as she is pushing the puppy outward. No. She settled down again. She went back to sleep. Don't take your eyes off of her. There! There is another contraction. She's awake. The uterus has been dilating as the puppies have gotten into position for their delivery. Look at her vulva. Has it enlarged? Dilated? All of a sudden! Whoosh! The water bag breaks. This discharge should be clear-colored telling you this is a normal delivery. If it is black or brown or green, check with your veterinarian (who you have on call). The water bag is the protective sac around the puppy. It smoothes the passage for the puppy into the cervix from one of the two uterine horns where it has grown. The cervix dilates and the puppy slides right down into the vagina. The vulva swells, becoming large, soft and pliable. Her contractions come more frequently. A bubble appears. Whoosh! Here comes the puppy.

She delivers her puppies during the third stage of labor. Most bitches usually have to work very hard expelling the first puppy if it is a big puppy. Sometimes there is trouble; the vulva has not dilated enough, the puppy wants to show up with its hind legs emerging first (which means harder work for the bitch). Head first is easier.

My Naughty posed a new problem attempting to push out her first puppy in her second litter. I've been helping bitches whelp litters for 30 years and I thought I had seen everything but I had never seen this one before. Only the puppy's head emerged. She exerted lots of effort but could not get the rest of it out. I removed the sac so the puppy could breathe and although I have pulled puppies out many times, I could not pull this one out. It was stuck. Stuck hard. I did not want to injure her or the puppy so after 20 minutes of looking at the puppy's head sticking out of Naughty's vulva, I picked her up, carried her to the car and away we went to the veterinarian at 6 a.m. on a Sunday morning. Halfway through town I heard

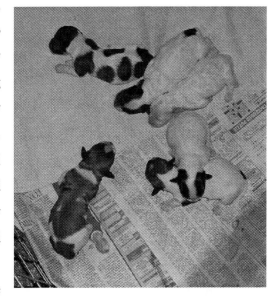

Naughty's puppies. The second from top was born in the car. The other five entered the world without any problems. Three boys and three girls.

the puppy cry. Glancing back to the rear seats, Naughty was cleaning her puppy. Car rides do help expel puppies that seemingly are emergency whelping problems! I had thought when carrying Naughty to the car that this puppy had already died. She and it certainly let me know otherwise. We did go on to meet the veterinarian whom I had awakened. She admired the puppy, we had a good laugh together, and Naughty, the puppy and I returned home. The remaining five entered the world without any problems.

Novice breeders really require the assistance of a mentor in case problems arise, because they often do. The bitch I would worry about would be one frightened at what was happening; the

one who would come running to you crying instead of pushing and helping the puppy come into the world.

As soon as the bitch has delivered the puppy, she will reach out to grab the sac in which the puppy is enclosed and remove the membranes, starting at its head. She then cuts through the umbilical cord with her teeth, consumes the afterbirth which is the placenta (let her, it is full of nutrients and hormones and she will only consume as many as she thinks she needs). She then begins massaging her puppy with her tongue. This gets the puppy's blood circulating. Leave the bitch alone. Instinctively, she knows exactly what to do. When she has finished ministering to her puppy, it crawls off to one of her nipples. As it suckles, it releases the hormone oxytocin in the dam's body and her milk comes down. (The same thing happens when her puppy cries. The dam's brain receives this sensory information and again the crying releases oxytocin and she comforts her baby.)

If she ignores the puppy, is frightened, or looks askance at the bloody membrane which contains the puppy, get hold of the baby and remove the membrane – tear it away quickly starting with the head. Do not allow a puppy to lie alone for more than 30 seconds with his head inside the membrane. The puppy will suffocate. It can also breathe in so much fluid from the sac that holds it that it drowns. As soon as the membrane is removed, hold the puppy with the washcloth, cut the umbilical cord, using the scissors (cut jaggedly which the bitch would do with her teeth; little bleeding occurs with a jagged cut). Tie the stump with thread. Then vigorously massage the puppy. Keep working on it if it is struggling to breathe and you see fluid coming out of its nose. Stand up. Take hold of it securely in both hands, its head towards the floor. Support its head securely. Raise your hands above your head, and swing them straight down. Do this several times, quickly, holding the puppy's head securely. You don't want to snap its neck. It's only a few ounces in size. Fluid should be expelled out of its mouth and nose. Then massage the puppy again. Roll it over and over. I have worked on a puppy for ten to 15 minutes and it has thrived.

Sometimes, puppies need mouth to mouth resuscitation. Blow hard enough to expand its lungs. Reaction from the puppy should occur after three breaths. Keep up the mouth to mouth resuscitation for a minute or so. Fluid should start foaming at its mouth. This, again, is the fluid it breathed in from his sac after it entered the world.

Another respiratory aid is Duprin. You should be able to purchase Duprin from your veterinarian. You only want a single drop of it. One drop in the puppy's mouth right on its tongue. No more than a drop, please. Duprin is a wonderful life saver used correctly, if you are able to secure it.

74

Many mothers work on their puppies bringing them back to life. They use their tongues as swabs, digging deep into the puppy's mouth and throat and nostrils, wiping up fluid. It is an amazing thing to watch, the mother's instinctive intelligent rescue of her newborn, cleaning out the fluid from its lungs in this manner.

Caesarean sections save many bitches and their puppies. Modern surgery has made this a very safe operation and amazingly, the mothers are nursing their newborns within several hours of the surgery. You'll know your bitch may require a Caesarean to save her babies and herself if she is in difficult labor for more than 24 hours; you can tell she is exhausted and she is unable to deliver a puppy. Get her to the veterinarian you have on call.

Be sure to watch your bitch carefully. Many times bitches become so exhausted after delivering and caring for several puppies, they don't even notice another arriving. Never leave the whelping box with the mother in labor.

Alita and family. Alita is Tmist Alita ROM and is owned by Janet and Scott Hicks. Breeder is M. Morris.

NURSING

Newborns waste no time in getting to their mother to nurse. Even the 4 ouncers have strength enough to get there. A weak puppy might not be able to nurse at first. It can survive 12 or more hours without feeding; however, the rate of survival increases if you hold the puppy up to a nipple and with your free hand massage the dam's teat and squirt her milk right into its mouth. I have done this rather than giving a formula since the first milk from the dam contains colostrum, which protects the puppy from puppy diseases for about eight weeks. If the mother's milk has not yet come down enough for it to make a stream, collect what you can get from massaging her teat into a small sterile syringe and inject the drops collected slowly into the puppy's mouth. Formulas should be used as a last resort. My suggestion is pasturized goats milk, warmed. Realize a newborn only takes several drops each feeding and it must be fed every two hours. It is sleepless time for at least several weeks if you have to feed a litter of puppies every two hours. I've done it three times in whelpings over the years. It's a sleepless interval, for sure. A tough time.

I emphasize that if a bitch is healthy and optimally fed during her last four weeks of pregnancy, she will produce an ample supply of milk that becomes available, if not several days before her whelping, within 24 hours post whelping.

Feed her lightly for three days post whelping. If she has consumed the placentas she has received from them ample hormones and protein to help sustain her protein requirements the first few days. My suggestion is to feed her cooked oatmeal or cream of wheat; a raw egg and a teaspoonful of karo syrup mixed in it, with a topping of goat's milk several times a day. Dams thrive on such meals for about three days. It takes that long for queasy stomachs to settle down. My Naughty, in both of her litters, pushed away the cereal dish that I placed down for her at the end of three days post whelping. In fact, her habit in each of her two whelpings was to pull newspapers with her teeth from the floor of the litter box and cover up the dish.

Naughty with her 14 day old puppies. Look at that famous Havanese smile.

She explained in no uncertain terms she did not want such a diet any longer. So I opened a can of chicken breast meat, served it 3/4 chicken to 1/4 kibble and it disappeared in a flash. During her lactation, I alternate one of her four meals daily with blended beef roast, and the other three meals are heavy with simmered chicken and a vitamin with a sprinkle of kibble. She relishes milk bones too.

Along with her intense fastidiousness – she did not like to lie on blankets when feeding her puppies – she preferred to lie on newspapers so she could chew holes where there was a trace of puppy elimination and thus in a corner discard the evidence! Naughty is a very intelligent matron and one who insists doing things her own way. What a wonderful brood bitch, such an intelligent dog!

You may have to take your bitch on collar and leash outside to eliminate after she whelps her puppies. I do for several days, so intent is my bitch on remaining with her puppies. At the end of that period she knows by your actions that they are safe when she is away. Although I have other dogs and they are always free in the house, I put up a gate to the puppy room and enclose the whelping box in a double x-pen. My bitches are praised every

Savannah and puppies are owned by Sandra Barnes, Mischief Havanese. Savannah's breeder is Lynn Nieto. Sire of the litter is Ch Los Perritos Re-Fried Beans, also owned by Sandra Barnes.

time I enter the room, when visitors come to admire the litter from outside the room gate; no dog is allowed to come into the whelping room where the puppies are. This, I believe, is this bitch's very special time. Each bitch in my house knows this and I have always had very proud, loving and attentive dams.

Towards the end of the first week, she will leave her puppies to go outside by herself, but not for long. Gradually her food dish should become fuller. One has to be careful not to overfeed. Newborns suckle only small amounts of milk at each feeding and overproduction of milk often leads to swollen or caked breasts, which are painful to the dam. Puppies then are unable to nurse from them. Check the two back breasts daily when you wash her breasts. If they become swollen and caked, take her temperature and check her out with your veterinarian.

Beef, chicken, eggs, beef liver and milk all stimulate milk production. An all purpose vitamin is a must. So is water. A bitch will often drink a full pan of water before going into the litter box to feed her puppies. So be sure to keep the water dish continually full with fresh water.

As the weeks go by, her breast milk becomes more concentrated. In fact, it reaches the richest concentration about the fifth week of lactation. So her food requirements should triple at the fourth and fifth weeks. Serious weaning of the toy Havanese by the dam usually begins during the sixth week. Milk treats are given until the eigth or tenth weeks, depending on the bitch and her diet during lactation.

Naughty's puppies do not begin eating the food I put down for them until the middle of their fifth week of life. That is how excellent a bitch's milk can be. It is usually a waste of time to offer Havanese other than dam's milk before the fourth week. Their stomachs must develop enough to handle digestion of other foods. The puppies need to be walking fairly well, not wobbling about. Activity encourages normal elimination, which is also important.

The bitch's coat thins during lactation. At Naughty's second pregnancy I left her coat full, only using clippers on her breasts. However, by the end of her lactation, while it did not thin greatly, it thinned enough to tell me that adequate weaning was essential by the end of the sixth week.

Pregnancy, whelping and lactation for your bitch should be a wonderfully rewarding period of her life. Good food, wonderful offspring and extra admiration and attention make for a brood bitch's complete happiness.

For the breeder, it is an emotionally rewarding, and at times a heartbreaking and very expensive hobby.

Good luck.

Chapter Eight

From Birth Through the Toddler Period

Have you ever seen the head of a newborn puppy? It may have been a purebred dog like a Havanese, a Greyhound, or a Portuguese Water Dog. It may have been the head of a mixed breed. In each case, the shape of the puppy's head is practically identical. It is globular. Eyes are sealed. Ears are sealed. The puppy at birth can only smell, taste, swallow and cry. Only as the puppy develops does the shape of his head, like the shape of his body, change. With the changes, the puppy develops into the type of dog it will become. Watch as the baby teeth disappear and permanent teeth erupt. Jaw lengths change. Then when the teeth are well set into the jawline and adolescence disappears, ah! There is a dog with a completely different aspect.

Let's share an up-to-date look at puppy rearing from birth through the toddler period - hour one through the 20 weeks of life. The experiences and lessons learned in this all-inclusive critical period are vital to a better way of life for both dogs and their owners.

Following through with sound litter and toddler socialization should remove many reasons millions of dogs each year are doomed to throwaway fates. It should eliminate some canine emotional stresses, thus lowering stress-related diseases and behavior problems.

Many of us, in this busy modern age, breed dogs as an avocation. We are not able to spend as much time as we'd like with the puppies we rear. However, quality of time spent with puppies is an important ingredient in shaping future behavior patterns.

American researchers, John Paul Scott (1950) and M.W. Fox (1971), in particular, performed studies which show the experiences puppies have during critical periods in their early lives influence behavior in their later lives. Their books have given us excellent insight into these periods. So too have Katherine A. Houpt, VMD, PhD and Thomas R. Wolski DVM in their book, "Domestic Animal Behavior" (1982).

Objective studies by ethologists show that vital animal imprinting begins in hour one of life. That puppies who are bonded to humans during both the neonatal (1-2 weeks) and transitional (3 weeks) period respond by developing faster mentally and physically. They also exhibit greater confidence throughout the entire socialization period.

This makes it obvious that preweaning (suckling) socialization of puppies is important to the emotional evolutionary progress of the dog just as is the practice of mating sound dogs important to the physical evolutionary progress of the dog.

Where early open behavior is fostered during the prime socialization period (4-12 weeks), few shy, backward, sound or touch shy puppies develop. This will not be true, of course, where temperament defects are genetically well established.

Millions upon millions of puppy buyers purchase puppies who have been adversely imprinted during their early weeks. These puppies have been programmed, often unconsciously so by their breeders, to grow up with behavioral problems. The faulty characteristics may not show up until the puppy is five to seven months old; oftentimes the behavior does not appear until the puppy becomes an adult. The affected dog is difficult to live with and extremely hard to train.

Built-in behavior defects are just as tragic as puppy deaths because they eventually alienate owners from their pets and pave the way to "humane" obliteration.

Other studies into canine behavior suggest that the majority of dog owners do not realize how important socialization is to their puppies during the juvenile period (10 weeks to sexual maturity), particularly in the weeks 10 to 20.

I say there are five critical periods:

1) Neonatal period (1-2 weeks)

2) Transitional period (3 weeks)

3) Period of Socialization (4-10 weeks)

4) Toddler period (10-20 weeks)

5) Juvenile period (20 weeks to sexual maturity).

Each new period builds upon the last one.

The toddler dog, unlike the toddler child, is physically adept. Mentally, he toddles (progresses slowly). He is as deeply influenced by experiences or lack of them in this period as is the child.

Puppies who do not receive a wide range of experiences in the toddler period often become emotionally deprived. As an example, if toddler puppies are subjected to sound or touch vicissitudes or are physically abused, the early positive imprinting done by the breeder is negatively modified.

What exactly is imprinting?

Webster defines imprinting "as an indelible distinguishing effect or influence," which "stamp the characteristics."

The Austrian ethologist, Konrad Lorenz (1957), established imprinting as occurring during a definite and short period of an animal's life.

Imprinting is not irreversible, yet the following statement made by Dr. Scott gives one pause: "While previous learning may be altered by subsequent learning, subsequent learning will never obliterate previous learning."

Let's take a sample healthy puppy litter beginning at its birth and cultivate it in several imprintable weeks, seven days at a time. We'll give the litter optimum human bonding and socialization. We'll divide the puppies' development and the breeder's prime duties into the following sections, where applicable:

1) General

2) Muscular and Nervous system development

3) Eyes, ear, teeth

4) Temperament development, including socialization and training needs

5) Breeder's prime duties.

Bear in mind that the development of a fetus is well documented. Development begins at the head and works backward. Thus, the physiological functions of the newborn healthy puppy are well established. While the newborn puppy's brain matter is bland, it is definitely formed. At birth the puppy can cry, he can crawl, he can smell, he can suckle and he responds to touch. The remainder of his motor responses are sluggish; leg muscles are undeveloped, therefore he cannot walk. He can push himself on his rear legs and does very well kneading his mother's breasts with his front ones. He can't see and he can't hear. His eyes and ears are glued shut and just as he is born before he can walk, see or hear, he's born before his heating mechanism has developed. At birth he is unable to generate warmth within himself.

Yet nature, prudent in everything, has made it possible for the newborn puppy to defend himself from the cold. He concentrates on remaining close to a prime heat source (his mother).

His response to heat is positive. Let him respond to your heat; let him feel you radiate affection. Just because he can't see or hear and can't be aroused emotionally through these senses, gentle fondling stimulates his heart muscles; consequently your contact quickens the development of both mental and motor responses.

As the pup suckles, emotional alliance of puppy to dam is bonded; as the pup is cuddled, emotional alliance of puppy to human is also bonded.

An innate prolepsis of nature is that nourishment must begin at birth for favorable development.

Let's set our scene.

Our four by five feet whelping box is deliberately placed in a laundry room, close to all normal house sounds. The laundry room houses a washer and dryer. Their daily use acclimates pups to modern machinery noise; so much a part of their future lives.

The whelping is over. The dam has been cleaned, fed and praised; the box has been scrubbed and turned into a puppy litter box. Fresh papers have been laid on the floor. Over these, a blanket has been spread (the blanket is wrapped around a square board which holds the blanket in place). The blanket will afford necessary soft traction (preferred by puppies) so body and leg msucles are able to develop correctly. Newborn pups should never have to crawl on newspapers, which give neither softness nor traction.

The pups, six of them, are being taken out of the small heater and towel lined box where they had been placed for safekeeping. As each pup is lifted out it is stroked and cuddled. It roots, sniffs and contentedly cuddles in the breeder's hands and arms.

The pups had been placed on the puppy scale when born. Here are the birth weights of the six: the three boys are 8 ounces each; two of the three girls are six ounces with the smallest 5 ounces.

FIRST WEEK - Day 1 through day 7. Puppies are one week of age on day 7.

General - First Week: To the uninitiated, newborn puppies look like rodents. The knowledgeable breeder, with an eye for a dog, sees in the simple lines of the wet newborn a glimmering of what future structure is going to be like. Then, when watching pups as they seek their first food, the breeder gains a glimpse of future temperament.

Muscular and Nervous System Development - First Week: While the central nervous

A newborn from a Roughrider litter.

82

system is not yet wired in to a heavy-duty plug, as it were, facial muscles develop as puppies feed. Towards the end of the first week, even the smallest pups are able to suckle lustily.

A Sweet Honesty litter, one day old, bred by Meta Von Hout. Her kennel is in the Netherlands.

Body and leg muscles develop as pups crawl to a nipple, root and push and support themselves while feeding. Sleep twitching stimulates muscles.

From the very beginning some pups turn themselves sideways and upside down as they nurse. They begin to hold their tails straight out when milk comes down. This marks the beginning of the use of tails as balance implements.

Newborn pups sleep close to one another, almost in a circle, all touching. If they are not warm enough, they sleep in a pile.

Contented pups do not cry. Crying is initiated when they awake and the mother is not near, when they are hungry, hot, cold or sick. Newborn Havanese are impatient when their mother is not at their side. "Mom, where are you?" they cry out. Havanese newborns have quite loud voices even at six and eight ounces.

The dam stimulates a great deal of feeding by licking her pups with her tongue. She also stimulates all elimination with her tongue, lapping it up, keeping her puppies clean and sweet smelling.

Two day old puppies of a Roughrider litter. Naughty refused to leave them on a blanket the first week of their lives. She would pick them up in her mouth to carry them away. That is dangerous, so they spent their first days on paper.

At about the fourth day of life, the puppies' temperature mechanism begins working. Pups can now shiver to gain warmth or move off by themselves if they are hot. However, they still chill easily. It is

vitally important to maintain temperature in the litter box room at 80 or 85 degrees the first week. Forget about the mother. Pups cannot thrive in cold rooms. Warmth allows them to use their nourishment to grow instead of using it to keep warm.

Eyes, Ears, Teeth - First Week: Eyes and ears are sealed the entire week. Teeth buds are growing in the gums, but not yet felt.

Temperament development, including socialization and training needs - First Week: Mental abilities can be seen during the initial suckling experiences. All newborn puppies instinctively gravitate to the nipples closest to the dam's rear - the linguinal area - where the most milk is found. Bigger pups remain there. Pups that cannot suckle well enough to bring down milk from large teats, scramble away and jostle each other for milk at the lesser teats.

You can gain temperament information as the pups move to the bitch to feed. While all pull forward with front legs and push with the back legs, each does so differently. One may prefer to push forward favoring the crawl; another slides along in a belly flop, still another propels himself with a version of the side stroke. They can stretch straight out on their tummies even at the first feeding. Some have the ability to grasp a nipple quicker than others. A few are not able to find a nipple even after repeated tries. They'll voice their complaint immediately. (Early suckling difficulties may point out health problems that often show up in the next few weeks.)

Future behaviors are so apparent at birth. Some puppies begin crying fresh out of mother, impatient to get to their mother's nipple. Others cry when they can't grasp a nipple quickly or when mother gets up and leaves them. A few are silent and root patiently, never uttering a sound of impatience. There is always one pup in each litter who likes to sleep with his head on the up curve - high up on the dam's breast. And he moves there quite deliberately after feeding, knowing exactly where he is going. Several lazily slide back to the floor after nursing and curl up. Still others move to their mother's hind or front end to cuddle in the warmth between her legs. Each one reacts differently in an identical situation. Each displays characteristics that set it apart from all the others as it adapts to the world.

Towards the end of the week, on the fifth or sixth day, well nourished puppies will spread themselves out in the litter box, never alone but with one or two others. Their mother (and you) are doing a great job.

All grunt, cry (whine) and squeal. They sound like baby crows or piglets and not at all like dogs. Each puppy has a distinct voice, even at birth.

Breeder's Prime Duties - First Week:

Place small puppies on larger teats periodically and massage these teats until milk comes down. Supplement weak puppies. While puppies do not establish definite nipple hierarchies as do the young in some other animal species, you're equalizing litter behavior as well as growth by changing nursing teat order.

Change blankets, sheets and papers at least twice a day. With a washcloth, warm water and a teaspoonful of Ivory soap, wash floor.

Give the dam a "back" bath daily as needed to wash away blood, stains, etc. Wipe her tummy with a warm water soaked clean wash cloth, then dry it.

Weigh the puppies daily. Use a kitchen scale, the type with a deeply cupped removable tray is ideal because it can contain a squirming puppy fairly well. Of course, place a warm, dry washcloth on the tray before placing the puppy on it. Hold your hands above the pup or on the pup without pressing your weight down; don't disturb the accuracy of the scale. The warm washcloth and your hand soothes the puppy. Some are going to squirm. Some sniff, investigating where they are. Be sure to hold the puppy close to your cheek after the weighing ceremony is over.

Pick up puppies several times a day: stroke, rock and nuzzle them. Your physical contact bonds them to you. Stimulation quickens the development of mental and motor responses. Newborn pups respond by moving towards you, rooting, sniffing your skin or clothes and nestling in your warmth. It's a good thing to know that stroking (even just touching) is very calming to a puppy. It is necessary for normalacy.

Be sure to take them to your veterinarian at day two, three or four to have dewclaws removed. (The only dog of mine which injured a dewclaw was a Havanese because hers were not removed by the breeder.) Dewclaws are very difficult to trim on Havanese. Why? They are difficult to find under hair and Havanese seem to regard nail trimming as a weekly abuse session. The task of trimming nails once a week is so much easier on both human and dog without dewclaws to search for and trim. Some complain that it is cruel to remove dewclaws, "very painful for the puppy." Nonsense. As each is taken out of the box away from their littermates, they begin to cry. They stop when held gently in the veterinarian's hand until the cut is made which eliminates the dewclaw. Then they cry out in anger, more than in hurt. As soon as they are placed back in the box, they become quiet. Dewclaw removal on a newborn is no big thing. Removing dewclaws at an older age is painful; in addition they then take a long time to heal. It would be cruel to remove them. Do it, please at two,

three or four days into life. At dewclaw removal my veterinarian also gives each puppy a thorough examination. He listens to their hearts, examines their mouths, umbilical cord remains, private parts, and checks for any congenital problems.

Weight gain of well-fed puppies on day seven is usually about five to seven ounces.

SECOND WEEK - Day 8 through day 14. Puppies are two weeks of age on day 14.

General: The rodent look is now giving way to a definite puppy look. Heads are still bigger in proportion to the rest of the body.

Cheney, 10 days old, is from Cherie Belcher's "Elections 2004" litter. The four puppies were born 11/03/04, election day! Mom is Ch Tejano's Hidden Treasure.

Muscular and Nervous System Development - Second Week: Front legs, because of constant kneading and pushing against their mother's teats as puppies nurse, are developing well. During this week, usually about the 12th to 13th day, puppies push their bodies up by their front legs and sometimes, stand for a brief moment before falling over. The back legs do not yet have the strength to keep them in a standing position. Most continue to attempt to stand, do stand and whoops! they wobble and fall down immediately. So puppies still must crawl to nurse. The mother during this week moves about be-fore allowing her puppies to nurse. She cleans one, then another, all the time changing her place slightly in the litter box. This greatly exercises leg muscles as the puppies attempt to remain with her. Her movement also stimulates voice muscles for the pups cry out, "Let me eat," until she settles down in one spot and each can grab on to a tit and nurse. A third benefit of her moving about performing her cleaning chores is that scent glands and hearing are exercised as the pups scramble to locate their mother. Healthy, well-fed puppies spend only seconds staying awake after being fed. Their long sleep periods are punctuated with movement - their bodies twitch, their legs jerk - they even squeal.

Eyes, Ears, Teeth - Second Week: We need to begin cutting toenails towards the end of this week. Long toenails are sharp against the mother's teats. I suggest the use of a cosmetic scissors because nails are still very thin. Eyes usually begin opening at about the eighth day, ears at the same time. The process is very slow in Havanese. Although you may see wide-open eyes, protective film has to be absorbed. This takes several weeks. Some puppies appear to hear sound during the latter part of this week but they do not yet react as puppies of larger breeds would. You can observe the minute widening of space where ears have been sealed together.

Temperament development, including socialization and training needs - Second Week: When awake, puppies begin to investigate blanket and newspaper textures. They also begin selecting places where they want to sleep in the litter box. There is usually one puppy in a litter who wanders off to sleep by himself unless he is too cold or too hot. Prime development this week is in body and muscle growth and in scenting where their mother is in order to feed and be cleaned. The puppies' grasp of their mother's teats are so strong that beginning this week one is often carried aloft as their mother departs the nest. The puppy drops someplace other than where the remainder of his brothers and sisters are. He'll probably go to sleep on the spot, but upon awakening an hour or more later, depending on how he is emotionally put together, he'll begin squealing in terror or frantically crawl this way and that searching for his mother. Then again, he may calmly rest where he has fallen until he hears or smells his mother's return.

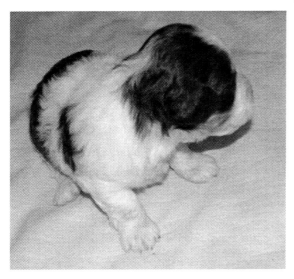

At the end of two weeks, as eyes are opening, a puppy can sit up. Front legs are strong enough to hold him in this position for an instant or two.

At each of your visits, pick up each puppy, rub its body close to your cheek and talk softly to it. You might not receive much reaction, however touching and being stroked is necessary, as stated earlier, for normalancy in a puppy. When someone touches you tenderly, you might not openly respond; however, your inner being absorbs the caress, making you feel good. So too does it to the puppy. Oops! The moment you place a puppy on a scale or other object, it begins squirming and squealing. A cold scale is not a soothing touch.

Weights: Healthy, well-fed puppies gain an average of from four to six ounces this week.

THIRD WEEK. Day 15 through day 21. Puppies are three weeks of age on day 21.

General: Puppies now look like dogs. They have developed a puppy smell. It is soft, furry-like and silky. It is a clean and cozy odor.

Muscular and Nervous System Development - Third Week: Depending on the litter, pups begin wobbling on all four paws by the end of the week. They place most of their weight on rear pasterns and hocks. They wag their tails as they walk. They begin to mouth one another. Haunches and back ends serve as seats as they learn to sit and turn their heads about. With their noses, they investigate everything they come in contact with. However, their periods of investigation are very brief. They wobble one second and the next fall asleep where they fell. They do seek out their brothers and sisters and the litter usually sleeps in a tight group. Awake, they seek their mother.

They melt against your cheek when you pick them up and hold them. But they do not like the scale on which they are weighed. Even with a cloth on it, they resist being placed there. Their mother still cleans them, vigorously so. It's fun to see one being carried aloft when their mother leaves her suckling brood, it latches so tightly to her teat.

Eyes, Ears, Teeth - Third Week: Eyes are open but glassy. Puppies see light but they cannot focus, objects are still blurs. If eyes are a lighter shade, the final shade will be a lighter eye. The darker a newborn's eye, the darker the final shade. Puppies still cannot discriminate where sound is coming from. It is still difficult for them to discriminate where the correct source of a smell is coming from. No teeth are felt in gums yet.

Temperament development, including socialization and training needs -Third Week: The puppies world revolves upon their mother. Suckle, sleep, wobble, eliminate; suckle, wobble and sleep. Sleep, both quiet and active sleep takes up the better part of each 24 hours. However, an astute breeder is discovering temperament. One puppy explores his small environment every moment awake; another shakes with fear when picked up; a third finds a corner in which to sleep away from the others; a fourth enjoys hearing himself yodel, which he performs quite loudly when off by himself - he's lost and lonely; the fifth and sixth are content to enjoy their long naps, suckling and wobbling expeditions without any open

At three weeks, Cherie Belcher's Dubya learns he has a voice. He could be saying, "Hi Kerry" to his littermate.

displays. Each action and non-action are signs of future dispositions: highly curious, shy, confident and self disciplined, open clownish, and laid back. Decisions as to temperaments are also dependent on how each puppy is developing. If weights are unequal, some puppies small and some large, compensation has to be made. Mental development at this stage of a newborn's life depends in large part on physical development.

Breeder's Prime duties - Third Week: Keep the litter box clean. Give the dam back baths as required to eliminate bloody discharge (normal for about four to five weeks). Groom her daily. At Naughty's first litter I cut her coat down to about two inches and with a number 10 blade on my clippers kept her teats clear of any hair. I left her hair long during her second pregnancy and lactation period, combing and brushing her coat her each morning. Her hair thinned only slightly; I was glad I left her coat in its natural length.

From the third day after birth until about five weeks, dams cannot be trusted to leave blankets or papers untouched. It is as if they have 'hot flashes,' and must scratch and tear to relieve these hormonal attacks. Their puppies need watching so they are not smothered or hurt.

Naughty is also a very fastidious dam; if she missed cleaning her puppy and a spot of urine was on paper or blanket, she would pull the blanket away and/or scratch up the paper into a ball and carry it over to the side of the litter box. She preferred her puppies to be on paper (I didn't!) I anchored blankets down on a board so she refused to lie on them.

Kerry, Dubya and Cheney are seeing what the world looks like. They are from the Elections litter bred by Cherie Belcher, Tejano Havanese.

Check your dam's breasts twice a day. Overfeeding swells them and makes them hard to touch. My Naughty demanded five meals a day the first several weeks so I always checked her breasts before and after she nursed. Caked breasts and masititus are very unpleasant times for both bitch and breeder.

FOURTH WEEK. Day 22 through day 28. Puppies are four weeks old on day 28.

General: Most Havanese are not ready to begin to be weaned this week. If they are still unsteady on their feet, just wobbling about, you do not accomplish much. Importantly, tummies are still very immature and the puppies will resist your attempts to teach them to lap.

Puppies first meal.

Try it only if dams are becoming exhausted. Whistle each time you bring food to the puppies. The first several attempts - you on the floor beside the pups pushing their noses into the dish to initiate their tasting and lapping - will be without much success. Let the mother in to clean up the dish. My Naughty does not like milk and after a few laps she walks away from the dish. Forget about beginning weaning puppies this week if dam and puppies are healthy. Keep the litter room warm. Remember, puppies chill quickly and easily.

Muscular and Nervous System Development - Fourth Week: Most Havanese puppies spend this week, as last, sleeping like zombies, except for muscle movement. Systems now allow them to eliminate by themselves. If they use their blankets for elimination purposes, increase paper in the litter box; decrease the paper area if all wobble off the blankets to use it to eliminate. Most dams continue to keep their nests clean. Pups do begin walking steadily a few steps before falling down although weight in rear legs is still placed on hocks. When awake they investigate everything they come in contact with.

Eyes, Ears, Teeth - Fourth Week: You can open the shades on the windows or pull wide the curtains in the daytime. Their sight is improving. They still have trouble distinguishing where sounds and smells are coming from. No teeth are felt yet, although tooth forms can be seen in the gums.

Temperament development, including socialization and training needs - Fourth Week: Most of each 24 hours is spent in sleep and consequent growth. Each time you enter the litter box room pups will awaken and wobble over to where the gate or entrance to the litter box is. Carry them several times a day to the second litter box which you have set up either in the kitchen or living room. Make sure their mother is waiting for them there.

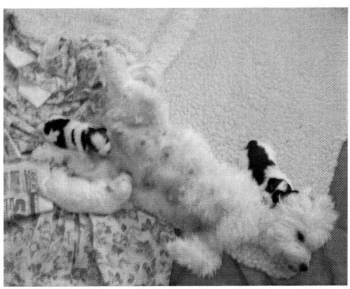

Naughty enjoying feeding time.

Their mother's presence instills confidence. Place brightly colored toys in this litter box, particularly balls of all sizes. They will leave their mother alone long enough to play with littermates and investigate the furnishings in this litter box.

In Naughty's second litter, as I picked up one puppy to carry it to the living room x-pen, she began shaking violently. It did not matter that I was gentle and held her close. She did not stop shaking. This puppy had reached the initial plateau of discrimination and she could not accept my moving her away from a comfort zone. I was dismayed. This beautiful puppy was saddled with a shy gene. As soon as I placed her in the x-pen with her littermates, she calmed, comfortable because she was with her littermates. I watched her closely for a minute thinking back on the many times I had held her since she was born. She was not fearful. She was shy, finding it difficult to cope with environmental changes. Not only would I have to single her out for extra tender loving care (TLC), I would have to get her used to all kinds of environment. Please let me digress for a moment. I am going to quote from my book, *"Devoted to Dogs."*

Shyness: Fear and shyness in an animal are two separate terms. Although dogs under human mismanagement may become fearful of many things and are called "shy," all creatures are fearful of certain environmental happenings. Many are afraid of the dark, fearful of the noise of thunder, yet are strong and stoic in all other respects. Exposure to certain environmental stimuli may produce fear in creatures just as exposure to certain chemicals may produce

allergen. In dogdom dogs that are shy are sometimes called dogs with 'wild genes.'

Dogs, like all creatures, have a full range of behavior and emotions as do humans. It's part of nature's sense of balance and symmetry. The package of genes in each dog helps determine its level of sensitivity to events and environments as well as its innate activity level - which may range from active to quiet. There are many, many dogs with high levels of sight or sound sensitivities that are not given the opportunity to adjust to a myriad of human environments in a positive manner. There are certain imprintable times when hormone concentration rises when these onslaughts permanently imprint the dog. This frequently happens to dogs with high intelligence.

Is the shy dog really forever terrified, cowardly, untreatable, thus untrainable? Or can it, in wondrous unfolding of character, exhibit strength and bravery and prove intelligently pliable once it is unburdened of its extremely reflexive sensitivity to outside stimuli?

J.P. Scott and J.L. Fuller ("Genetics and the Social Behavior of the Dog", 1965) in close scrutiny of the social problems afflicting dogs, proved in numerous studies that both genetic and environmental conditions affect the personality of the dog. Many other experiments in breeding attest to the fact that patterns of behavior are inherited and that innate shyness is the result of more than one inheritance factor. What they are is mainly undetermined at this time for so complex is the brain, with its billions of cells and myriad nerve trails, each weaving its own destined path through the body, that the mystery of how any living creature moves and breathes and thinks is not easily surrendered to man's probing.

There are many researchers who believe that color of the dog is, in part, responsible for the dog's temperament. The late great Obedience pathfinder, Blanche Saunders, believed color affected a dog's temperament and its ability to be trained. But she emphasized that since color dominants vary with breeds, "one must first determine the dominant color in a breed to know what the color influence may be."

Although shy dogs may arrive in our world whelped from nervous, frightened, anxious parents and exhibit the same tendencies, other shy dogs are whelped out of normal parents and have come down through strains in which no nervous-tainted behavioral reflexes have been displayed for many generations. Also, offspring of a shy parent may show no tendency towards shyness at all.

To breeders, the spook in the canine breed closet is the shy dog. Open the door and they tumble out in every conceivable type of coat and in every pad size - these behavioral disorders are strangers to no particular breed.

These are scenes from the
Eukanuba dog show, 2004.
This show is one of the most
prestigious dog shows
in the world.

Shown above top is a group of
Havanese being judged.

The middle photo is of Sheryl
Roach with American Dutch
French Luxembourg Belgium
Champion Alan V.'T. Leurse
Hoefpad on the table ready to be
examined by the judge.

The bottom photo is a close-
up view of Alan with Sheryl
at the Eukanuba show

A

Top: Cheryl Drake is the owner/handler of Mia, who was the Number 1 Havanese in Canada 2003. Mia's full name is Am/Can Ch BPIS Mia V'T. Leurse Hoefpad.

Middle left: Beanie is a black Parti and his registered name is Ch Los Perritos Re-Fried Beans. Beanie belongs to Sandra E. Barnes, Mischief Havanese.

Middle right: This black Irish Pied bitch, who goes by the nickname of Scorcher is Ch Los Perritos Paws of Fire. She is handled in this photo by her owner Natalie Armitage. The judge is Mrs. Lydia Coleman Hutchinson. Breeders are Lynn Nieto and Troy Lewman. Natalie's husband Russell is co-owner.

Bottom right: Smudge. Ch Tapscott's I'm A Hottie. Bred by Pamm and Jeanne Tapscott and owned and always handled by Gloria S. Dittmann, DawnGlo Havanese.

Bottom left: Ch Janizona Elegance in Motion, who goes by the call name of Elle, is owned by Janet and Scott Hicks. Breeders are Janet Hicks and Terri Pike.

B

Top: Jenny, Ch ERAS Camelot's Hope of 3V'S, went Best of Breed at the Elgin KC in 2004 with owner Lynne M. Van Slyke showing her. Judge was Mrs. Carole A. Beattie. Jenny is owned by Lynne and breeder Marjorie L. Staniszeski.

Middle: Phoebe, Ch Los Perritos Overlook Salsa, was the first Havanese bitch to earn an AKC championship. Phoebe was sired by Falco V. Nonpariel out of Los Perritos Jodi Guacamole. Her breeders were Lynn and Jose Nieto. Her owners are Russell and Natalie Armitage.

Bottom left: Feliz, Ch Tapscott's Feliz Navidad winning a Group 3. Sire is BIS Ch Westcreek Hot Shot Tapscott ROM and dam is Beautiful Carlita von Salzetal. Breeder/ owners are Pamm and Jeanne Tapscott.

Bottom right: Sasi, AKC/Can Ch Wincroft's Double Stuff and More is owned by Barbara and Michele Johannes. She was bred by Renee Jarboe and Jeannette Stark. Sasi was six months and one day old when awarded an Award of Merit at an HCA National Specialty. She was also the first puppy to win Best Puppy, Winners Bitch and an Award of Merit.

Bydand is Daisy's breeders' kennel name.
Ch Bydand Upsy Daisy Tejano is
owned by Joel and Cherie Belcher.
Bred by Bill and Diane Klumb.
Judge is Mr. Thomas Daniels.
Handler is Ms. Lois DeMers.

Tito!
Ch Tejano's Senor Puente
is owned and was bred by
Joel and Cherie Belcher.
Judge: Ms. Jean Lade.
Handled by Cherie
Belcher with John Belcher
assisting. Cherie Belcher
is HCA president 2004-
2005.

Waldo was Number 2
in the U.S. in 2002. He
is shown here with his
owner/handler, Tara
Martin. In the AKC
registry Waldo is known as
Ch Precioso Canelle One
in a Million. His breeder is
Sharyl Mayhew.

D

Top left: A group of Sweet Honesty dogs owned by Meta von Hout of the Netherlands.

Below: Louie is Ch Los Perritos Hellzapoppin owned by Adam King and Lynn Nieto and bred by Lynn Nieto and Natalie and Russ Armitage.

Top right: Icee belongs to Gloria Dittmann. His formal name is Tapscott's White Xmas DawnGlo. Icee is Major pointed and a son of Ch Yes Giorio vom Salzetal x Ch Couture's Princess D'Tapscott. Bred by Pamn and Jeanne Tapscott. Gloria handles Icee in the ring. This photo was taken by Gloria Dittmann.

Middle left: Rylie is a daughter of Cheryl Drake, Ashtone Labradors and Havanese. She excels in Junior Handling.

Middle right: Amanda Johannes, six years old, handles Bonnie, Ch Silverdale Star of Wincroft ROM, owned by Barbara and Michele Johannes. Bonnie was bred by Rita Stern (Silverdale Havanese). Sire is Katrina's Charmer of Manfred and dam is Witty Lady De Cuba.

E

Top: You've seen Bailey before. Here he is again with a sly wink in his eye and all dressed up for a new adventure. Ch Pocopayasos California Star is always hugged by owner, Karen Ku.

Middle left: Jomaran's Little Miss Muffet who goes by the call name of Mitzi, was bred by Cathy Enns and is owned by Suzanne McKay. She is shown at five months of age scaling the piano. How did she get on that bench? She hopped into a planter, then onto the bench then across the keyboard and off onto a table to sit by the window.

Middle right: Gloria Dittmann's Smudge, Ch Tapscott's I'm a Hottie, bred by Pamm and Jeanne Tapscott changed color from Sable Parti to almost white. Smudge doesn't care about color. Retrieving is what Smudge likes to do.

Bottom left: Havanese just love to investigate table tops. This is the author's Tawney, Shelly's Spectaula Roughrider, enjoying watching the world below her from the table.

Bottom right: Maggie, from Heavenly Havanese, breeder Mary Williams, wonders why people have trouble with computers. "They work well when I sit by one," she says.

F

Top left: Beth Johnson, Feliz Havanese, with Cori, Ch Feliz Correa Patiaculos. Lizbeth and Bob Johnson are owner/breeders.

Top right: Rumble, a black Irish Pied dog with the formal name of Ch Overlook Utter Chaos is owned by Lynn Nieto and Russell and Natalie Armitage. He is handled here by owner Lynn Nieto. Judge is Mrs. Clover Allen.

Middle: Aimee, Ch Mucho Bravo Amore De Wincroft is owned by Barbara and Michele Johannes. She was bred by Mirabell Woudman (Mucho Bravo Havanese of Holland). Sire is Don Zaddeq De Cuba of Cuba and dam is Dutch Ch Mucho Bravo Spectacular Red.

Bottom: Seven year old Cody is owned by Carol Campbell of Terra Cotta, Ontario, Canada. Registered as Belvern's Cody of Bayleux, Cody is trained in Obedience, Flyball and Agility, the last being his favorite. His breeder is Wanda Backus-Kelly of Port Rowan, Ontario.

G

Top left: Martha Hayes, niece of Cathy Wiley, shows off the show ribbon won with MoJo, Tapscott's MoHair Jo. Breeders are Pamm and Jeanne Tapscott.

Middle: Charlie, with a registered name of Ch Janizona MyPal Charlie Brown, was bred by Janet and Scott Hicks, Janizona Havanese. Charlie is owned by Nancy and Bill Whitaker and Janet Hicks.

Ch Sebring Sorcerers Stone, better known as Max, winning Best of Breed at Chico, CA KC. Co-owned by the late Tamara Rutters (on the right) and Elaine Cirimele (on the left).

H

Top: Tinker, Ch Gingerbread Starkette Sprite winning Best of Opposite Sex at the 2004 HCA National Specialty. Shown in this photo are Nona Dietrich, breeder; Elaine Lessing, Judge; Jan Stark, co-owner; Michelle Johannes, Trophy presenter; and Fredith Holt, owner/handler.

Left middle: Ch Roughrider Hallmark Hot Jazz, winning third in his class at the 2004 HCA National Specialty. Handling him is his owner, Tanya McDonald. Jazz is co-owned by Tanya's daughter, Tamara Carey.

Middle right: Winning Best of Opposite in Sweepstakes at the HCA 2003 National Specialty is Selena. Selena's registered name is Ch Janizona's I'm Too Sexy. She was bred by and owned by Janet and Scott Hicks.

Bottom: Ch Overlook Leaps and Bounds, a silver parti bitch, who goes by the call name of Hamster, is shown going Reserve Winners Bitch at the Toy Dog Club of Central Florida in 2003. Judge is Tom Baldwin and breeders/owners are Russell and Natalie Armitage. Natalie is handling Hamster.

I

Top: E. Ann Ingram, sister of owner Cathy Wiley, is posing Tootle, Fairway's I Think I Can on a grooming table. Breeder is Joyce McCracken.

Middle: Buster, Am/Can/Mex/FCI International Ch Starkette Pride of Wincroft ROMX. Owned by Barbara and Michele Johannes and Adam King. Bred by Jeannette Stark (Starkette Havanese). Sire was Ch Voila Prime Time and dam Ch Starkette Cookies and Cream. Buster was top HCA top stud dog for 2003. He ranked No. 3 Breed and No. 4 All Breed for 2002. He was in the Top Ten in 2003 and Top 15 in 2004, all with limited showing. He was also shown at the 2002 World Dog show in Amsterdam and placed second in his class with all excellent ratings and thus received a World Dog Show Winner Trophy.

Lower right: Overlook Firelight's owner is Amber Vallee and Russell and Natalie Armitage. Her sire is Ch Los Perritos Wee Pantaloons. Her dam is Ch Los Perritos Paws of Fire. Lily was bred by Russell and Natalie Armitage and Lynn Nieto.

Bottom left: Susan Nelson showing a Brace at a Palm Springs show.

Bottom right: Lucy, Waltron's I Love Lucy. Her owner is Jerry Tate. Lucy was bred by Ron Walters. Her sire is Ch Snowcrests Coby By Lejerdell and her dam is Ch Flame La Cuba CAo.

Martin Cabral with Punxsy, Ch Meme Zee's Spirit O Roughrider CD. Punxsy is owned by the author. Breeders are Mike and Martha Burns.

Middle right: Ch Feliz NiceN Naughty Roughrider CD winning a Major with Martin Cabral handling. Breeders are Beth and Bob Johnson. Co-owners of Naughty are Kathryn Braund and Mr. David W. Haddock.

Middle left: Judge Sandra Goose Allen awarding Sassy, Ch Roughrider's Sarsaparilla a five pt Major at the Richmond Dog Fanciers show in 2004. Sassy is owned by Kathryn Braund and Mr. David W. Haddock. Beverly Wilson handled Sassy to her championship.

Bottom: Judge Robert Sturm awarding Sassy, Winner's Bitch for a five pt Major at the Capital Havanese Club of Northern California in 2004. Her brother, Jazz, Ch Roughrider Hallmark Hot-Jazz is beside her, having just won Best of Winners. Tyson Pate was Best Jr. Handler at the show and showed Jazz for owners Tanya McDonald and Tamara Carey.

Top: Ch Recuento Dante by Lejerdell. Dante is owned by Lizbeth and Robert Johnson. His breeder is Jerome Podell and Anja Bours-Van Haarlem.

Middle left: Mars, a Cuban dog, HU Ch Pequeno Principe de Lariomr is owned by Maria Paterne and Zsusanna Gazso-Podell.

Middle right is a Sweet Honesty Havanese, Miss Cinnamon Girl Sweet Honesty. She is owned by Meta von Hout of the Netherlands.

Bottom left is Mr. Wacko Jacko, also owned by Meta von Hout.

Bottom right is Ch Moorea's Rodeo Cowboy owned by Mary Cane.

L

Top: The puppy sitting beside her mother is Shallowbrook Starlet O'Hanna (she was a singleton puppy). Mom is Ch K.B.'s Star of Havana-Hanna. Both are owned by Joan Ambrose.

Middle: Punxsy, Ch Meme Zee's Spirit O Roughrider CD owned by Kathryn Braund and bred by Martha and Mike Burns. Punxsy is showing off the famous Havanese smile.

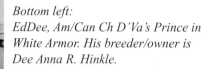

Bottom left: EdDee, Am/Can Ch D'Va's Prince in White Armor. His breeder/owner is Dee Anna R. Hinkle.

Bottom Right: A show prospect belonging to breeder Mary Lopez, Amor Havanese, named Twister. In this photo he is 12 weeks of age.

M

Top left: Ch Roughrider Hallmark Hot Jazz as a puppy with Jett Carey.
Top right: Sue Zeckel with Roughrider's Justice. Justice is owned by Sandy and John Zeckel. Kathryn Braund is breeder.
Middle: John Belcher kissing Daisy, CH Bydand Upsy Daisy Tejano, owned by Joel and Cherie Belcher. Daisy was bred by Bill and Diane Klumb.
Bottom: Hailey and Megan. Sharron Davis submitted this lovely photo showing the joyous affection Havanese have for children.

N

Top: MoJo, Tapscott's MoHair Jo, shows his love for Anna Arnett. Anna is granddaughter of Cathy Wiley. MoJo's breeders are Pamm and Jeanne Tapscott.

Left Middle: Patrick Fournier laughing as the author's Punxsy and Tawney kiss Pat's son, Reid. Pat is the author's son, and Reid is her grandson.

Bottom left: Here is Lucy, Waltron's I Love Lucy AX AXJ, going down the Agility A-frame. She is loved, trained and owned by Jerry Tate.

Bottom right: Sage Ellefsen, step-granddaughter of Kathryn Braund, is ready for another kiss from the author's Naughty.

O

Top left: This precious charmer is eight weeks of age and is being reared by his breeder, Vicki Walton.

Top right: At seven weeks of age Mia finds a dumbell. She is Mimosa's Midnite in Havana bred by Suzanne McKay and owned by Susan Bell.

Middle: Ch Roughrider's Sarsaparilla, is shown here as a puppy. Sassy was bred by Kathryn Braund and is owned by Kathryn and Mr. David W. Haddock.

Bottom: Left is puppy Tanzy, Feliz Tanzonite Tango who was bred by Lizbeth and Robert Johnson.
Right is Annie, her coat in cords. Her name is Los Perritos Lil Sure Shot. She was bred by Lynn Nieto and Troy E. Lewman and is owned by Tami and Curt Parde.

P

Experiences in the whelping box with faster developing puppies lording it over slower developing puppies encourage timidity in the slower developers. Negative litter interaction in the litter box imprints many slower developing puppies. That is why dam and/or breeder supervision is necessary for sound puppy development.

And thankfully, dogs with either inherited or acquired shyness often come to life when exposed to normal environments and given lots of TLC. Obedience training is also essential. The trained dog understands what he can and cannot do in the human's foreign world. Training builds confidence. Confidence means a happy, well-adjusted animal and an excellent pet and canine citizen. Just as psychologists cure people of shy psychosis, dog breeders and owners can cure most pets of shyness.

Breeders duties - Fourth Week: Having two litter boxes makes for easy change of papers and blankets and scrubbing of floor. Whistle softly when approaching the litter box. Cuddle, rock and fondle pups frequently. Mute house voices until puppies become accustomed to the change in scenery. Don't yell. Sound shyness often begins in the litter box. Sound aggressiveness, such as that imprinted by constant human quarreling or yelling by children, may also be imprinted here. Keep sound stimulation positive - soft, calm.

FIFTH WEEK. Day 29 through day 35. Puppies are five weeks of age on day 35.

General: Although many breeds spring to life at about 21 to 30 days of life, Havanese nervous and immune systems are slower to become fully operable. Dalmatians are leaping out of the litter box at 14 days, Portuguese Water Dogs, Poodles and Havanese wait until they are four weeks or more to become active. It just takes longer for nature to put some systems in "go" order!

At the beginning of this week you wonder: why aren't the puppies more active? They are up and about for 10 minutes or so, mouthing each other, sniffing the environment and examining toys in the litter box but they do not seem to be aware of anything going on that does not concern where they are and where their dam is.

All of a sudden! Baroom! They come alive with a bang! "They squeal, they howl, they squeak as loudly as they can, "Let me out of here!" You rush to see what the matter is. You find them with their sweet little muzzles pressed hard against the wires of the x-pens in which they are housed. They are clamoring for attention. It is amazing. It is as if they had been paying rapt attention to everything you were doing for and to them these past weeks and wanted to surprise you on how much they knew. They know exactly what they want. These little sturdy one and two pounders want out of the environment in which they are in. They want to be running all over the house in which you live.

Human babies and puppies have one delightful and sometimes frustrating trait in common. They spoil in the wink of an eye.

Muscular and Nervous System Development - Fifth Week: The puppies now actively play with one another, pulling on each other's ears, fur and legs. Their nervous and immune systems have become fully operable. They awaken at the least sound and in high

The puppies know what they want. They want to be running all over the house.

pitched squeaks and squeals beg to get out of where they are. Their developing sphincter muscle control allows them to move off the blankets and eliminate a distance from where they sleep. Several are fastidious and when their front feet touch the paper, they let go. Several do not care. Help teach clean bowel habits. Reduce blanket space and enlarge newspaper space accordingly. Remember to pick up and replace newspapers as soon as they are soiled.

If liquid food has been introduced during this period, many bitches stop ingesting excrement. Others continue to do so. A meticulously clean litter box encourages housetraining and discourages coprophagy (feces eating). When feces is allowed to accumulate while owners work, curious pups often mouth and taste it as well as smell it. They initially don't know what it is. It's an object in their small environment.

Teaching puppies to lap milk is fun. First, whistle as you approach. Within two days, all puppies will respond to the whistle and hurry to where you set down their food dish. Place the weaning formula in a large, almost flat dish like a glass pie pan. Insert a milk-dipped finger into each tiny mouth. Then dip noses into the formula. Most will begin to lap immediately. If not, they'll turn to a littermate and lick its muzzle and face before returning to the dish to sample a bit more. Bring their mother back to the litter box. She'll lap up the rest of the formula and wipe each of her babies clean. The pups learn to lap by observation of how their mother does it.

The puppies in Naughty's second litter refused to drink either the goats or evaporated milk formula and continued to suckle their mother's teats for their complete nourishment until almost six weeks old. I did not at first understand why. But when I put down a dish of baby meat and crushed kibble and watched them gulp it down it dawned on me why. They had been well supplied with milk from their mother; they did not need milk from another source.

Clipping pups' toenails now becomes a weekly task. Since weighing of pups has been a daily occurrance, some pups are used to being held rigidly; they may accept paw holding without fussing. Be sure to massage each paw soothingly before and after you clip nails. You can still use scissors since nails are so delicate. However, don't expect them to take this grooming necessity without a great deal of squirming and fussing. Refer to the Grooming chapter for complete information.

Eyes, Ears, Teeth - Fifth Week: Some eyes fill with matter at the inner corners. Havanese are very close to the ground and pick up debris quickly. Bacteria forms. This isn't cause for concern if the bitch still cleans them. But be prepared to wash the matter away with warm water each morning if it begins to accummulate daily.

As an interest of note, coyote pups remain in dimly lighted dens until the fourth or fifth week of life. These pups will then be able to be outside in bright sunlight without squinting. Development of canine eyes undergoes a similar time factor.

Some puppies may show evidence of some milk teeth appearing through gums. Pups should have 28 milk teeth by seven to eight weeks. (These erupt in larger breeds by six weeks.) The emergence of teeth is one reason mothers wean their puppies. Milk teeth are very sharp.

Watch jaws as teeth erupt. The lower jaw will grow for several days and then stop while the upper jaw grows. Jaw alignment influences tooth alignment. Most puppies become restless as they teeth. They are exhibiting normal pain response. Gums are sore. Teething pain is relieved by mouthing and biting at one another, pulling each other's hair and by biting at blankets, papers, litter box walls as well as any other object within reach.

It's a common phenomonen that whatever object one pup will bite at, another pup coming along will mouth and bite at also. He smells his littermate's scent on that object. Pups and dogs do this even though a mouthed object hasn't been touched for weeks. If you find puppies biting at objects you do not want touched, scrub these objects to remove scent and saliva deposits.

This fifth week of life is the ideal time to present your pups with teething aids. Excellent ones are hard rubber (English rubber) balls with bells inside. For a tiny Havanese, balls should be at least 1-1/2 inches in diameter; old pieces of toweling and damp wash cloths are great for irritated gums as teeth push through. Never offer soft rubber or plastic toys. If you place a fresh marrow bone in the litter box, watch the pups scramble to locate it with their noses. Soft cloth toys are also excellent. Toys help imprint on pups which objects belong to them and which do not, discouraging later destructive mouthing.

Temperature development, including socialization and training needs - Fifth Week: Friends will want to see the puppies. Have them sit on the floor and allow the puppies to approach and investigate them before they stretch out welcome arms. Pup confidence is achieved in small steps.

It's a good time to introduce the puppies to the room beyond their litter box. In my house their mother precedes them down the hall from the bedroom where their nighttime sleeping quarters are into the living room where two huge x-pens are set up. Of course they piddle on the way. Carpet is always the nicest texture for puppies to piddle on. I string several sheets of newspapers along the way and am always happily surprised when I see a pup rush over to the paper and then squat. How intelligent with so little knowledge of the world around them. They'll play in the living room for several minutes and each gets picked up and hugged. Just like larger breed puppies, this is the week they begin to untie your shoelaces.

Keep everything low key. If there are hesitant puppies in your group, common sense holding and stroking is the right thing to do. Don't push them into the world too fast. Too early a move may set up stress and cause adjustment problems later. Studies have proved negative personality traits such as touch and sound shyness as well as fear of strange places are often caused by the way pups are introduced to "space" in these helpless weeks outside their litter box territory.

I noted my shy puppy displayed caution as she explored the new environment. And she stayed very close beside a bolder littermate. However, she was doing better. Her actions were natural and desirable. I began to be assured my TLC was taking effect.

Caution in new environments at this age signifies thought developing processes. Predictable actions are crouching, gathering together with peers, nosing new areas tentatively, roaching backs, peering about guardedly, and finally - backing up.

Wow! Most puppies, when discovering they are able to move backwards, abandon all cautiousness. They're agog with their new-found muscular coordination. They then spend long moments repeating the backing up action - from other pups, from objects and from absolutely nothing! They back up with the sheer joy that they can do so. Many squeal in delight as they back up over and over again.

If one is picked on by its littermates, pick up the abused puppy. More developed littermates can easily turn one which is slower to develop into a shy puppy. The shy gene can be overcome with lots of tender loving care.

Breeder's Prime Duties - Fifth Week: Change newspapers as soon as they are soiled. Change blankets often. Keep sounds and noises low. Cuddle, kiss and talk to the puppies. Allow them to explore several areas in the house. You can now lower the temperature of their sleeping quarters to 75 degrees. Puppies chill easily.

At the end of this week, introduce children to the puppies. I hire what I call "Socialization Engineers." Each weekend several groups of youngsters and/or teenagers spend an hour or two playing with the puppies. It's a heady time for both. It's wonderful socialization.

During this period you are setting up veterinarian appointments for the first vaccinations and worming of your puppies. Most puppies are born with roundworms. They are prevelant in the soil in many parts of the country. Hookworms and whipworms are not as common. When I lived in the state of Washington, the ground in the area in which I lived was so saturated with roundworm eggs that each litter of puppies I had needed to have their first worming at four weeks of age. Here in dry Montana my puppies have always been found negative for internal parasites. Neither are dogs in Montana (unless not cared for) afflicted with fleas which impart tapeworms. I do have a veterinarian check a puppy's stool at the age of four weeks just to be certain. And I do have them wormed at six and a half and eight and a half weeks. The medicine is safe.

As far as vaccinations so many people do not realize puppies have received immunity from their dams with the first milk they drink after birth. The colostrum in her milk is a gift from nature designed to protect the puppies against puppyhood diseases. This immunity usually lasts until the puppies are about eight weeks of age. However, the protective titers are falling then. In my opinion, the first of the four puppy vaccinations should be given by the breeder's veterinarian when the puppies are six weeks of age. Novice breeders often refuse to allow visitors to see their puppies until after the first vaccination. This is a commendable practice but not necessary. The puppies will not pick up human diseases. Of course common sense tells us not to admit visitors with colds or infectious respiratory diseases.

SIXTH WEEK. Day 36 through day 42. Puppy is six weeks old on day 42.

General: Each puppy's face has taken on its own unique expression. Expressions grow eloquent as eyes reflect emotional development and creativity in thought. Each is a miracle of response.

Muscular and Nervous System Development - Sixth Week: All systems are go! Pups now run, although unsurely. So they run. They run all over. They run straight through (if possible), over and up and down objects.

This wonderful playpen belongs to Mary Lopez, Amor Havanese. It occupies puppies and older dogs for hours.

I like to introduce a small stand for them to jump on and hide under. The stand has a ramp attached so they can climb up and down and play "king of the mountain."

This week they are ever curious, bold and fearful - all at the same time. Every moment they are awake, they are busy. They are bold, nosy, fearful of every new environment they encounter. They manipulate bodies fairly well, although they often tumble or slide when running fast on smooth surfaces.

Since they are companion dogs, they hate to be just with their littermates. They beg to be held, to be kissed and be touched. They scream if you leave them alone too long.

They now detest their litter box (as babies do their cribs). They carry on when gates are closed to keep them inside.

Naughty and one of her puppies sharing a kiss.

They wet constantly. Liquid goes out faster than it goes in.

Pups can now be introduced to food as well as liquid. By six weeks they should have a milk drink in the morning, a fresh simmered meat or cottage cheese lunch, an afternoon kibble and meat drink and a second milk drink in the evening.

Eyes, Ears, Teeth - Sixth Week: If there are tear stains on fur under the eyes and the bitch does not remove them, wipe the corners of eyes clean with a clean warm water dampened washcloth. Don't get water in the eyes or rub.

Ears are wide open. Pups hear well. Even if you don't suspect hearing problems this is a good week to give each pup a simple hearing test. How? Isolate a pup. When he isn't looking at you rattle a bell, sing a few words of a song, whistle, rattle a pan. Do this on the right side of him and then on the left. Watch his ears. A "Uni" pup, one who hears in only one ear, will raise the flap of that ear when he is listening to sound. When he's away from his littermates, he cannot follow the movement of heads. If you suspect a pup's hearing isn't what it should be, repeat the simple hearing test at seven weeks. Deaf afflicted puppies normally lose all hearing ability at about five to six weeks. Screech in pretended alarm. The alarm gene is well instilled in Havanese puppies. Those with hearing will respond immediately. Be sure to test hearing in a different, yet familiar area to each pup. He has to be comfortable when being tested for it to be successful. If possible, BAER test at eight to 10 weeks before pups leave for their permanent homes.

Pups scratch their ears. This is natural. It's not a sign of ear problems; however, this is a good time to begin checking ears daily for cleanliness.

Teeth continue to erupt.

Temperament, including socialization and training needs - Sixth Week: Now that the pups are accliminated to both the litter room and the living room, allow them to explore beyond it. As quickly as they exude confidence, increase their world view. Allow them to wander into the kitchen (be sure their mother is with them for comfort and confidence and yes, a few milk treats). Oh, what a delicious place is the kitchen in which to study smells.

Some, on these exploration journeys, will dash back to familiar confident territory, or hover close to a favorite littermate. It is important to mark these pups for especial cuddling. Others will be bold and if you're not watchful, you'll have to hunt them under beds or behind chairs or in closets. Whistle twice. They'll reappear.

The bitch's maternal instincts are diminishing. If other dogs live in the house, most mothers no longer fuss when they come up to the litter room gate to nose her infants through the wire. In fact, she wants them to play with her puppies now. As a matter of fact, those bitches who enjoy nursing their pups at this age, most often are the ones who welcome other dogs' attention.

Never allow animals to be rough with the puppies in play. As a rule, most adult dogs are marvelous baby sitters. They are enormously tolerant as the puppies climb all over their

bodies and try to reshape them by pulling on their fur and tails.

Havanese puppies should learn how to get along with a variety of dogs. Teaching puppies to play with dogs who have different coat textures, faces and bodies than they do is a great aid in helping them adapt to the world they are going to live in. Havanese are naturally friendly with other dogs just as they are with people. Of course, you never allow this play unless you are present and on guard.

Even so, nature protects puppies. She gives them a puppy scent that informs adult dogs to be ever gentle with puppies. Only when this scent disappears in late adolescence do adult dogs feel privileged to growl and snap. In my experience, adult dogs are ever tolerant of the Havanese. With one exception. If a breeder has a male dog of a larger breed in the house and that dog becomes jealous of a Havanese male, it is best to keep them separate once the Havanese loses his puppy smell.

The whole of your house and part of your yard becomes a puppy school room this week. Follow the puppies about wherever they go and remove them from dangerous obstacles. As you remove them, talk to them calmly. Set them down in a safe place so they can continue their explorations.

Your yard becomes a puppy schoolroom.

This is a heady time for both puppies and breeder. They are examining, you are delighting in their discoveries. Most pups will halt and wet someplace along the route. If they are in the house, its good to know much of this liquid is dilute; the wetting won't damage rugs and carpeting. They are so busy, they are not aware of what they are doing - not that it would matter to them. If you are adamantly against this happening, limit exploration adventures to two pups at a time. The phrase "safety in numbers" applies here. In the sixth week of a Havanese life, confidence lies in numbers, even if the number is a mere two with Mom tagging along. Every exploration is a rich learning experience. Every early and positive contact with intimate house surroundings helps each puppy develop an open, outgoing disposition.

My shy gene puppy was doing well. The "socialization engineers" I hired for weekends to play with the puppies always singled her out for TLC. Her attitude in comfortable surroundings was bold. In a group she was as daring and investigative as were her littermates. Her tail wagged for every visitor. She begged to be picked up and played with.

Was the axiom "hormones influence behavior and behavior influences hormones" settled? I would learn more about her adjustment to new environments when I got her out for walks on the streets in town.

Outside temperatures in the 60 to 70 degree F range, winds not too strong, are just great for puppy adventures as they reach six weeks of age. And when they eliminate outside, the praise you give says housetraining has begun in earnest. So has adaptation to the wide outside world, a necessary prerequisite for optimum canine learning potential.

During these excursions, a breeder learns a great deal about a puppy's personality. As Bruce Fogle DVM MRCUS says in his fine book, "The Dog's Mind," "To understand the dog's mind we need to understand the complicated relationship that evolves between littermates during this formative socialization period."

If there is a wild little puppy in the litter, highly excitable, it requires extra socialization. Despite its active personality, it usually is an extremely sensitive puppy.

Prime Breeder's Duties - Sixth Week: Make a two-whistle sound each time you offer food to the puppies. Provide fresh water as soon as food is introduced. Clip toenails weekly, massaging paws before and after.

SEVENTH WEEK - Day 42 through day 48. Puppy is seven weeks old on day 48.

General: Expressions grow eloquent as eyes reflect emotional development and creativity in thought.

Muscular and Nervous System Development - Seventh Week: Pups are now well up on feet.

Begin stacking (standing) each pup daily. When you first place the puppy on the grooming table, he might show fear of the height. If he roaches his back and tenses his front legs, gently rub his tummy as you stand him, holding his head and neck securely with the other hand. Massage his back with your fingers. Give him a small meat treat and place him back on the floor.

The initial introduction to the grooming table should take no longer than 20 seconds. Lengthen the time each puppy is held there as the days go by, but don't keep him on the table longer than 40 seconds at any one time. Condition each puppy to look forward to this quality one-to-one time, having its belly soothingly touched and back rubbed and massaged and receiving a tasty food treat. Only when it is thoroughly comfortable in a standing posi-

tion on the table, may you begin to groom - brush and comb. That should occur sometime during the latter part of this week. (Refer to the grooming chapter.)

Puppy play now becomes intense. Play fights, necessary learning experiences which teach pups how to inhibit their bite and give and take, become intense. Interrupt them if they become too intense. Lift up the aggressor and talk gently to it. Manners training begins this week.

This is the week you'll want to take pictures for potential puppy adopters. Havanese are

in good physical balance during the seventh week of life. You'll require assistance as you take these pictures. One holds the puppy in a stacked standing or sitting pose while the other snaps the picture. If you are going to stack the puppy on a table for the picture, focus the camera on an object stand-in. Place the object at the exact place you'll stand the puppy. Although the picture will be of the puppy, not you, wear a contrasting soft-toned

outfit - blue or green works well. Mute the background. Direct the puppy's eyes on a one-third angle to the camera, so the camera does not pick out red eye tints.

Puppies are better able to control their urine and bowel movements long enough to move to preferred spots to perform them. This is the week to introduce a puppy box with a lining of newspapers or piddle pads. Catch the puppy when you see him turn-

These delightful seven week old puppies belong to Janet Hicks, Janizona Havanese.

ing or squatting, place him in the box and say gently, "Do your chores." If he does, praise highly. Of course he doesn't understand what you mean. Give him a few days and he will. He'll still eliminate other places, nevertheless you have begun his housetraining.

Eyes, Ears, Teeth - Seventh Week: Examine each puppy's teeth by lifting the side corners of his lips. Are they coming in with a scissors bite? Can you tell if his jawline is slightly over or undershot? Are there any obvious mouth problems?

Temperament, including socialization and training needs - Seventh Week: Pups taste everything within reach of their mouths. Allow their mother to continue their behavior lessons. She usually begins to do this during the sixth week and intensifies her training this week. As she plays with a pup, she teaches. In her play, she exhibits profound tenderness towards her puppy in her hugging and nuzzling, yet never hesitates to chastise to improve its conduct. She chastises in such a tolerant manner, the observer isn't always certain if her corrections are mock or real. If, however, there is not ample room for her to give these lessons to her pups, she doesn't. Some people claim, "My bitch never played with her puppies." Perhaps the litter room was too small and crowded for her to stretch out and feel free.

Here's a suggestion: Allow her to nurse pups or give them a milk treat, one at a time, in a large familiar area, like the living room or on a lawn outside. Keep the other pups away. Observe. She'll mouth the pup while he feeds, licking him thoroughly just as she did when he was newly born. She'll take a pup's whole head into her mouth and shake it gently. If it becomes overly boisterous, she'll push him away roughly, perhaps growling at him. If so, she immediately turns around, figuratively speaking, and nuzzles him lovingly. She's teaching him cooperation, how to inhibit his bite, how to observe leader body language. She's explaining to him that if he can't do one thing, there are always acceptable substitutes. She's helping him develop confidence in his innate abilities.

As for the puppies, they are busybodies even when they are sitting still, looking up into the sky at birds. They dash up to trees, eagerly sniff the different barks and scratch at the earth. Insatiable examiners, they dig at cement and eat everything edible - dandelions, berries, field mushrooms, grass and flowers. Stone items disappear down their gullets as well as do bits of paper, cloth or wood. If it is wintertime, snow fascinates them. They may get cold but still they will rush up and down little snow banks, dig big holes in the snow, and then thoroughly soaked, enjoy your toweling. In the house they dash into the kitchen to smell roasts or cakes baking in the oven; they nose every inch of floor and carpet; they crawl under tables and play hide and seek under chairs. They harass their mother constantly. They grab her nipples and tug. They jump up to pester her. With happy little puppy voices, which incidentally have begun to lose the delicious high tones, they beg to be lifted up; they paw to sit on laps and be held in arms. When satisfied in their pleasure, they grunt in comfort and fall asleep.

Prime Breeder's Duties - Seventh Week: Take a clue from the dam. She knows when her pups are leaving the helpless age. Remember, the transition from a helpless pup to one who will possess a sound and open temperament has been forming. It is now up to you to make this period a telling one. This week begin imprint training. Remove a pup from an object he must neither touch nor chew. As you remove him, admonish him gently, "No." The way you say the word makes it meaningful to him. Divert his attention by immediately fondling him and giving him a small object he may touch or chew.

Encourage good housetraining habits so that when the pups go home they'll know what is expected of them and will begin to cooperate as long as the new owners cooperate. Emphasize these lessons by taking the pups outside each awakening, if at all possible. They enjoy eliminating outside.

As an enticement, place their food dishes outside and use your whistle recall command to get them there. After only several calls they'll dash outside to their food bowls like a gaggle of baby geese rush to water. The pattern is beginning to be set. Open the door to the outside, whistle and the pups immediately rush outside to eat or eliminate.

While each pup must be allowed to assert himself so he learns his sense of identity, pups should not decide amongst themselves who is going to be boss. No pup should be forced to accept a low status. While each pup's basic temperament has its origin in genes, we are beginning to understand the complex development of disposition; in studies supervising litter play each pup needs to learn to interact with one another in a healthy, outoing manner. In this way, no pup in the litter becomes timid or overly dominant.

EIGHTH, NINTH AND TENTH WEEKS: We have covered the mental and physical growth in the helpless weeks and in the prime socialization weeks.

During these last weeks that the puppies remain with you, the breeder, you are very busy talking to prospective adoptees; writing contracts, taking the puppies to the veterinarian for their first and second vaccinations and worming, as necessary; and performing all the myriad duties associated with raising a wonderful Havanese litter.

Puppies are very active during this transitional period. It's fun, if you have time to give kindergarten lessons, first with the whole litter participating and then with one pup only. A few suggestions:

1) Play whistle recall. I use a field whistle such as a Thunderer or Gonia whistle. When you sound the whistle, make the whistle talk. Don't just toot on it. Watch the pups rush to you when they hear the whistle.

2) Play retrieve with balls and tiny dummies.

3) Try to fit at least one five minute period with each pup on a one-to-one basis. It's loving time.

4) Take each puppy for a walk in town.

My shy puppy, bold and energetic in comfortable surroundings, froze in each new environment. If I took her to a mall, she would not move from the spot where I set her down. She surveyed each new landscape wide eyed. While she did not shake when I picked her up, her heart would be racing.

Socialization of a puppy like this takes time. Confidence must be slowly built with each new experience. When confidence was developed, she would be able to conquer her fears (I hope).

If a puppy is going to travel to his new home in a crate, whether by plane or car, prepare it for the trip by placing open door crates in the x-pens several weeks beforehand. However, never put or leave a small puppy in a crate by itself. Isolation of a puppy from the rest of the litter in this fashion is detrimental. When it embarks on its new home adventure, sights and sounds along the way will occupy his mind. In its present environment, panic sets up a base for future separation anxiety attacks. Don't do it.

Puppies who have had optimum behavioral training in the litter box, go to their permanent homes with confidence. Perhaps they'll be cautious as they set foot on their new adventure. Cautiousness is a good trait. However, when they arrive at their new homes they will have tails wagging merrily in minutes.

Importantly, if only one or two puppies remain with the breeder at 10 to 12 weeks, these last will be reluctant to leave. At these ages the puppies are settling into a house routine. They are already becoming devoted to the breeder. Bold and happy as they may appear, they are loathe to depart from their customary routine. Unlike humans, who can break and change habits, dogs

Isolation of a puppy from the rest of the litter as shown above sets up future separation anxiety attacks. When it embarks on its new home adventure, the different environment will occupy his mind. But to isolate a puppy from the rest of his litter in the breeder's home is detrimental.

cling to theirs even though adaptable to environmental changes. Havanese are extraordinarily sensitive and perceptive to change.

Example: I kept one puppy from Naughty's second litter until 11 weeks of age which is when his owner could pick him up. On her arrival and her joy at seeing him - her arms reaching out to him - he turned and ran from her and looked at her from behind the protection of my legs.

My other dogs were instantly and constantly on her lap or playing with her as she sprawled on the floor with them. Not this puppy! He avoided her, tagging along with me the whole weekend. He left with her, of course, but unhappily so.

"He was comatose the whole flight," she later told me, laughing. "I was worried. However, the moment we stepped inside my home and he met his future companion, my other Havanese, his tail began to wag. He then took it upon himself to explore the whole of his new home. When he was satisfied, he came to the couch where I was sitting and begged to be lifted into my lap.

"He now is, as you said he would be, a lover. He just never leaves my side and is as happy as a Havanese should be."

Give the permanent owner clues on what you have been working for with the puppy. Perhaps he can do one of the following before he leaves the nest: a) remains quiet on table while being groomed; b) holds stand position with your hand only at head; c) holds sit position as collar is placed around neck; d) sits quietly on lap while riding in car; e) starts for door to go outside to eliminate; f) does his best to remember where the inside piddle box is. If he can accomplish just one of these things on his way to his new home, you have done wonders with your puppies.

Offer the new owners a statement like this to remember: Visualize what you want your puppy to be. Then imprint his behavior towards that goal. Never take puppy behavior socialization for granted. Like love, renew it daily.

Terri Bergan says, "He is happy as a Havanese should be."

HAVANESE SIZE AND LENGTH OF COAT

Prospective owners want to know what size, color and length of coat their puppy will be and have as an adult. Variation in size from 8-1/2" to 11-1/2" is not always predictable. A large bitch and a small stud or a large stud and a small bitch could well produce both small and large puppies. If birth weights are approximately five to seven ounces adult height should fall within the standard. It has been estimated that puppies which weigh four lbs. or more at the age of eight weeks could go oversize. This is not always true. One characteristic to look at is the bone of the newborn, not just weight. Sandra Barnes, owner of Mischief Havanese Kennels and a Havanese breeder since 1996, writes: "Certain pups have surprised me and grown larger than expected. I can now pretty much guess their size by determining the size of their parents. I also look at the pads of the feet. If pads are small then the puppies usually remain smaller. If the pads are on the large side then these pups usually grow to the larger end of the standard."

Ch Los Perritos Wee Pantaloons x Ch Silverdale's Amazing Grace are the parents of this litter. Breeders were Adam and Tina King and Renee Reiherzer.

Length of coat varies. The standard states that the *"coat will not be so profuse nor overly long as to obscure the natural lines of the dog."* Meta van Hout of the famous European Sweet Honesty Havanese Kennels says, "Straight coats can grow very long. My Whitney had a very long coat which reached the floor. I had to cut it shorter so she could move freely. Curly, wavy, fluffy coats will not reach the floor, yet the condition of the coat all depends on the owner. I think when Havanese reach the age of two years, you will see the coat's maximum length." Other breeders believe coats reach their maximum length and profuseness when the dog reaches three years of age. Sandy Barnes feels that "the maximum length of coat is achieved at five years of age. I think the Havanese is at the peak of maturity by then," she says. "Genetics does play a role in the type of coat the dog has."

Dams, with space in which to move around, do a great deal of work socializing their puppies. Cricket, shown in the top photo at seven weeks pregnant, explains to her seven week old puppies (in the photo below) how to navigate a deck step. Cricket's registered name is Mimosa Midnite Medley. Cricket was bred by Penny Will (Havana Canada) and is owned by Suzanne McKay (Mimosa).

Cricket didn't tell her seven week old puppy to upturn the toy basket; however, this bright youngster is immersed in her own socialization activities. "You have to upset the toy basket if the toy I want is at the bottom," she says.

Cricket did show this ten week old how to go in and out of the dog door. It's a very important housetraining function and this puppy has the hang of it very well.

Chapter Nine

Rainbow Colors of the Havanese

by

Suzanne McKay

Havanese come in a delightful assortment of colours in both solid and two or three colour combinations as well as innumerable variations of each. You will find Havanese in solid colours of White, Cream, Champagne, Gold, Red, Chocolate, Sable, Silver, Blue and Black. Any of these colours can combine to create many eye catching two and three colour coats. Colours develop and change as the dog matures. In many cases the difference between puppy colouration and adult coat may be quite dramatic. Many Havanese lighten significantly from birth to young adulthood. Some darken again later on with maturity, though not usually to the depth of colour they had as puppies.

WHITE: Crisp and bright; pure snow white from birth (no colour allowed on any part of the dog, including ears).

CREAM: Is Ivory or creamy yellowish white, the colour of dairy cream or almonds.

CHAMPAGNE: Is a pale tawny yellow, the colour of champagne, from light to deep intensity with yellow undertones. In some registries, Cream and Champagne are combined as one colour, while in others they are separate.

GOLD: This is a rich warm colour in various shades of medium gold from honey to apricot. There are very definite reddish highlights to the coat. True Gold dogs retain much of their colour throughout their lifetime, though the colour may soften with age.

RED: Red is also a rich warm colour, similar to Gold with deeper and more intense colour, ranging from Orangey Red to deep Mahogany. Some registries combine Gold and Red while others have them separate.

FAWN: Fawn is a cool colour ranging from tan, beige and buff to light brown shades.

SABLE: Sable coats are distinguished by darker tipping on a lighter coloured underfur. The amount of tipping may be very heavy or very light. The underfur can be brown, fawn, red, gold or silver. Tipping is generally black but may also be shades of brown, gold or silver. Sable coats often lighten or progressively silver as the dog matures. Some sable dogs lighten dramatically almost all the way to a pale cream or off-white leaving just subtle shadings and highlights of colour. A true sable will always retain the dark tipping on the ears and tail (even if it's just a few hairs). Sable is the most changeable of all the Havanese colours. The degree of silvering is dependent on the other colours and modifying genes in the genetic makeup of the dog. If the tipping is cut off, generally it will not return except on the ears and tail.

BRINDLE: Much confusion surrounds brindle markings. Brindle is one of the more complex coat colours. The classic brindle combination gives dark bands, more or less regular tiger striped on a lighter background any shade from cream, champagne, tan, gold or silver (i.e. similar to brindle coats of the Boxer or Dane). Tiger stripes are apparent at birth and may run all over the body in streaks or stripes of black or brown. Not all brindles have this classic striped look. Some have agouti hair, where the hairs are banded in rings of colour like rabbit or wolf fur. There can be three or more rings of colour. Brindle may also appear more subtly as a combination coat where two or more different colour hairs are mixed throughout. Black, brown and auburn hairs intermixed may make a dog appear a tobacco colour all over. In some registries this colour is called Havana Brown, in others it is known as Black Brindle. A brindle can also be an intriguing blend of the agouti hair along with intermixed solid hairs. The base colour may lighten as the dog matures but the overall pattern will remain. Some lighten and then darken again. Brindle dogs often have a dark mask on the face and may have black ears and tail as well as a dark dorsal stripe. Brindle is not the same as sable where the coat is only tipped in colour.

CHOCOLATE: Puppies are born chocolate. True chocolate dogs will have self-coloured liver or brown pigment; they cannot have anything black. They usually also have lighter coloured eyes in warm brown, amber or golden shades. Chocolate coats may vary from milk chocolate to a darker bittersweet chocolate colour. Some chocolate dogs may turn silver. These would correctly be called a "Chocolate Silver." Chocolate refers to the coat colour, not only the pigment colour.

SILVER: Puppies are born black and start to lighten at about four to six weeks of age. The colour change usually begins on the face and head. As the dog matures, the coat will lighten to varying shades of silver from pale platinum, sterling and pewter to deep grey. The coat change is complete at approximately 12 to 15 months of age.

BLUE: Puppies are born black or so dark as to appear black. The black is dull rather than glossy like a true black and may have a dark reddish cast. The coat may start turning as early as six to eight months or as late as three to five years. Once it starts turning, the coat colour will continue to develop until it takes on a definite blue/grey cast. The in-between colour is often a muddy brown or reddish colour. Final blue colour may be any shade from medium to dark silver/gray/blue and charcoal. Pigment is black. Some consider silver and blue to be lighter and darker variations of the same colour while others see them as two distinct colours.

Recently there has been notice of some light blue dogs being born blue that also have blue eyes and blue pigment. At this time, until we learn more, we do not know for sure whether this is a previously unidentified combination in Havanese with similar genes at work as found in the blue colour of the Weimaraner or if perhaps it is Merle genes at play. Again, this is another colour combination that appears ambiguous and controversial.

BLACK: Deep jet black. No reddish or brown tones and colour does not lighten.

HAVANESE MARKINGS

PARTI-COLOUR or **PIEBALD**: Two colour coat. Coat is predominantly white (over 50 percent) broken with irregular patches or spots of a second colour. These patches may be any other colour. Lightly marked dogs with less than 10 percent colour are usually considered extreme Parti or extreme Piebald. An example might be a white dog with one or both ears partly coloured and no coloured patches on the body.

PIED: Also known as **IRISH PIED.** Two colour coat. Over 50 percent of coat is coloured. Coat pattern is laid out as follows: the underbelly and lower legs at least up to the elbows are white. There is also white on the chest up to the bottom of the chin, as well as a full or partial white collar or shawl around the neck. The tip of the tail is always white. There may be a coloured mask on the face. The colouring on the back is solid and appears as a large saddle or cape covering the shoulders, back and sides. Topline is coloured while the underline is always white. Pied is basically a heavy marked Parti and some registries call them all Parti variations, with simply more or less areas of colour.

TRI-COLOUR: There are variations. Three colour coat. A classic tri is basically a parti or pied dog with the addition of a third colour. This third colour can be any shade of tan or

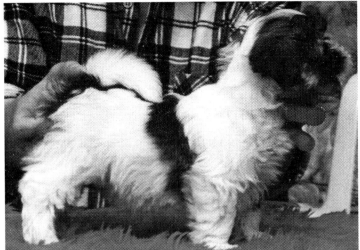

These three pictures show the coloring change in Meta von Hout's bitch,
Silly Miss Sally Sweet Honesty.

Top: eight weeks of age.
Middle: five months of age.
Bottom: five and one-half years of age.

Courtesy Sweet Honesty Havanese, Netherlands - Meta von Hout.

gold and is laid out following the typical point pattern. Tan Points are found on the muzzle, eyebrows, cheeks, ears, chest, legs and vent.

Another variation is the **HOUND MARKED TRI.** The markings are similar to a Beagle or other hound breeds. Three colours; generally Black, Tan and White. These dogs may display a classic saddle pattern. They do NOT have tan points. Typically the markings are Black and Tan or Sable appearing on the head, legs and saddle.

Some registries do not recognize the tri-colour patterns but rather refer to these dogs as Bi-coloured Partis or Bi-colour Pieds, i.e. Black and Tan Parti indicates patches of black and patches of tan on a white base coat.

TAN POINT: Predominantly dark coat overlaid with a colour point pattern and with or without white trim. The classic Black coat with Tan Points without any white trim at all is known as the Black and Tan. Though the most common background coat colour is black, it may also be Sable, Blue, Silver or Chocolate. Colour points are laid out in the following pattern: lighter markings appear on the muzzle, eyebrows, ears, cheeks, legs, chest and vent. The point pattern is similar to the markings on a Doberman or Rottweiler. Colour points may be any shade of tan or gold (Tan Point) or silver (Silver Point). Points often lighten to silvered pearl or creamy white as the dog matures. White trim is permissible on the chin, chest and feet.

WHITE MARKINGS: Two colour coat. A predominantly coloured coat. Solid colour with small patches of white trim found on the chin, chest and feet. Trim may also be cream, tan or silver.

VARIANTS

Many Havanese carry the TICKING gene. A parti-coloured dog with this gene will have flecks of colour throughout the white coat, giving it a salt and pepper appearance. Dogs without this gene will have a white that stays crisp and pure. Ticking only affects areas of white coat. Some registries identify this as Belton.

Another prominent gene is the SILVERING gene. The majority of Havanese carry this gene to some degree. This gene is responsible for colours that progressively silver and lighten as the dog matures much like prematurely graying hair in humans. In the Havanese, this premature graying may start soon after birth. Some colour changes can be quite dramatic going from a very dark puppy coat to a pale cream or champagne adult coat.

The **CHINCHILLA** gene masks the colour red and does not allow it to fully develop. This is most noticeable on **Tan Point** dogs and is responsible for the points appearing silver

rather than tan. This causes some confusion as a number of Tan Point dogs (as adults) have no visible tan on them at all! Depending on the intensity of the gene, the points can be as dark as pewter or as light as pale platinum. Tan Points may lighten and then darken again with maturity.

Some Havanese also have a SADDLE gene. This is where the coat colours start fading from the front towards the back. The colour fading usually stops around the shoulder area, leaving the front, face, head and neck lighter and the shoulders, back and rear darker like a saddle. Similar pattern-wise to a Yorkshire Terrier. Where these Havanese also have the Chinchilla gene, any gold or tan areas will fade to creamy white.

Common Points of Confusion

Many people get confused about the **Parti** and **Pieds.** Genetically they are the same but one simply has a greater degree of visible colour. Both are a two-colour coat but, where differentiated, it is according to the difference in the coat marking patterns. **Parti** being considered 50 percent or more white with irregular spots or patches and **Pied** being considered 50 percent or more coloured where the colour follows a distinct pattern.

Silver vs Blue. As adults, some of these dogs may have very similar colouring, though generally Silver dogs are the lighter silver/grey shades while Blue dogs are the darker charcoal/blue shades. You would need to know when the coat change occurred to accurately determine whether it is a silver or a blue. The big difference between the blue colour and the silver is that silver dogs start turning silver at the roots at a very early age, four to six weeks. They first show signs of silvering around the mouth and eyes and may take up to a year of age to become completely silver. Blue dogs remain black at least up to six to eight months or longer and then start turning towards the silvery blue colour later in life. Though, as mentioned above, controversy exists, as some consider silver and blue to be variations of the same colour, and there appears to be another blue variation that is not currently understood.

Dogs that are Havana Brown or Black Brindle can be mistaken for chocolate as the overall appearance may be similar as adults. The easiest way to tell the difference is to look at the pigment and eyes. Chocolate puppies are born chocolate, and most have liver pigment on the nose, lips and eye rims. They may also have lighter brown or golden eyes. Havana Brown puppies are born black, or so dark brown as to appear almost black. They gradually change to various shades of tobacco brown as the dog matures. Their coats are a combination of black, brown and auburn hairs intermixed. Pigment must be black.

These colour definitions are as accurate as possible with the current information available. As we learn more about the complexities of Havanese colour genetics, some of these definitions may be deleted, expanded or changed and perhaps other new ones added.

Havanese colours are intriging. Please refer to the HCA for the most up-to-date information.

These three pictures show how profound a color change can be. The photos are of Susan Nelson's Tippy. At birth she was dark brown. Her color changed to champagne with black tips and ended up with reddish gold tips. Tippy is shown here at three weeks, eight weeks and at 11 months.
Courtesy Susan Nelson.

Chapter Ten

Care and Mannering of the Puppy

A Havanese puppy requires these things when he comes to live at your house: food and water; a bed or crate to sleep in which is placed close to his owners until he is at least four months of age; housetraining to a definite place; a box of toys all his own kept in a place he frequents; a fenced yard where he learns he can play in all kinds of weather while being supervised; love including lots of lap holding and hugging and lastly mannering.

Let's go over these items one at a time.

DIET:

Puppies eight weeks to three months of age usually require four meals a day with fresh drinking water available during waking hours. Your puppy's breeder undoubtedly will offer you a suggested diet. If not, the following time-proven diet can be fed.

Be sure to feed high quality puppy kibble and increase portions as the puppy grows. Blend the kibble in a small amount of warm water prior to each feeding. Milk teeth are not completely erupted and by blending the kibble it does not sit in the stomach for hours before being digested. Some Havanese puppies will turn their noses up at blended kibble. They enjoy munching dry kibble.

Breakfast: blended kibble with an equal amount of evaporated milk and warm water

Lunch: cottage cheese and/or yogurt with a small amount of blended kibble

Dinner: blended kibble mixed with a small amount of baby beef or baby chicken

Bedtime snack: an equal amount of evaporated milk and warm water

Puppies three months to five months of age usually require three meals a day with fresh drinking water available every waking moment. Some, particularly if there are other dogs in the household, only want a midday snack. In fact, many Havanese puppies don't want a noonday meal. Shortly after three months he will be on a two meal a day routine. Your puppy will tell you when he is tiring of the noon meal. None will refuse a midday snack! Your puppy will also tell you if the portions you serve are too little or too much. Be careful not to overfeed. Once he leaves his mother and siblings, lean is better than fat.

At three to four months you may wish to substitute canned foods as topping on his kibble. And when all his milk teeth have erupted, he does not need his kibble blended. A teaspoonful of warm water along with a teaspoon of canned food does make his kibble more appealing in taste and halts compacting in the stomach. I do not suggest leaving a Havanese dish available all day. Scheduled feedings makes for predictable timing for elimination. Those that do leave their dog's dish available all day should never add supplements to the dish. Supplements can sour in a few hours time.

If you wonder why dogs are content with the same food day in and day out, in contrast to humans who have approximately 9000 taste buds, dogs only have 1706! That is one reason if you have a fussy eater, the odor, texture and taste will become enhanced if you warm his food before serving.

Many owners like to cook for their Havanese. Meats suitable are baked or simmered chicken and beef meat from stews and roasts. Portions can be blended or minced and packaged to be frozen or refrigerated, being used as needed. Vegetables? Havanese enjoy canned or fresh peas alternated with another chopped green vegetable like string beans as toppings on their kibble. Many Havanese delight in munching raw broccoli heads, small slices of carrots and fresh fruits such as apples, pears and tomatoes. A raw egg yolk mixed in with kibble is gobbled down readily. Seek out the book by Donald R. Strombeck DVM, PhD entitled "Home Prepared Dog and Cat Diets - The Healthy Alternative."

Some owners feed the newly popular raw diet to their Havanese. If you are interested in pursuing what constitutes a safe raw diet for your Havanese, homework is involved for both safety and health reasons. The internet has excellent sites available on "canine raw diet formulations." Two of them are as follows: Amore, wwwpetfoods.com; Alternatives 4 Pets, Inc., www.alternatives4pets.com.

We are fortunate that Susan Nelson, a long-time breeder, exhibitor and trainer of Havanese, has generously given us her story on why she feeds raw. We present her story here.

WHY I FEED RAW by Susan Nelson

I have been feeding my dogs a raw food diet for almost nine years. Sadly, I look back with regret at the 30 plus years I had been feeding my faithful companions a kibble dog food thinking that this was actually good for them.

A serious, unidentified virus affecting all my dogs was the turning point in my life. The Alternative Health Care Veterinarian who was successful in returning my dogs to good health showed me how important a good raw food diet was in keeping my dogs healthy in the future.

Like so many others, I was worried that my dogs or I would come down with E.coli or Salmonella from preparing or feeding raw food, especially from the raw chicken I was feeding them. I gradually overcame this fear as I learned more about the digestive system of a carnivore/omnivore. I learned that the short digestive track in dogs and the high acidic level in their stomach made it almost impossible for the food, even if it were bad, to cause my dogs any harm.

Back when I started feeding raw, I had to make up my dogs' diet from scratch including grinding up raw chicken necks and backs. I had many good books and articles to refer to which helped make it possible. Today, there must be 30 or more companies who have come out with complete frozen raw food diets. Many of them contain no grains. They use 100 percent USDA inspected and approved meats and bones and many use organic fruits and vegetables. I now primarily feed one of these diets instead of making it up from scratch. I change brands often so my dogs are getting a variety of meat sources. They love these diets.

I often find myself bragging about the differences I have noticed in my dogs these past 10 years. For starters, I find that I am no longer taking my dogs to the veterinarian for this problem or that. At one time, I had all my dogs covered under a canine health insurance plan. I discontinued this coverage when my dogs were no longer getting sick. I now take my dogs to the veterinarian once a year for a health check and a complete blood panel. I no longer vaccinate my dogs either. I discontinued this practice when I started the raw food diet. I do have my veterinarian take an annual titer test to make sure they are still protected and have never come across an instance where they had to be vaccinated. I think the combination of these two changes is what is contributing to the exceptional good health of my dogs.

Interestingly enough, I noticed that when my bitches had a litter, all the pups were large, healthy and uniform in size at birth even those that ended up at the bottom of the standard. Out of the 17 puppies born since switching to raw, all averaged between seven and eight ounces and this included the litters with five pups. Best yet, the bitches never ran out of milk. They were still allowing the pups to nurse well into the eighth or ninth week.

Prior to feeding raw, my original sire had a low sperm count. Afrter switching to a raw food diet, his sperm count jumped to a healthy level. Even today at age 13, his count has not shown a decline.

Another benefit: my three youngest dogs, which have always been raised on raw diets, have teeth which never require professional cleaning. Their parents who started out on kibble diets, did.

Many dogs as they age lose the spark they once had. My oldest Havanese, Sparky, soon to be 13, is still running Agility courses and doing Obedience. His activity level is that of a youngster. My second oldest Havanese is Tippy. At the age of 10-1/2 years, she returned to the show ring after being out for five years and she took a Best of Breed over three dogs in the Top 10 and then went on to take a Group 3 at a Toy Breed Specialty. The next weekend she took High Scoring Rally Obedience title over 40 other dogs. Tippy and Sparky will

Here is Susan Nelson's Sparky surfing! Sparky is AKC/ARBA Ch Shaggyluv's Energizer ROM OA OAJ. Sparky's date of birth was January 15, 1992.

continue showing in Obedience and Agility until such time it is no longer fun for them. While I cannot prove to you that their exceptional health and vitality are the results of feeding raw and not vaccinating, I wholeheartedly believe it myself.

If you are interested in finding out more about feeding raw, there are many good books and interesting sites on the web. I will warn you in advance it is not easy to make the switch. Talk to those who have done it and stay away from those who have not tried it yet tell you how dangerous it is. If and when you get to that point and start feeding your dogs and cats a raw diet you will quickly see the positive effects this change has on your pet.

Thank you, Susan Nelson.

VITAMINS

Do purchase puppy vitamins, either from your puppy's veterinarian or from a pet store. Some puppies ignore the vitamin if placed with their food or offered as a treat. If so, crumble the vitamin and mix it in with its food. Vitamins aid in building straight bones.

AILING PUPPY FEEDING

Puppies (and dogs) recovering from a diarrhea attack often bounce back quickly by drinking barley water. Barley is strengthening and digestible. Simmer a quarter of a cup of barley in a quart of water for an hour, strain the barley until the liquid is clear, mix a teaspoonful of karo syrup in with the water and serve. This is a recipe handed down from my grandmother for both children and pet animals who have had stomach or bowel distress.

Wire crates allow puppies to see out yet are safe havens and puppies need to be right beside your bed at night.

It is not a panacea for puppies who suffer a serious illness.

BEDS

A wire crate placed beside your bed containing a nicely warmed blanket for the newcomer is a good start. No Havanese puppy should be put in a kitchen or other room far from where the family sleeps. The puppy needs to be close to his family. You can calm him down with voice and hand from your bed through the slats of the wire crate. You are also right there to get up and take him outside when he becomes restless during the night. Night restlessness in a puppy means he has to eliminate. I fail to follow the common sense rule, "Don't put the puppy in bed with you. Even if you are a light sleeper there is always the possibility of rolling over on the puppy while you sleep or the puppy falling off the bed." I do place a puppy in bed with me. The Havanese knows he is at a high place and I trust his puppy judgement: "I won't fall out!" I am also an extremely light sleeper. True, the first night a new puppy sleeps in bed beside me I do not sleep much. I worry. However, the instant the puppy stirs and cries (and it will), I grab my clothes and take it outside.

Do place a robe or cold weather clothes, slippers and a flashlight (if necessary) beside your bed, put them on quickly as soon as your puppy stirs. Take the puppy out of his crate and carry him outside. Don't allow him to walk, his bladder or both bladder and bowels are bursting.

We have always found the best weather in which to housetrain a puppy was in the wintertime, when it's good and cold outside. We have taken our puppies out in below zero weather, when it is snowing or raining or the winds howling. The puppy eliminates quickly, gets back in your arms and when you return him to his crate right beside your bed, he snuggles up for a good sound sleep. On warm weather nights a puppy might decide that after he eliminates it's a good time to play.

Set up a second bed in the living or dining room for daytime naps. A good choice is a round bed with a soft cushion in the center.

HOUSETRAINING

I prefer to housetrain puppies to go outside to eliminate. A small "litter" box can be used inside during inclement weather while puppies are very young. But often puppies become confused and decide for themselves that a carpet or floor is just as good as going to the litter box. There is no confusion in their minds if taught from the beginning that outdoors is where they must eliminate.

Puppies usually find an area in the yard they prefer. This preference is due to their profound territorial instinct. It may be right in the middle of your prized flowerbed and no matter what you try to do, that's the area they insist on using. Accept their preference. Happily, as puppies grow, they enlarge their territorial area and several areas suit this necessary purpose.

If you insist your puppy must eliminate in one definite area, be sure to take him there each and every time you take him outside. After he becomes 'sort of reliable' take him there on leash. Leash training for elimination is sound practice. Often a puppy will refuse to eliminate when away from home. He's unconfident. Teaching a puppy to eliminate while on leash gives him a secure feeling and helps him not to be so selective.

Do check with your puppy's breeder what has been done to aid your puppy in housetraining. Unfortunately, some breeders say, "Nothing. That's your job." I was appalled when I first heard this from a Havanese breeder. After I picked up a nine week old puppy from another breeder she told me, "Oh, she's never been outside. It was too cold." Young puppies are shaped and molded by experiences in early rearing. That puppy bitch certainly had been imprinted to eliminate inside. She was over 10 months of age before she learned that "outside" was the only place for elimination.

I grant you being a hobby breeder is hard work. And breeders cannot be expected to have your Havanese housetrained. That is the permanent owner's job. It is very difficult to begin

housetraining four or more puppies at one time. However, puppies six and seven weeks of age begin to urinate and defecate away from their bed. Their territorial instinct influences their decision to keep a certain area of the x-pen clean for their sleeping quarters. Therefore, a good start in housetraining can be made at this age.

In daylight hours, Havanese breeders can begin taking their six week old puppies outdoors after a meal. Yes, they may have to be carried. Once outside, within five to 10 minutes, cold or hot, raining or snowing, with you at their sides, they'll eliminate. Carry them back in. After several outside excursions, six and seven week old puppies will rush to the door when allowed out of their x-pen. They are being imprinted with the correct elimination place. Even if breeders cannot get them out at night, habit adjustments permanent owners need to make are comparatively easy.

It's good to remember a fresh supply of urine enters the bladder every six minutes in humans, even more frequently in a puppy with a tiny bladder. And a Havanese has a tiny bladder. It simply cannot hold much urine. That's the reason owners should pick up their puppy every 20 to 30 minutes and take it outside. Don't close the door on it. Go with it. Stay with it. Praise AS (not before or after) it eliminates. Carry or walk the puppy back inside.

Movement stimulates elimination in any animal. After each play period, a puppy will squat and eliminate. You must be on guard to anticipate this. The reason puppies can hold it during the night is because they do not move around enough in their sleep to stimulate the body's supply of fresh urine which, while they sleep, is filling up the bladder. That's why, once a puppy awakes, that tiny bladder is bursting.

Even though metabolism slows in all living creatures during rest periods, Havanese puppies may have bowel movements in their crates at night if owners have not seen to it they eliminate before going to bed. Whatever happens in that crate is the fault of the owner. Patience along with moving the dog is essential. Dog handlers at dog shows can often be seen walking a dog around in big circles. They are moving the dog in order to stimulate both its bladder and bowels so that the dog will perform its "chores" before going into the ring to be judged.

The longer you wait before starting housetraining a puppy, the stronger the odors will become on carpets and floors.. These odors re-attract the puppy.

If you go out of the room and the puppy cannot tag along beside you, be sure to have a papered x-pen set up where you can place it.

Dogs are creatures of habit. Getting them outside to "do their chores" at specific times of the day really helps these lessons sink in. *Consistency* in doing sets the habit. Housetraining of toy dogs has been called difficult because, I believe, they are so quick to squat without our noticing it. Odors permeate the floors, enticing repeats.

Some owners believe that if a dog can sleep in their crate during the night without having an accident they should be able to do this in the daytime. All animals eliminate if it becomes physically uncomfortable for them to hold it.

A good schedule to follow is this: Take the puppy outside when awakening in the morning, after every meal, after every playtime, after every nap –automatically every 30 to 45 minutes during the day. You must remain outside with the puppy until it eliminates. Give it praise as it eliminates, each and every time. Some owners offer treats to their puppy after it completes its chores, however the act of elimination is a reward itself. Offering treats can confuse.

For six, seven and eight week old puppies, a small litter box can certainly be utilized by the breeder. I have one I move from the night sleeping quarters to the living room play quarters. However, when at six weeks (rain or cold or shine) they are introduced to the outside, I take away the litter box except at nighttime. It may take two to four weeks for a Havanese puppy to become "kind of reliable." Medium sized dogs are not deemed reliable in housetraining until five months. Toy dogs, which includes the Havanese, are not deemed reliable until eight months!

While the puppy Havanese is enormously receptive to new experiences, their attention span is extremely short. Training instills habit at this age. It does not necessarily instill remembrance of what went on a moment earlier. That's one reason housetraining for elimination is not reliable. Be patient. Guide the puppy. Don't chastise the puppy.

When breeders follow common-sense housetraining procedures most puppies housetrain quickly. Here are two examples of how influential early imprinting is:

A Havanese puppy owner, Kay Barnum of Anchorage, Alaska writes: "The first clue that Tango was an exceptional puppy was when I began house-training upon his arrival here at 10 weeks of age. I was expecting a long, intense training process knowing the reputation toy breeds have for being very difficult to house train and in fact being a total impossibility in some breeds. Not to worry. Tango from the very first day used the "litter box" which I lined with wee-wee-pads. October being quite cold in Alaska, and that year we had snow early, I was pleased that he adapted so quickly to the litter box and fully expected that he would use it for his entire life. He had other plans. I had placed the box by the back door convenient for him to access. One morning while I was upstairs working in my office, I kept hearing

Tango making a little "woof" noise. Thinking he was playing with the cat, I ignored it for about 20 minutes and finally went to check on them because this little "woof" continued.

"There was Tango standing at the back door woofing to get out and as soon as I opened the door he raced outside to go potty. I could not believe it! He was only 11 weeks old! Thinking it was just a one time thing, I kept the litter box at the back door for him to use. He did not ever use the box again but always came to get me to let him out and he never, ever had an "accident" on the floor. Even when he was totally engrossed in playing with one of the cats, he would suddenly run as fast as his little legs would carry him to the door and make his little whisper "woofs" to get my attention. And at night he would put his cold, wet little nose on my face to wake me so he could go out."

Second owners, who picked up their puppy at eight weeks of age, called on the telephone several hours after they took her home. "Maybe this is a one-time thing," said Bill Larson, "but after we took Emma on an exploration adventure of house and yard, she ran to the patio door and barked. Jane and I once again let her outside. She jumped off the patio and promptly did her 'big chores.' Amazing!" While Emma did perform her "big chores" outside, it took two months before she could be trusted to run freely in the house without stopping to empty her bladder when it became uncomfortably full.

Warning: It's a common phenomenon that puppies around 14 to 15 weeks of age test owners. Perhaps at the moment they haven't had enough attention or perhaps they are just telling you, "I'm a precocious puppy and I want to do what I want to do when and where." They will suddenly and without warning, piddle right in front of you on your best rug. Don't scold. To scold would be giving attention. Instead, exclaim indignantly, pick up the recalcitrant silently, put him outside and close the door on him. When you bring him back in, get him in your arms and cuddle together on the couch. Tell him, "I know you'll do better next time." And he will.

Then one day, when he is about 15 weeks old, he runs to the door, sits down and looks back at you. "I need to go to the bathroom," he says with those eloquent eyes and expression. His attention span is lengthening. He's growing up. He understands. And unless he's kept inside too long, outside is where he performs his chores. Happy day! Wonderful puppy!

TOY BOX

If when the puppy enters his new home, he finds he has a toy box with several toys and sterilized bones inside it, he will be reluctant to chew or destroy yours. He has his own. This is not a guarantee he will not investigate ends of carpets or chair legs while teething, however, a toy box with dog toys helps a puppy understand what is his and what is yours.

FENCED YARD AND ROOM TO RUN AND PLAY

Dogs become bored in their own yard when put outside for long periods to while away time. When there is nothing to do, they begin to dig or tear at bushes and bark at traffic and people going by beyond their fence. Your puppy needs you to play with him. Take 10 minutes a day to play with your puppy outside on his terms. The bond between you becomes stronger, his willingness to please you becomes stronger, and his joy is everlasting.

My yards have chicken wire attached all along the fence lines covering the lower part of my no-climb fences. Havanese find it irresistible to learn what is on the other side of any

Roughrider Cooper, at age 10 weeks is investigating this piece of paper. Cooper's owner is Patricia O'Shaughnessy-Clark.

fence. Neighbors horses graze in my pastures during the summertime and horse leavings are delicious tidbits to dogs. So are the different weeds and wild flowers that decorate the pastures. My Havanese escape artists like to push their bodies under chicken wire, so I have had to have it anchored well.

LAP HUGGING

A chore you and he will delight in. A time not just to cuddle and touch, but also for a one-to-one talk.

MANNERING

All puppies need to learn mannering in order to gain confidence in themselves and the environment surrounding them. The grooming chapter introduces the basic commands of sit, stand and down commands and suggestions on teaching them to your puppy while he is on the grooming table. But that is not enough. Training and socialization of your puppy, as stated earlier, is an ongoing project.

INVESTIGATION

As I wrote in my book *"The New Complete Portuguese Water Dog,"* (1997), a "puppy constantly craves information about everything it sees, hears or touches. Exploring via touch or taste by mouth is an ideal way for it to gain information. We have hands as well as mouths; puppies have only mouths."

We keep an eye on our puppies not only because we need to housetrain eliminations but also to housetrain investigations. Your Havanese will follow you wherever you go in the house; that's good. When he stops and begins to nibble on a protruding edging of a carpet or the rung of a chair, a low, soft "grrrrrr" from the bottom of your throat will lift his head. Reach into your pocket for a toy he can bite at or try to pull apart. Praise goes along with his acceptance.

Nibbling of your clothes, the untying of shoelaces, or the stealing of clothing items from closets or beds all fall under the category of investigation of the center of his life – you. So don't scold. Growl. Distract. Growling is effective because that is what their mother does when her pups annoy her. Distracting is effective because the Havanese puppy attention span is short – well! Except for food, your lap and a nap.

TEETHING

Milk teeth are not always fully erupted until a Havanese is about 10 to 12 weeks of age. It's a period when chewing is essential to the puppy's comfort. The toy box serves as a reminder to him that he has possessions he can chew. Other items good for him to chew are dampened and frozen washcloths, small sterilized bones purchased at pet stores, sticks of celery and carrots, and large holed marrow bones. I keep a supply of refrigerated celery sticks, carrots and marrow bones when I have a litter of puppies. I simmer a few marrow bones in a pan of boiling water for five minutes, cool them down and remove the marrow. Heavy fat such as is found in the marrow is too rich for Havanese. The large holed bones are then clean and healthy bones for Havanese to teeth on. Never use the narrow ringed marrow bones. They are dangerous. They can get caught in the puppy's mouth or jaw.

A puppy gets his permanent teeth between the ages of four to seven months. Chewing becomes more pronounced after these teeth begin to settle in its mouth. He has to chew to relieve the discomfort. There are products on the market which sprayed on to surfaces deter chewing for a few hours. I once had a Dalmatian puppy finish off a cabinet door after the odor and taste of a product called "Bitter Apple" wore off. He was fine during the morning hours after an initial spray, but when I left him after lunchtime, unless I resprayed, he chewed.

PROOFING

Just as parents must baby-proof a house, puppy owners must puppy proof. Don't leave shoes, purses or paper lying on a low table or chair. An agile Havanese puppy's reach is exceptional. Puppies and dogs also have a penchant for finding a loose thread on a carpet or from a cushion on a favorite chair and working at it until it unravels. I don't mind a roll of paper from the bathroom strewn in a line down the hallway floor. Misbehavior like this is enchanting to us and delightful to the puppy once it discovers what fun it is to roll the paper off the roll. Just growl when your puppy gets hold of something he must not have. Be sure to wrap or tie electric cords. Cover them with a pillow. Or offer something he can munch on. Havanese learn mannering quickly because they are so willing to please.

WHISTLE COMMAND

Young Havanese puppies seldom leave your side. It's when they reach the toddler age (just like human toddlers) that they feign deafness when you call. They are busy! Doing something or nothing. They are learning to be self-fullfilling, to do what makes them happy and comfortable. Yet when they hear the whistle (if they have been weaned with a whistle announcing their food dish), they will come running. This is a wonderful command. Once learned, you will discover the whistle is as necessary a tool when walking the dog as is the collar and leash. It is described fully in my book, "Devoted to Dogs." A short lesson is to use the whistle each time you put down the puppy's food dish. You do not want to use a silent whistle. You want to speak to the puppy with the whistle. Whistles with far-reaching, shrill and solid tones are the Acme Thunderer and the Genie Commander. Both can be purchased at sport stores. Place it on a lanyard and hang it around your neck. Each time you feed the puppy, blow the whistle. Don't just "toot toot." You want the puppy to understand that when you blow the whistle it means his food is ready for him. It will only take several feedings for the "whistle imprint." Then use it to command him to come when you are in the yard with him. Give him a treat when he responds. Practice several times a day with your puppy. In a few days the whistle command becomes part of the sounds he always responds to.

Now repeat these lessons without a whistle. Be sure to use a high lilting voice when calling your dog and always be consistent with a command. A good one is "Come," the command used in obedience training. Treat when he gets to you.

MANNERING OF THE OLDER PUPPY

Here are several suggestions.

Havanese, whatever their basic temperament, love to show off. A conformation class offers them this opportunity. It gives pets as well as potential show dogs a burst of confidence. In

A conformation class gives pets as well as potential conformation dogs a wonderful opportunity to show off and to be given praise and treats. This is a Susan Nelson handling class.

addition, these classes aid in mannering. Locate and call your area's local kennel club to inquire about these classes. The reason these classes are valuable for pets as well as potential show dogs is that dogs and puppies are moved around a simulated ring walking by their owners' left side. They are given praise and treats as they turn corners. They are touched, praised and treated by the instructor as they come to a standing halt in front of him/her. There isn't a nicer way to teach a puppy to accept hands-on examinations by strangers or to walk on leash and stay close to an owner's side than in one of these classes.

There are a multitude of excellent training books available at your local public library. Reading these will help you decide if you want to enter your *older* puppy (five or six months) in an obedience class. Taking your dog to a positive taught basic obedience class is a must in my opinion. These are some of the things I tell my students who sign up for my classes.

TRAINING HINTS

All animals are self-fulfilling. They do what makes them happy and comfortable. They avoid things which are unpleasant.

In all dog training, trainers harness the dogs' three basic survival drives –the food drive, sex drive and avoidance drive. We harness this power by channeling each drive into positive actions. For example, you have a friend hold your Havanese and you tease him with a ball and run away. You then turn and call your dog to you. The person holding your dog lets him go and your dog runs to you faster than he ever has before. When he reaches your side you give him the ball. He is loaded in drive and we have begun to channel the drive into an obedience exercise, the recall.

The drive of avoidance, is one we do NOT want the dog to use. A dog can change from any other drive into the avoidance drive the fastest, without any warning. The avoidance drive is based on fear or confusion. Teaching heeling to a dog using the avoidance drive makes for unhappy, sluggish dogs.

We do utilize the avoidance drive in exercises such as sit, down and stay. Example: you tell the dog to sit as you push his rear to the ground. As soon as he sits, you praise him. To a novice trainer, a push on the rear may not seem like pressure, but to our pets this is unpleasant. However, by repetition of the exercise the dog learns that when he hears "sit," pressure comes. To avoid this he sits and is praised. In time he forgets the pressure and sits to receive the reward, a treat and praise.

Dogs learn by association, repetition and through play. Yet no dog or human learns or retains what he/she is studying if he's overstressed. In obedience, the goal is to teach your dog that training is fun. It leads him towards fulfillment.

Breaks: We give breaks to load our dogs with drive. During breaks students must play with their dog and get him excited. You want the dog to jump in the air in pleasure, to tug on a toy. The moment the teacher says "sit," you unload the dog. He must immediately sit and not move until released to do something else. Loading and unloading are important steps in sound training. For example, someone rings the doorbell at your house. The dog becomes loaded with excitement. You command "sit" and the dog sits. That is an example of loading and unloading.

Just as loading and unloading are important tools in training, your tone of voice is a highly important tool. You use a confident and clear voice when giving commands. You use a low growl tone when your dog is doing something he should not do. "Uggg" coming from deep in your throat is like a growl. It becomes the only correction (punishment) ever needed with a Havanese. A high lilting tone tells your dog you are pleased with it. Praise is effective given in a high tone of voice.

In training you need to praise your dog frequently. Praise tells him he is doing something kind of right and as he grasps what the exercise is all about, all right. He does not know this if you do not praise.

When heeling, talk to your dog in a happy, positive tone. Heeling is a difficult exercise for a dog to learn. Therefore, the trainer must always be upbeat when teaching heeling. In training a dog to move correctly, you must move your body correctly. The dog is a great observer and imitator of movement. Do not walk in uncertain, awkward steps. Walk with a purpose. Walk in a straight line when heeling. Take long, quick, happy steps. When teaching your dog to turn, turn sharply and happily, saying to your dog, "Wow, isn't this fun!" as he turns with you. He will then think turns are great fun.

When you take your Havanese for a walk, keep him by your side. If he pulls forward, stop and wait for him to look back at you. Remain still until he returns to you. Then begin walking again. Each time he pulls, stop. A few walks like this and he will watch you and remain beside you. He soon will become an expert heeler. You as a leader allow him to sniff and explore only on your terms. When you allow him to sniff, give him an OKAY command. He can then do what he wishes as long as he does not pull you when he gets to the end of the leash. If he does, be ready to either turn around, back up or stop until he stops pulling.

Taking your Havanese for a walk around the block daily may get to seem mundane to you after a while. Not to your Havanese. Each walk is full of new smells, sounds and objects he can investigate with eyes, ears and nose. Walking your Havanese is also a great time to teach him the meaning of sounds he'll remember which will become habit. For instance, when you turn a corner at the end of the block, command "Turn" in a happy, lilting voice. When you come to a crossing, command "Stop" in a firm voice and push down on his rump as you say "Sit." It will only take several walks for him to begin doing these things on his own. And you never know. This might prove a life-saver sometime.

Each experience you give your Havanese will increase his knowledge. Your Havanese will learn by watching you attentively. To him, sounds and body movement are canine school books just as is the collar and leash.

Your puppy automatically develops great memory for sounds. The swish of a plastic bag, the noise of an opening refrigerator door, your car's engine as it turns the corner for home

Your puppy wants to be a part of what you are doing. Selena does. This is Ch Tapscott Tickled Pink owned and loved by Sheryl Roach.

- these are sounds that bring him right to your side with a smile and a look in his eyes that says, "I want to be a part of what you are doing" or "How happy I am you are home."

You need only respond with a hug, a touch, a caress or a "Good dog," and his heart bursts with joy.

PUPPY MANNERING REMEMBER RULES

When puppies (and dogs) know what you want, they have the ability to respond. By mannering and training them you help make them happier, more confident and easier to live with.

Consistency, patience and positive attitudes are the best rules for training your Havanese.

Puppies are like small children in that they test you. Be sure when a dog isn't quite certain what you want, that you encourage and praise each correct step. When he knows what you want, when you give him a command, follow through and enforce it.

Never get angry at your dog. If you become frustrated (and we all do), go sit down and pet your dog while you think through the problem. Then get up and have him do something he knows well, so you can praise him. If the dog is confused, *you* have caused the confusion.

You must also pay attention to how your dog reacts in any situation. Each Havanese is different. Some require lots of praise while another needs a firmer hand.

A well mannered Havanese is trained, not born.

Chapter Eleven

Grooming

Remember Rule: When you own a Havanese, correct grooming
becomes a responsibility.

We're going to talk about grooming. If you don't like to groom a dog, please do not adopt a Havanese. True, there are those of us who take our four-legged animal children to groomers for this task; however, you still have to do maintenance grooming on, preferably, a daily basis. So think about the chores of grooming before you take one of these toy dogs to your heart.

ENJOYABLE GROOMING

Since daily grooming of a Havanese is necessary, it's up to you to make these frequent sessions enjoyable. Grooming puppies should be an endeavor full of kisses and hugs - a relaxing activity for both of you. If it isn't, grooming will soon turn into a chore not looked forward to by either of you.

Enjoyable grooming depends upon how you start. And correct grooming has its rewards. Your dog's coat will shine and develop into a coat of great beauty. You both will be proud of the way he looks; he'll strut and you will have many compliments on his appearance.

As soon as your Havanese has investigated his new home, get him back in your arms and place him on his grooming table. Give him a treat as you hold him there and he looks down at a new vista. Exclaim how wonderful he is. (Always treat an older dog or a visiting dog as you would a young puppy.)

GROOMING TABLE

You may decide his grooming place will be on the top of your washing machine or dryer or on a small sturdy table (never use an unsteady table) which you also use for other things.

It's best to give a dog his very own grooming table. By doing so, you give him a possession he treasures. Starting him out on his very own table, making the spray bottle, the brush and comb experience a fun time, he'll thoroughly enjoy this very special time. He'll quickly learn his grooming table is a place where he gets complete attention from you. It becomes a bonding table, a comfort table, a fun table. With those precepts installed, he will be eager to be placed on it, even when at about eight to nine months his puppy coat changes to an adult coat and his drop coat mats!

TRANSITION PERIOD

During this two to five month period he will begin to develop the rich, thick outer coat which helped attract this breed to you. (It should be in its full glory when he reaches three to five years of age.) He will also develop a dense undercoat; in some dogs this undercoat starts off as wooly or cottony. It quickly becomes a mess if not cared for.

One reason the Havanese is called non-shedding is that his hairs don't fall on the floor or grab onto couches or people's clothes as those of shedding breeds do. So-called non-shedding breeds, of which the Havanese is one, don't drop hairs off the body. They retain them. But if you do not brush and comb the non-shedding Havanese frequently, the dead hairs resting in his undercoat become tangled with the hairs on the forming voluminous, gorgeous top coat. Mats form. Then it is "ouch time" for your Havanese as you attempt to unravel them. Dematting is lots of careful, gentle work. During this period your Havanese may begin to dislike being groomed. Can you blame him?

GENTLE TOUCHING

Begin your grooming sessions with gentle touching. Touch is one of the dog's most important senses. The dog's need to be touched and petted is important in its bonding to humans and in play with other dogs.

After setting him on the table, hold him with your right hand under his head, your fingers touching his ears. Remember this phrase: *control of the head is control of the dog.* Your left hand will hold his back up. How? Place your left hand between his back legs under his rump and raise the rump. There. He is standing. With your left fingers fondle his tummy. Now take your left hand away and massage his whole body with your fingers, including muzzle, head, legs, feet, chest, back, flanks and tail. As you massage, sweet talk. "Oh, you are wonderful. What a good puppy." Then take away one of your hands, give him a treat and place him back on the floor. Two to three sessions is all it will take for him to enjoy being lifted onto the table and massaged.

INITIAL SUPPLIES

Now that we have begun our grooming sessions, let's go over the supplies that are needed.

1. Grooming table, a sturdy table that will not wobble, preferably a commercial canine grooming table. Laps, while watching TV or enjoying R&R, are nice for quick brush-ups.

2. If you like, place a rubber backed mat or towel on the grooming table to prevent slipping. I place a towel on the table after bathing my dogs.

3. Two combs, greyhound type, which have both wide and narrow teeth.

4. Two pin brushes (be sure the tips are not raised). Expensive pin brushes are worth the money.

5. Two bristle brushes.

6. Two spray bottles, each filled with 3/4 cup water and 1/4 cup rinse or conditioner.

Why two sets of the above? It is convenient to keep one alongside your special chair in the living room. Many Havanese owners like to brush and comb while relaxing or watching TV.

7. Treats. Puppy treats should be those your dog's breeder suggests. Tummies of young Havanese puppies are still in the development stage. It's advisable not to give a variety of treats and supplements until the puppy is at least four months of age.

MIST AND BRUSH

On the third grooming session, after a gentle massage, introduce him to the spray bottle and contents by lightly misting his body and legs. Take the brush and brush him. Make the brushing fun. Talk to him. Tell him how handsome he is. Lift a rear leg and brush it, lift one front leg, brush it, turn him so you can lift the other front leg and brush it. He'll fidget and wiggle when you start on his legs, particularly his front legs. Most dogs protest when their front legs are combed or brushed. Legs are sensitive body parts. Also, front legs have almost invisible hair feelers to aid in scent explorations. Toy dogs are notorious for not wanting these feelers disturbed, thus they pull away their front legs when their coats need to be brushed and combed.

If he tries to turn around or lean down and mouth your hand or brush, laugh and tell him matter of factly, "This is something you have to have done every day." Don't stop when he protests. It is normal for a dog to protest when he does not know what is going to happen to him. Your manner should display confidence in order for him to become confident under your hands. Finish brushing with your left hand as you hold him under the head with your

right hand. Keep the session short. One minute is long enough. When you have finished, praise him, offer him a treat and place him back down on the floor.

MIST AND COMB

Next session add the comb. Combing gets down to the skin. It also helps dislodge mats. No, he won't have mats as a puppy if brushed and combed every day. But both brush and comb are essential grooming tools. It is easy for the comb to get down to the skin and it is easy to brush and not get down to the skin if you do not know the correct way to brush. Here's the reason brushing is necessary. Brushing brings out sheen. It stimulates oil in his coat. Brushing also stimulates growth of new hair. Therefore both brush and comb are essential grooming tools. You will soon understand that Havanese grooming must begin at the skin. Right now, since he is a puppy, both brush and comb slide easily through the hair to the skin.

COMMANDS TO LEARN

In these initial grooming sessions spend time teaching your puppy (or older dog) what the commands sit, stand, side down and belly up mean. Use them in your grooming sessions. Teaching these commands is easy. And your dog soon will retain the commands and actions he has been taught and be proud to comply. He knows it shows how smart he is!

So let's have some fun. Here are suggestions in teaching these commands.

Sit: Hold a treat above the puppy's head and as the puppy raises his head to see what you have in your hand, sit him with your other hand on his croup with fingers underneath his tail. As you sit him, not before or after, gently command, "Sit." With repetition, he soon learns that when he sits, he hears the "sit" sound. Within a few days, when you command "Sit," he'll automatically sit without any physical pressure from you.

Stand: Hold a treat straight in front of his head. If he is sitting he will rise and lean forward to see what you have in your hand. *As* he stands, not before or after, gently command, "Stand."

Side Down: No dog, puppy or adult, likes to be taken off his feet. Their defense instinct protests, sometimes mightily. However, when your puppy becomes an adult, combing and brushing him while he is lying down makes the job easier on both of you. So teach him now. To place him on his side, do as dog show handlers do. He is standing. Gather him to you, wiggly or not, wrapping your arms around the length of his body firmly, holding his legs and gently and swiftly lift and place him (don't shove him) onto the table, lifting his feet, commanding, "Side down." It's as simple as that. Quickly massage his tummy as he wonders how he got to where he is. Then take the brush and brush his tummy with nice long, gentle strokes. Tell him, "See, it's just to brush you nicely here." Laugh and let him up. It may take a few days or even a week for him to understand the reason for "Side down." He will. In fact, after a few sessions he'll more than likely lie down before you tell him to do so. Havanese are bright. They like to be comfortable while being brushed.

Belly up: This is simply a continuation of side down. It's an easy command for him to learn after he learns "Side down." Be sure to massage, then quickly brush and comb before you allow him up. Of course, reward his cooperation with a treat.

MEASURING STICK AND SCALE

Your grooming sessions, while he is a puppy, need only last one to three minutes a day. I like to introduce a measuring stick and weighing scale after the initial week of grooming. Use these once a week. You want to see how your puppy is growing. Write down the figures on his puppy notepad. He'll learn to accept these "odd to him" tools easily now that he has learned what grooming sessions are all about.

BATHING YOUR PUPPY

Advice given dog owners by layman dog owners in bygone days was that bathing should only be done several times a year. Bathing dogs with the harsh soaps then available could eliminate the oils in a dog's coat and thus damage a long-coated dog's hair. Many dog owners bathed their dogs in cold water, using canning jars or bowls or pans to rinse them with. This made for unhappy baths, inadequate rinsing, limp, dull, sticky coats and irritated skin. We've come a long way since "lumps of soaps" (usually white curd) were the only soaps available. Next came Ivory soap, which now, in its liquid form, is often used for soaping dogs (as well as people), and because of its purity, cleans and rinses off well. (Dawn Antibacterial, used to remove oil from birds soaked in oil, is another liquid soap popular for bathing dogs.) Today, there are excellent sweet smelling shampoos, cream rinses, conditioners, oils, fragrances, insecticides, etc., available in every price range for grooming dogs. It's a billion dollar business. Some groomers scoff at canine grooming products, preferring to use people shampoos and conditioners. Your breeder will suggest several brands. Other fanciers will tell you which ones they like. Pick and choose and use the ones that enhance your dog's coat.

FREQUENCY OF BATHING

Frequent massaging, combing and brushing will maintain your puppy's coat in superb condition. As far as bathing twice a year, even in the late 19th century, knowledgeable

English dogmen advocated that "dogs kept in the house should be washed once every week or ten days." Vero Shaw, author of *"The Illustrated Book of the Dog"* (1870), added that "washing is not so necessary where grooming is strictly attended to." I certainly agree with Shaw's statement that grooming should be "strictly attended to," and although the Havanese coat can look great for more than a week when it is groomed every day, because of sticks and dirt and weeds and mud which cling to his coat, I suggest he be bathed every week or 10 days.

While the Havanese is one of over 20 so-called "non-shedding" breeds, it is also a "non-shedding" breed of sticks, weeds, grass-cuttings, sand, mud, snow, rain, water, etc. My five Havanese enjoy the "run-like-hell" game, chasing each other at full gallop over the Montana prairie's dry grasses or frozen soil on my ranchette. Many interesting weeds (or snow and iceballs) cling to them when they traipse back into the house, breathless from their fun excursions. These need to disappear by both grooming and/or bathing.

Author of the book, "A Dog Of our Own" (1979) stated, "You should NEVER BATHE a puppy under six months old." Other writers insist no puppy should be bathed more than once a month. If so, these writers claim, you dry the skin and break the hair. How absurd! Responsible breeders bathe puppies once or twice before they go to their permanent homes at eight to 12 weeks. Sickly puppies often need to be bathed. I once had to give baths to seven four week old puppies for three days straight because they had raging diarrhea after catching a virus one of my other dogs brought back home from a

This puppy belonging to Beth Johnson, Feliz Havanese, is getting a bath.

dog show. My veterinarian gave me explicit directions: "Bathe those puppies and dry them well." Puppies must also be bathed if infested with fleas, ticks, etc. And exploring puppies can get quite dirty. Clean skin and hair is important for a dog's health. And what is prettier than a sparkling, cleanly bathed Havanese puppy? Nothing! With warm bath water, common-sense toweling, warm (not hot) blow drying and house privileges for the remainder of a cold day, puppies and their coats thrive with once or bi-weekly baths.

BATH SUPPLIES

What is necessary to have on hand when bathing a dog? A bathtub, of course. It is first on

the list. The kitchen sink makes a great bathtub for a Havanese. A raised tub, so you do not have to bend over, is ideal. Not ideal is a shower stall even if you are in it with your Havanese and you are holding him in your arms. That would certainly be uncomfortable (although many owners do bathe their dogs just like that); it sometimes makes the dog dislike being bathed (not that many are ever happy being bathed)! If a shower is all

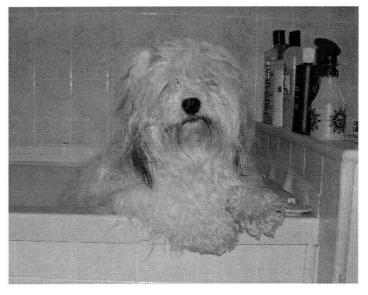

The author purchased a bathtub from a trailer company, had it installed on a platform and there is no stooping involved.

you have in your house, I suggest you purchase a small plastic table or bench and a rubber backed mat. Set those in the shower stall. Place your puppy on the table with the mat covering it while you bathe him. I have done this in an emergency. It doesn't frighten the puppy as does water sprayed from way up there to way down here. A dear friend of mine fills her bathtub with water every Friday evening, plunks some baby water toys in it and then her Havanese, who is jumping up and down with excitement beside the tub waiting to be lifted into it. What fun that little Havanese has in the nice tub of warm water on which float toys she can mouth and push about until her mistress is ready to soap her.

Other bath supplies are:

1. Shampoo
2. Cream rinse or conditioner
3. Soft sponge or wash cloth
4. Cotton balls to place in ears to keep them dry
5. Three towels; one to wrap the wet puppy in and two to dry him

6. Hand sprayer.

TUB ORIENTATION

The water should be warmer than lukewarm and your hands should be ready to hold your squirming puppy tightly so he cannot wiggle out of them as he attempts to climb out of the bathtub. He will try. One tip to make this first bath adventure a bit more pleasant for the puppy; place a treat on the floor of an empty tub and place the puppy in the tub. Show him the treat and allow him to eat it in the tub. Then let him explore the tub. Do this several times a day for a week. This will aid in acquainting the puppy to this very strange place.

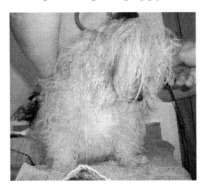

Although it is not necesssary to have water in the tub to bathe a dog if you have a hand sprayer, I suggest adding water so it reaches the top of his hocks in order to soak his feet well. Place the puppy in the tub and with sweet talk hope for not too much wiggling and splashing to get out.

SOAPING AND RINSING

Every groomer has his/her own way of doing things. These are my suggestions. Begin soaping behind the puppy's ears and work backward. He'll be less frightened or wiggly if you wet and soap his head, face and ears last. When you do, place a hand over his eyes to keep soap and water out of them. Shampoo, empty the tub and rinse well. Shampoo again, then rinse and rinse and rinse being sure to get all the soap out. Use the dampened sponge or wash cloth to gently clean around his eyes. Then pour either creme rinse or conditioner into your hands, smooth it over the puppy's body and legs. Let it settle into his coat (follow the instructions listed on the product), then rinse thoroughly. Note: On badly matted

My socialization engineers enjoy giving my Tawney a bath and drying her as seen in these three photos.

138

adult coats, many owners leave the conditioner on the dog until the mats smoothly leave the coat. Then it is rinsed out. Sometimes, the conditioner is left on the coat until mat "season" expires.

SHAMPOOS

"The purpose of shampoos for dogs, as well as for people," a well-respected barber friend told me, "is to cleanse skin and hair and leave it in good condition. The reason water alone can't do the job is that water molecules aren't equipped to pull dirt and dust free from the outer layers of skin and hair - the cuticle. Shampoo molecules are. Each little shampoo molecule has a head and a tail. The head is attracted to water (but does not like dirt) and the tail is attracted to dirt, grease and oil but does not like water. Working as a team, both parts of the shampoo molecule cleanse the hair.

"That is why it is so important," he continued, "to properly massage shampoo into the skin and hair of your dogs. The little tails of the shampoo molecules roll the dirt and grease up into tiny globular shaped balls and lift them away from the skin and hair cuticle.

"That's why it's also necessary to have the correct Ph balanced shampoo for your dogs (as well as for humans). A too-alkaline shampoo has an excess of these shampoo molecules. Too many molecules open imbrications and cause tangles.

"Hair overlaps just like shingles overlap on a good roof job. Excess shampoo molecules separate the layers of hair when you massage; the hair rubs together and forms tangles and mats."

Two scientists who studied hair molecules of many mammalian species, found that canine hair was the most alkaline of all species tested. Draizee (1942) took samples from six areas of each dog's skin tested. The Ph range was 5.18 to 9.18. Ninety-five percent of the samples fell within the range of 6.2 to 8.6, and the average of all readings was 7.52.

In 1954, Roy found the "skin of normal dogs had a Ph of 5.5 to 7.2." Roy felt that dogs with acute moist dermatitis had hyperhidrosis (excessive amounts of apocrine secretion on the skin suface). In 92 percent of these cases, the Ph ranged between 8.2 and 9.0. "It is not clear," he said, "whether Ph has an influence on skin disease in the dog."

Acid Shampoos: A shampoo with a Ph balance of 5.5 would be a mild shampoo for dogs, one you could use often. That's an acid shampoo. Acid shampoos range from 4.5 to 5.5 Ph. They cleanse out dirt and debris but not to the point that they remove the natural oils from the hair. As we know, shiny hair comes from oils left behind. Shine also comes because the cuticle layer of the hair lies flat when it has been shampooed. You get more

"shine" reflection from a flat surface.

Acid shampoos (low Ph balanced) don't remove oil and there is no necessity for extra conditioners to be added to them. Most professional human beauty salon shampoos are acid - 4.5 to 5.5 Ph - since the normal human skin Ph balance is 5.5. They do a very good to excellent job on most people.

Neutral Shampoos: The higher the Ph balance in a shampoo, the more cleansing action there is and the more drying the shampoo is. In the supermarkets the Ph balance used in most national brand shampoos is 7, which is neutral. Baby shampoos are 7 Ph. Baby shampoos are made primarily so babies don't cry when shampoo gets in their eyes. But baby shampoos may strip out oil from hair. Then the user needs a conditioner.

"There's another thing to remember," my barber friend told me. "The cleansing action of the shampoo depends, not just on the alkalinity, but also on the contact time with the skin, scalp or hair. Many alkaline products work beautifully without damage to the skin, scalp or hair because their contact time - if the label instructions are followed - is short.

Alkaline Shampoos: "Any shampoo from 7.5 to as high as 9 Ph is an alkaline product. The higher ones burn eyes. Many supermarket shampoos burn eyes because these products strip all oils from the hair. These shampoos have to have conditioners put back into them. If you have dry hair, or if your dog has dry hair, you are probably using a high Ph balance shampoo, 7 or over," he said.

"A dog's owner," he added, "has to find the Ph balance of their dog. My suggestion is to start out with a mild shampoo, say one with a 5.5 Ph balance, and work up."

He suggested I go to the drugstore and ask the druggist for Ph paper. "The paper comes supplied with a scale with a color code. Touch the dog's shampoo with this paper and it will turn color. Check the color against the color code on the Ph paper. It tells you the Ph balance of the shampoo, not that of your dog."

"Those little molecules with their heads and tails really fascinated me," I said. "What happens to them during rinsing?"

My friend laughed. "The reason you have to rinse hair well after it's been shampooed is that the shampoo molecule heads, which are attracted to water, follow the warm water currents and the shampoo molecule tails which are holding these little globules of dirt and grease, are attached to the heads. They have to follow the heads.

"So the dirt is removed by the rinsing when the dirt loving tail follows the water loving head. It is never removed during shampooing. It is just held together in a little glob by the tail. If you are shampooing with an alkaline shampoo (high Ph balanced), you have to rinse thoroughly and then thoroughly once again because alkaline shampoos contain an excess amount of those little shampoo molecules."

"What about brushing of the hair?" I asked. "What are the best types of brushes for humans, and how about good brushes for dogs?"

"It used to be," he told me, "that women spent a long time brushing their hair each day. But that was back when people only washed their hair every two weeks or so. Boar bristle brushes were commonly used for brushing. The hair had to be brushed well to bring the oil out to the ends of the hair, especially if the hair was long. Remember, the oil was deleted by the shampoos. Practically all shampoos were highly alkaline in those days.

"Things have changed. We understand a lot more. We have learned that if we use an acid (low Ph balanced) shampoo, we should add conditioners. Either way, we don't have to brush, brush and brush to get oil to the ends of the hair. Modern brushes of nylon and wire (for dogs) are now made with a lot more space between the brushes. These spaces allow the bristles to get down to the scalp (or skin of the dog). When the brushes get down to the scalp or skin, circulation is stimulated almost immediately.

"My recommendation," my friend finalized, "is to shampoo with a canine Ph balanced shampoo for the dog, rinse well, and brush with a wide-spaced brush so the brushes get down to the skin. Finish with a massage of the dog's skin. This ought to help keep the skin fresh and the muscles firm."

Remember, start with a low Ph balanced shampoo and work up until your dog's hair is clean and shiny. When it is, you will have matched the Ph balance of your dog's hair and skin. Part of the reason you wanted a Havanese is because of the beauty of his coat. Therefore, it has to be taken care of on the outside as well as on the inside. For dogs to be shown at dog shows it becomes critical to use the best and most correct (for the dog) shampoo possible.

SUPPLIES FOR GROOMING AN ADULT HAVANESE

We come now to supplies needed for the lifetime grooming of your Havanese.

I've already given you suggestions for the table, combs, bristle brushes, pin brushes, spray bottles and their mixtures, towels and treats.

I suggest you add these items to those listed earlier:

1. Small jar to hold water

2. Cotton balls or clean moist wash cloths (to clean stains on hair around eyes daily and also to clean ears when necessary)

3. Jar of half alcohol and water or half vinegar and water or commercial ear wash (weekly chore). Don't become overly worried about surface dirt in the dog's ears and clean and clean and clean or continually pull little hairs out of the ear. In many cases doing this sets the stage for ear infections.

4. Canine (not human) toothpaste. Human toothpaste contains detergents not suitable for dogs to swallow. (I confess I do not clean my dogs' teeth. It is desirable to do so, however.)

5. Nail clippers (a weekly chore)

6. Mat removers

7. Scissors: (regular and blunt end scissors for tidying). The standard states: *"Minimal trimming of the hair at the inside corner of the eye is allowed for hygienic purposes only, not in an attempt to resculpt the planes of the head. Minimal trimming around the anal and genital areas, for hygienic purposes only, is permissible but should not be noticeable on presentation. The hair on the feet and between the pads should be neatly trimmed for the express purpose of a tidy presentation. Any other trimming or sculping of the coat is to be so severely penalized as to preclude placement. No other scissoring is allowed."*

8. Hair dryer: This can be a hand-held department store dryer instead of a canine hair dryer. Ideal is a stand canine dryer because you will not be encumbered by having to hold a dryer in one hand and comb, brush and perhaps hold the dog with the other. Pretty difficult to do with a squirming dog. A stand dryer leaves both hands free. It is a worthwhile investment in drying a Havanese. Importantly, never use the high heat switch on a department store dryer. Coats will not only look dried-out and limp; high heat strips oils and natural moisture.

9. Don't forget the treats. Since your adult Havanese should be groomed daily or at the least several times a week so that his coat does not mat, treats reward him for his cooperation.

COAT TALK

Hair is protein. It gives warmth. It gives protection from heat. It also protects against injury.

Tactile Hairs: Tactile hairs, found on lips, cheeks, front legs, elbows, flanks, above eyes in the nose, are extremely sensitive to touch. Tactile hairs help the dog feel its way in the dark or through narrow places. The sensitivity of tactile hairs on the dog's elbows and flanks are the main reason most detest having their legs groomed.

Hair Shaft: A hair's shaft, root, growth rate, texture (thick or thin), color, length and whether it is straight, wavy or curly depend on its genetic influences. These genetic influences vary from breed to breed. In the Havanese, curly is recessive to wavy.

Affects: Hair is affected by climate, seasonal and other environmental conditions such as dirt, dust, dampness and static. Static can cause matting and breakage of the hair shaft. Both damp, moist weather with high humidity and hot, dry weather can affect coat with tangles. Extremely dry weather, dirt and dust may cause splitting at the ends of each hair shaft.

Hair Follicle: The root of each hair lies in a sac (follicle) below the surface of the skin. At the bottom of the follicle, a projection called the papilla contains an artery from which it gets food. "A hair," wrote Vero Shaw in 1879, "is simply a quill on a small scale, being supplied with nutrition and colouring matter from the papilla on which it grows."

Hair Shapes: Hair varies in shape from flat to round. The flatter the hair, the wavier or curlier it will be; the rounder the hair, the straighter it will be. Color, determined by heredity, comes from a pigment in the hair root called melanin. Melanin produces the variety of colors you see in Havanese.

CONCLUSION

As obvious by the above brief summary, environment, diet, climate and maintenance, as well as heredity affect hair; in this instance, the Havanese coat. Therefore, the Havanese requires consistent grooming to keep him looking and feeling his best. Along with an optimum diet, grooming will also aid in keeping him healthy, because under your watchful eye and work, his coat is less susceptible to mats and his skin less susceptible to infestations of fleas, ticks and other vermin when they are prevalent in your area.

WHY DOES THE HAVANESE ADULT COAT MAT?

As stated earlier, when a Havanese puppy reaches adolescence, between seven to nine months, he begins to grow a dense and sometimes wooly undercoat. The texture of the outside coat becomes stronger as it too develops. During this change of coat, mats often form because the growing and loose hairs of the undercoat tangle with the hair of the top coat. During this period, which can last from two to six months (yes, that long), the Havanese absolutely requires daily brushing and combing. Correct brushing and combing! I assumed one of my Portuguese Water Dog owners followed my suggestion that she groom down to the skin. However, when she took her puppy to a groomer when it reached nine months of age, the groomer quickly discovered mats covered most of the area right against the skin. The puppy owner had brushed and combed but never got below the surface.

When this period of coat change is complete, mats do not form as frequently. And most

dogs lose the cottony or wooly undercoats, thank goodness. It happened with one of mine. Some dogs sail through the puppy coat change with hardly any mats. I hope you are that lucky with your Havanese. As stated earlier, when you own a Havanese, grooming is one of the responsibilities of ownership.

COMPANION CUT

Grooming your Havanese need not be as frequent as it must be if you intend to show your dog in the conformation ring. We'll describe the Companion Cut shortly. We first have to get through the grooming responsibilities as the adult coat develops.

Here we go.

ADULT GROOMING

Be sure when you brush, to brush with long, firm strokes and comb gently with the wide teeth of the Greyhound comb.

HOW?

You are going to brush each side, belly, legs, rear and tail, then the front chest; finally the neck, head and ears. Your dog will get used to the routine quickly. Some people like to brush starting at the legs or head. It's an individual call.

USUAL PROCEDURE

Lay your Havanese on its side as explained earlier. "Side down."

Mist his coat lightly with the water and conditioner mix.

Make a small part of the body hair and hold in your hand the section above it. Hold it away from the part. Using the pin brush and then the greyhound comb, brush, then comb the small section beneath the part from the skin out until the brush and comb slide through the hair easily and there are no mats. Remember that the more thoroughly you brush, the fewer knots you will find. Continue grooming in this fashion parting the hair in small sections until the dog is

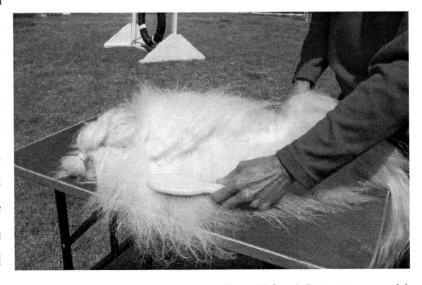

Susan Nelson's Buster is our model.

thoroughly brushed and combed from the skin out on that side. Include his belly. Then raise the back leg on that side. Oftentimes, leg hair is covered with tiny mats. They get the most wear when your Havanese is playing, so be certain the brush and comb can slide through the hair from the leg skin out.

He'll be tired now. Praise the dog, give him a hug and a treat as you allow him to stretch and relax. Then turn him around, groom the other side and the other hind and front leg. Again, give him a few moments to relax while you praise and treat. Now the chest and private parts. On males, do not trim the hair at the front of the penis. If you do, when he urinates, the flow can splatter instead of

AKC/UKC/INT Ch Shaggyluv's Blockbuster NA NAJ CGC is having his leg brushed.

flowing straight forward. Urine stains can discolor a female's anal area and also be sticky so trim the vulva area slightly with thinning shears so the female's flow will not splatter. If you intend to show your Havanese, remember that trimming of private parts should be done, *"for hygienic purposes only"* as the standard requires, and must *"not be noticeable on presentation."* Groom the rear, including the tail; then groom the head. Finally, take the scissors and neaten his feet by first combing and then scissoring neatly around the outside of the complete foot pad. Do not overdo. You only want to remove straggly ends.

In this grooming session you probably have half filled a small wastebasket with unwanted hair, some of it containing tangles and mats. If you tightly wad the unwanted hair into a ball, it will surely be baseball or larger in size.

Your dog feels so good when you finally place him down on the floor that he must dash about, and with a flurry of happy motion here and there, lie on his back, fling his legs into the air, roll over, and delightfully press different parts of his body against the floor. While he probably did not care for his bath and grooming, he certainly enjoys the feeling they gave him. You know he is proud of the way he looks when he smiles that wonderful Havanese smile and comes to you for approval.

"Aren't I handsome!" he exclaims by his actions. You agree enthusiastically.

FUN TIME

Now it is time to do something with your Havanese he thoroughly enjoys. Play ball with

145

him or play another game he likes, while you keep exclaiming how great he looks.

REMINDERS

When grooming without bathing, be sure you use the mist bottle and mist as you groom. If you brush with the hair dry, you encourage mats to form and the splitting of ends. I admit I sometimes begin to brush and comb dry; as soon as I remember Havanese coats should be glossy, I mist.

SHOW BATHING

If you are going to show your dog in a conformation dog show, bathe him a couple of days earlier, then brush and brush and brush until his coat lies smoothly against his sides and on his legs. That is a rule I learned from a top winning show handler. "Why do you keep brushing?" I had asked. "The more you brush before you take your dog into the ring the better his coat shines and the better it stays in place," was the answer.

Brush and brush and brush until his coat lies smoothly. Our model for this photo is Bailey, Ch Pocopayasos California Star CGC. Bailey is owned by Karen Ku, Kokomo Kennels.

HEAD PRESENTATION

Havanese have beautiful eyes. It is essential to show them off in the breed ring. The standard states head presentation well: *"The long, untrimmed head furnishing may fall forward over the eyes, naturally and gracefully to either side of the skull, or be held in two small braids beginning above the outer corner of the eyes, secured with plain elastic bands."* Learning how to make braids is not easy. One may require a helper to make them right, particularly with a wiggly Havanese attempting to watch what you are doing. Make a center part of the skull hair, divide it into three small sections and braid the three sections down (not up) to the outside corner of each eye, fastening each braid with a small rubber band. Remember what the standard says, *"small braids."*

COMPANION CUTS

After my first Havanese, Punxsy, won his championship, I decided to cut him down. It was summer. Since I also own Portuguese Water Dogs and clip them, I own clippers. I clipped Punxsy's entire body, legs, chest, rear and head down to about 5/8 inch using a #4 clipper blade. I trimmed his ears only slightly, keeping their length in balance with the rest

Punxsy, Ch Meme Zee's Spirit O Roughrider CD, owned by the author.

of his body. He looks very attractive in his Companion Cut. I receive many comments about his good looks when we go walking downtown. And he is comfortable, being free of all that hair and frequent grooming.

If you wish to keep your Havanese in a Companion Cut, reclipping should be done every five to six weeks. Most groomers like to start at the rear, clipping the rear legs, sides and body. Be sure to lift the leg on a male as you clip near the groin area. Be careful around the penis and anal regions on dogs and the vulva and anal region on bitches. I use a blunt end scissors in these areas and a #10 clipper blade. The back and front are done next, leaving the head, ears and neck for last. Hold the skin taut as you clip these areas so you don't nick the folds of skin close to the neck and face. The blunt end scissors should be used around eyes and nose.

COMPANION CUT SUPPLIES

To clip your Havanese, you require these supplies:

1. Clippers

2. Number 4 blade (will clip to approximately 5/8 inch)

3. Number 10 blade (will clip to approximately 1/8 inch)

4. Blunt scissors to neaten feet, private parts and eyes and nose

CONSOLATION NOTE

If you make a mistake in clipping, be consoled. Hair grows. Snip off the spotty excess. In as short a period as a week,

Roxie and Dooley in their Companion Cuts. Both are owned by Monica and Terry Hubbard.

you'll not see your mistake. Neither will anybody else. And your Havanese could care less.

NAIL TRIMMING

Every dog has 16 toenails, four on each foot. If the breeder has not had dewclaws removed from your dog's front feet, your dog will have 18. A few dogs have rear dewclaws as well as front ones. If your dog does, he'll have 20 nails for you to clip each week. Each week? Yes. Carpets, grass, tile, cement, asphalt - no matter what material he walks on, will not trim his toenails. Nail growth in some parts of the country (depending on minerals or lack of them in the water he drinks) will vary. Diet also plays a part in the growth of nails. In my opinion, clipping nails once a week is a good rule to follow.

LONG NAIL PROBLEMS

If you do not clip, you'll hear the clip clip clatter as his feet move on bare floors. Long toenails will soon destroy his beautiful movement. Long nails spread the toes. Long nails force a dog to push weight back over the pastern and walk in a flat-footed manner. The quick also gets thinner as nails get longer; they can then fracture. If left unclipped for many weeks, nails can grow into the back side of the dog's pads. It's happened many times and if you see such a sight, you'll cringe for the dog as well as for the sight of it.

NAIL QUICKS

Like human nails, each nail has a quick. As our nails do, the dog's quicks recede when nails are cut frequently. Look at your fingernails and toenails. You can see the pink quick. It happens sometimes that you cut into a dog's toenail quick, especially if they are black or dark colored or if he is protesting.

STYPTIC POWDER

A big seller - alerting you to the fact this problem happens often - is styptic powder. The powder puts an immediate stop to the profuse bleeding of injured quicks. Be sure to purchase a jar of this product. You also need canine toenail clippers. You can use cosmetic scissors while your Havanese is a puppy; his nails then are very fine. However, you must advance to toenail clippers by the time he is two or three months of age.

A DESPISED CHORE

No puppy wants or likes to have his nails clipped. Puppies make such a fuss in the initial sessions that many owners give up and take the dog to the veterinarian or groomer to cut his toenails. Don't do that! You are the boss. The first two or three times may make you feel the Havanese you love is a hellion on legs.

As you begin taking a foot in one hand, toenails clippers in the other, the puppy takes one look, screams, tries to force his way out of your lap, turns to nip you, and in fact, does everything to make it well nigh impossible for you to clip even one toenail. Do it! Without yanking his leg off, begin clipping a toenail on a rear foot. Hold the foot tightly. The rear foot is further away from his noisy head. If you persevere long enough you will somehow clip one nail without cutting into the quick. Good! You did it. Congratulations! Now clip another. Don't stop because he is bleating like a little lamb. Don't stop whatever this puppy does. His protective instinct is at work. He's fighting this chore just like he should. When humans have no idea what is happening to their bodies, the protective instinct takes over. That is what is happening here. You are telling him by your matter of fact attitude in a way he can understand that this is a necessary chore and he'd better get used to it. Keep saying that aloud if you feel you are weakening and allowing this small puppy (with the strength of an ox) to win this battle - which is right now. It might take you 15 minutes before all 16 or 18 nails are clipped and, hopefully, none have been clipped past the quick. If that does happen, immediately apply styptic powder with your finger right on the injured nail. It will immediately stop bleeding. Of course, your puppy has now been hurt. His tantrum will intensify. Don't, for goodness sake, coddle him or even think about saying you are sorry you hurt him. That would start another tantrum when you attempt to finish the task. Forget about the hurt quick. Turn up the sound on the TV or radio. Sing a song. Clip!

PROMISED SUCCESS

I assure you that by the third session - three weeks down the line - when you have him on your lap and the clippers are in your hand, he'll protest for a moment, and then (more than likely) turn his head away so he can't see what you are doing and you can clip from here on in with comparative peace and quiet.

One thing not to do, well, at least until he is an adult. Don't clip his toenails on the grooming table. While he becomes accustomed to this weekly chore, it will imprint dislike of the grooming table.

Clip on your lap.

EAR CARE

Be sure to place a cotton ball inside your Havanese' ears to protect them when giving him a bath. If you forget be sure to towel the inside of his ears thoroughly after the bath with cotton balls wrapped around a finger. Do not poke your finger or cotton deep into his ears.

EAR INFECTIONS

Havanese seldom get ear infections. Nature gave them a nice protective ear flap. If you

pluck hair from a Havanese ears, he may. Don't allow groomers to pluck hair from their ears. Nature put hair inside dogs' ears for protection.

Yeast is found on both human and animal bodies at all times. If our immune system is low in resistance, yeast can attack the ear or any other part of the body. A favorite place for yeast to attack is on front foot pads. Only when a yeast infection gets a good hold will a dog begin scratching his ears or chewing hair on his foot. So if you see toenail scratch marks on his outer ear and you extract a bit of dark, smelly material on a cotton ball when cleaning his ear and his ear emits a slight odor, take him to your veterinarian. A yeast infection on feet and legs? His chewing will make the hair turn pinkish and of course the hair will get thinner there. Your veterinarian will prescribe a product which will clear the yeast infection in about 10 days.

Many Havanese have a minor yeast growth on their lips. Saliva browns the hair there; a minor yeast infection blackens the hair. Nothing need be done if only several strands are black. You might want to wash and thoroughly dry this area more often.

Ear mites are not usually a problem on dogs with such good hair and flap protection but these little white critters which choose to live at the bottom of any dog's ear drum they can get at, are highly contagious. If your dog is infected, he probably picked these up from another dog or from a kennel environment if he has been left in one. His ear will emit a strong, musty odor. You will extract huge amounts of black material from his outer ear. He will shake, scratch and rub his ears against whatever he can find to rub them against. Take him immediately to the veterinarian for treatment.

EAR ALLERGIES

Allergies of any kind often first show up in ears. Your dog's ears might have a slight odor; you'll extract some blackish material when cleaning them and the dog's scratching is endless. This can lead to chronic inflammation. If the veterinarian's examination clears him of yeast or other infections and no ear mites are discovered under the microscope, your dog is undoubtedly allergic, either to something in the environment or in his food.

EAR HYGIENE

Hygiene for the ear? Dampen vinegar or rubbing alcohol mixed half and half with water or use a commercial ear cleaning solution on a cotton ball. Wrap it around your finger and gently clean the external ear canal which is the only part you can thrust a finger into. Only clean what the finger can feel. Never use Q tips. Misjudge when using Q-tips, or the dog moves his head quickly, and you can scratch or otherwise harm the delicate tissues of the middle ear. There are over the counter ear washes on the market. One, as mentioned above, is rubbing alcohol. It is a versatile product and death to ear wax.

Never overdo cleaning a dog's ears. If they appear clean on your weekly visual inspection, they do not need doctoring.

TEETH CARE

Your puppy sheds his baby teeth when he is between four to six months of age. In their

place come the second or permanent teeth. The puppy should have all of his permanent teeth at approximately six to seven months of age. If a baby tooth does not come out before the permanent tooth that takes its place appears, sometimes the retained tooth needs to be pulled. Most veterinarians will tell you to be a bit more patient and to give the puppy sterile bones to chew on to help dislodge that tooth (or teeth). One of my Havanese at six months had two baby canines which refused to budge. It looked as if it was necessary to pull them. However, the day prior to surgery one came out by itself. I dared

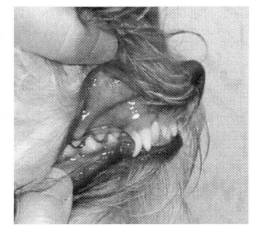

This photo shows the retained baby tooth which had to be pulled.

not wait much longer for the other retained baby tooth could have caused misalignment. My veterinarian pulled that one. In most cases, waiting is exactly the right thing to do. We breeders are worry worts when it comes to retained canine teeth. A good rule to remember is this: when you can see a slight coloring of that former glistening white baby tooth, you can be assured it is loosening and its exit from your puppy's mouth is only a matter of time. Only in rare instances does a retained tooth have to be extracted. If it is necessary, have a veterinarian pulled the retained tooth. Baby teeth have extraordinarily deep roots, extending down to the bottom of the jaw. Pulling out baby teeth is not a job for the amateur.

CHECK THE MOUTH

It's good to check your puppy's mouth every several days. It not only tells you what is happening inside his mouth but also teaches him you can look into his mouth and check his teeth anytime you want to do so. Mouth care is one of those necessary chores he has to endure.

TOOTH BRUSHING

Little thought has been given to brushing dogs' teeth until the past several years. If you have looked into older dogs' mouths and seen the condition some of their teeth are in, you'll

take on this task for sure. Infected teeth can set up infections in other parts of the body. You may choose to start tooth brushing when your puppy is young. Be sure to use only canine toothpaste, never human toothpaste. As an alternative to a commercial product, you can use salted water.

ANAL CARE

This is one job I leave to my dogs' veterinarian. You may choose to do so also. Still, we need to acquaint you with the anal glands and why they may have to be squeezed periodically to clean them out. The two anal glands lie alongside the anal opening, one on each side. While not every dog requires anal glands to be expressed, you'll know your dog has to have this job done if he scoots along the floor or licks his anal area often. If anal glands become impacted they must be treated by your veterinarian with antibiotics.

On the initial veterinarian trip with your puppy, learn from him how to empty anal glands. Then you can clean them out while preparing your dog for his bath. With your thumb and forefinger on either side of the anus, holding a paper towel against his rear (and a clothespin on your nose), squeeze the ill-smelling fluid which comes out against the towel. It has an exceptionally rancid smell. You'll want to dispose of the paper promptly.

EYE CARE

Necessary moisture (tearing) from the eye usually passes through a canal to the back of the nose. In small dogs these tear ducts plug up easily from inflammation and/or from assorted irritants like dust, pollen, shampoo, etc After all, the Havanese is a toy dog and low to the ground dogs are prone to picking up irritants. The tears then pass through the inner corner of each eye. This corner is also an ideal place for dirt and bacteria to collect which the dog encounters with each step he takes. Some Havanese have an increased flow of tears and need to have these corners washed and cleaned carefully each day. Use warm water. If this is not done, the moisture combined with dirt, etc., makes reddish brown stains that travel well down the cheek and coat the hair. The stains penetrate each hair shaft, sticking together in clumps. They are difficult to eliminate.

Unsightly eye staining may have several causes.

1. Hair that gets into the eye accidentally or hangs around the eyes can cause tearing which, in turn, causes staining

2. Hereditary influences (genetics) can cause staining

3. Certain folds cause staining

4. A high mineral content in the water the dog drinks, particularly iron, is a culprit. In-

stalling a reverse osmosis water system or using distilled water in the dog's drinking dish may help eliminate stains caused by hard water

5. Excessive tearing may be caused by teething, defective tear ducts, allergy and improper diet.

A majority of Havanese are afflicted with this unsightly problem; it is common among the smaller breeds. This staining is not observed easily on dogs with dark coated heads yet any excessive tearing should be treated.

Saturate a cotton ball with warm water and gently cleanse the hair on the outside of the eye at least once a day. When using commercial eye lotions be extremely careful not to get these into the dog's eyes.

GROOMING THE ELDERLY DOG

Scissor or clip the older dog to a manageable length. Don't make the dog stand or sit on the grooming table too long. Enjoy the dog for the great love and pleasure it has given you all of its life. Admire its coat, even when it thins as it may as he ages, or when it thins because of medication he must take to maintain quality of life.

As when he was a puppy, make each grooming experience a relaxing activity for both of you - an endeavor full of kisses and hugs. And, hey, don't forget the treats!

QUESTIONS AND ANSWERS

Question: If my dog gets "hit" by a skunk or is terribly muddy, do I have to brush him out before I give him a bath?

Answer: Of course not. However, water will set any mats already in the coat and make untangling them difficult. This is the time mat removers come in handy. So do coat conditioners. Sliding the end of the greyhound comb through the snarls also helps remove them.

Question: You say to begin brushing on a side. My groomer tells me to start grooming with the hind legs.

Answer: The standard grooming pattern is as follows: back legs, front legs, tail, top of body, sides, belly, chest, head and ears. Start and finish where it suits you.

Question: How do I make a decent part when I want to make a pony tail on my dog's head?

Answer: Use the narrow end of the greyhound comb to make the part. There are special commercial "parting combs" on the market. (Manufacturers think of everything!) Make a line from the top outside corner of the eye to the middle center of the skull and back around to the other top outside corner of the eye. Gather the hair and use the band to hold it together. Be careful you do not make the topknot too tight, causing the dog discomfort. He'll let you know he is uncomfortable when he gets down on the floor and tries to rub the band off his

head by pushing his head onto the floor or carpet.

Question: I had to go away for two weeks and my house sitter neglected to groom my Havanese. She is terribly mated. What do I do?

Answer: Most groomers will not spend the time untangling a heavily matted dog, no matter how much you plead. They will cut them down. It could be a job several days in duration, with time outs to keep the dog comfortable. Here is my suggestion:

Plan on spending an hour several times a day for two or three days, misting and untangling, slowly surely and gently. Then place your dog in the bathtub and give it a bath, rinsing thoroughly. If there are any mats left, you can see or feel the hairs clinging together. Those mats hurt the dog. Put a super duper conditioner on your dog, massage it into her coat and skin and LEAVE IT ON HER. Take her out of the tub and blow dry on a medium or low setting brushing and combing with long, gentle strokes. Most of the mats will untangle, helped along in turn, with the coat conditioner, the mat untangler, the end of your greyhound comb and your fingers. If the matting was absolutely horrendous, you might want to give her a second bath in a few days, repeating this procedure. Friends untangled a long-haired cat this way, although the cat was decidedly unfriendly throughout the entire process. You can leave conditioners on a dog who easily mats after baths without problems. Conditioners are skin soothers. If your dog's skin is badly irritated, obtain a soothing commercial lotion from your veterinarian.

Question: A friend told me that I'd have to give my Havanese a "back bath" often. What is a back bath?

Answer: A back bath is necessary if fecal matter becomes stuck on hair around the anal region. This does not happen often to dogs in a companion cut. However, the standard states the normal trimming of private parts must "not be noticeable on presentation." Most back baths are necessary if the dog has eaten an unusual treat, overeats, has temporary diarrhea caused by food changes, illness, etc. This fecal mass will cling to his rump hair. The odor will be strong. He may come to you for help or keep rubbing his rear end along the carpet or floor. Pick him up, take him to the tub, put on a plastic glove. Use the warm water sprayer on his back end which after a few minutes should remove most of the fecal matter. Spread shampoo over the area, shampoo well, rinse well, wrap him in a towel, dry and comb the area. Back baths take only several minutes to accomplish. I do admit they usually happen at five or six in the morning and giving back baths when you are not quite awake are not desirable.

Question: My Havanese has a continual yeast infection in one ear. The medication I get from my veterinarian doesn't seem to ever clear it up. Any other suggestions?

Answer: Some groomers claim that splitting an acidophilus tablet in half and inserting half the powder into each ear and then dousing it with a vinegar and water mixture followed by a thorough cleaning will get rid of yeast infections once and for all. Acidophilus bacteria cannot live long in an ear environment but before they die they eradicate yeast infections. It worked on a Portuguese Water Dog of mine.

Question: I read the grooming chapter for you for proofreading purposes. I do not find information on cording a Havanese. Why not?

Answer: I am not an expert or even a novice cording fancier. You will find Cording a Havane article in an issue of the Havanese Hotline, the Havanese Club of America quarterly magazine.

Question: My Havanese used to be wavy. I have cut him down. Now he is curly. What happened?

Answer: If you allow his coat to grow long again, you will probably find the curls to straighten out into big loose waves. Straight haired or wavy dogs of other breeds, not just the Havanese, have similar coat types.

Chapter 12

Health, Etc.

Two of the most important characteristics people want in a dog are stable temperaments and good health Thank goodness, the Havanese has both. Of course the Havanese is subject to diseases which afflict all dogs. Many of these afflict humans also. Several genetically derived diseases which Havanese may suffer from are cataracts and orthopedic abnormalities such as bowed legs, hip dysplasia, luxating patellas, and elbow dysplasia. Rarer are liver abnormalities, heart problems and deafness. These are discussed by veterinarian Joanne V. Baldwin (a former president of the HCA) and the Havanese Club of America Health Committee on the Havanese web site, www.havanese.org. If you do not have access to a computer, your local library will have one. I suggest you print out and study the health information.

The Havanese Club of America recommends Havanese breeders refrain from breeding dogs who exhibit several of the health problems listed above. This is not always followed by general hobby breeders and certainly not by commercial breeders.

If you plan on becoming a breeder, adhere to the ethics of the HCA. Never become a breeder who insists to a heartbroken buyer who has discovered an unbreedable fault in a "potential" show and breedable dog that there is nothing wrong with the dog and rant and rave in denial. Always listen with a sympathetic ear and remedy where possible, with good grace. Don't believe there are not breeders like this. There are too many!

When you take possession of a Havanese puppy or adult, it is essential to make an appointment with a veterinarian for a preliminary health examination and for follow-up health checks. Modern veterinarians are skilled in diagnosing and treating many diseases. Some veterinarians specialize in reproductive areas, others in areas such as opthamology, orthopedics, allergies and dentition.

A general care veterinarian gives your puppy the four vaccinations needed for protection against puppy diseases. He also can perform preliminary and adult OFA x-rays for hips, patellas, front legs and elbows. Your general care veterinarian can also refer you to the closest opthamologist who performs the necessary yearly CERF eye examinations and a veterinarian skilled in the one-time BAER (hearing) test. At your first visit to your chosen veterinarian, ask about after hour emergency services or a clinic he recommends. It's good to take along a copy of the health information which you perused on the Havanese Club of America web site so as to acquaint your veterinarian with the specific health problems this breed is subject to.

This chapter gives you a brief synopsis of several general health problems common to all dogs.

Canine Allergies

Allergies are treated, never cured. There are two types: contact and inhalant. *Contact* allergies occur when a dog, genetically predisposed to allergies, repeatedly comes in contract with the allergen. Chemicals in carpets are a common source; so are shampoos. Grasses and bushes often harbor fungus which can affect an allergic dog. *Inhalant* allergies include dust, molds and feathers. Fleas cause summer eczema as well as flea bite dermatitis. Spring and fall are the worst months for allergy sufferers; in winter most, not all allergies are dormant. Dogs react to allergens with eye, throat and skin irritations. Food allergies show up in swollen and infected ears. A puppy or dog who scratches or bites at himself occasionally is not necessarily allergic. Scratching and biting are natural reactions in all animals when annoyed by temporary skin irritants. It is when scratching and biting become intense that treatment by a veterinarian becomes essential. Antihistamines give relief as do prescribed veterinarian treatments with cortisone or diet changes. (For more information, please refer to the grooming chapter.)

Anorexia

Loss of appetite is often seen in Havanese puppies shortly after they arrive at their permanent homes. One reason is because they have been sharing a food dish with their littermates. Eating alone is daunting. It might take several meals before they feel comfortable eating by themselves. And owners should not immediately add their own supplements to the breeders' recommended diet. Some foods are too rich for developing tummies. However, proven diet enhancers for older puppies are peanut butter, spaghetti, and baby meat with vegetables added to kibble, blended together and warmed. Warming food enhances flavor because it stimulates taste buds. Liquid vitamins must be given daily. A Havanese puppy will outgrow anorexia unless it is a response to an illness. If anorexia continues for more than a week have the puppy given a health check by your veterinarian.

Bowed Legs

Each of the Havanese standards have called for "straight legs." The 2001 AKC Havanese standard states: *"The elbows turn neither in nor out, and are tight to the body. Forelegs are well-boned and straight when viewed from any angle."* Bowed legs, prevalent in the breed, are discussed in the Havanese Health section on the Havanese Club of America web site. Responsible breeders are trying hard to eliminate this condition although they are using dogs with bowed legs for breeding on the premise that "You can't

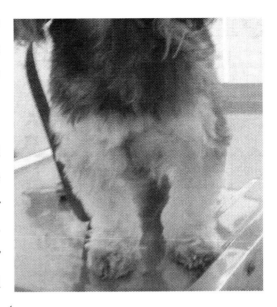

A photo showing bowed legs. There is dysplasia (deformity) seen in the right elbow. These photos are of a bitch co-owned by the author.

throw out the baby with the bathwater," meaning that if you only breed dogs with straight legs, the gene pool will shrink dangerously. Will the baby, in this case the Havanese, become deformed if drastic steps are not taken to abide by the Havanese standards?

It appears that somewhere in the past bowed legs entered the gene pool either by the use of street dogs for breeding or by the result of a dominant genetic mutation affecting the bones of the front legs. There are other pure-breds with bowed legs. They are normal for these breeds. I could go down a list of the statements in these standards: "as straight as possible," "reasonably straight," "forelegs short, strong and slightly bowed around chest," "may show a slight bend in the forearm," "forelegs straight or slightly bent with elbows close," bones of forearm bowed," etc.

Meta von Hout of Sweet Honesty Kennels in the Netherlands makes this observation: "The short leg in combination of a long back cannot have straight front legs in combination with well-bowed ribs." Obviously, the bow in the legs compensates. When one refers to the Skye Terrier standard, one reads: "Legs short, muscular, and straight as possible. 'Straight as possible' means straight as soundness and chest will permit." Another long and low and rectangular breed, the Sussex Spaniel, carries this statement in its standard: Forelegs, "both straight and slightly bowed construction are proper and correct." And the Cardigan Welsh

Corgi standard says, "The forearms should be curved to fit spring of ribs."

At present, it is deemed okay to breed a bowed front legged bitch to a straight front legged dog. Is this sound reasoning genetically? A straight legged dog can certainly be a carrier for the genes for bowed legs. If the condition does not turn up in the siblings, it does turn up in the grandchildren.

Do we follow the standard or not? Should the standard be changed to reflect the present day conformation of this lovely companion dog? Did the revision of the standard in 2001 do a disservice to the breed? Since we must follow the standard until this dilemma is resolved, I pose two suggestions: 1) When a dog or bitch used for breeding has bowed legs, sell the puppies only as pets. Early spaying (puppies from 8 to 16 weeks) has been proven *not* to be detrimental to a dog's health or longevity. 2) When puppies from parents who both have straight legs are sold as show and/or breeding potential, the new owners must somehow agree that even though they can show their puppies in the conformation ring, the puppies cannot become breeding potentials until cleared at the age of one year for this condition. Why this wait? Bowed legs do not show up until growth plates are closing. And the ages for growth plate closing are approximately six to nine months.

Many puppies currently being shown win championships before they reach a year of age. "In the Netherlands," writes Meta von Hout, "a dog must be 27 months to earn the championship title."

Bowed legs are not unhealthy legs nor do they pose movement problems to the dogs which have them. (Look at all the people in the world who have bowed legs and move around okay.) True, an extreme case could or may present future problems.

An example: I purchased a show potential and therefore breedable female at the age of nine weeks. At that age her front legs were perfectly straight. They seemed straight to me when I sent her off to be shown at a year of age. Her long and luxurious leg hair hid the bowed legs from me even though I bathed her regularly. She won her championship because she is a perfectly lovely tempermented, exquisitely happy, and a breed-typy bitch. When she returned home I saw her legs bowing Should she be spayed since straight forelegs are called out in the standard? Is this as bad a fault as an undershot mouth? lack of pigment?

I sat down with a group of veterinarians recently. I posed the problem. I produced my bitch with bowed legs. The veterinarians present were well versed in orthopedic problems in the canine. The concensus of opinion was that it would be normal for long, low and rectangular short-legged breeds (such as the Havanese) with wide chests to have such cor-

rection in the forelegs by nature. It would only be abnormal if the dog was slab-sided or had a narrow chest. Since my bitch has a narrow front along with bowed legs, not *"deep"* and *"rather broad in front"* as the standard calls out, there was a strong possibility her bowed legs were proof of an abnormality. An OFA-x-ray revealed dysplasia in one of the elbows. She also proved to have moderate hip dysplasia.

The above example proves that not all champions should be bred. I had purchased her as both a show-potential and breedable bitch. I adhered to the contract in obtaining her championship and performing all the health checks. I could not perform the last health check, the OFA X-rays for hips and elbows, until she reached the age of two years. The OFA report showed her to be moderately dysplastic in her right hip and well as moderately dysplastic in her right elbow. Therefore she had to be spayed. No responsible breeder will breed these faults so they can be passed on to offspring. Nature again had the last hurrah! Remember the bag of 100 marbles, 50 black and 50 red? Such are the heartbreaks. And again, a good reason not to breed until a dog or bitch has all their health checks performed.

Brucellosis

Brucella canis, causes brucellosis. It is a bacterium which causes infertility. It can take several forms including swollen joints in those infected, late term abortions in bitches, abnormalities or early death in newborns. Brucellosis is an uncommon disease but lethal to breeding kennels since it spreads by contact with infected tissue. Breeders should have each bitch or stud given a special test by a veterinarian before being bred. Written proof of the latest test results are then exchanged between breeders.

Cancer

Cancers are malignant tumors and each breed is susceptible to distinct forms of cancer. The Havanese is still in its revitalization period. It is too early to tell what forms of malignent tumors strike the Havanese more frequently. The most common cancerous tumors in a intact bitch are mammary gland tumors. These usually appear when a bitch ages. I lost two Portuguese Water Dogs to mammary gland tumors at ages 11 and 13. Modern treatments and surgeries for cancer can prolong a dog's life if quality is assured.

Car Sickness

Nausea is a common problem when puppies travel in cars. A prime cause is because the inner ear is not fully developed. There is resulting imbalance. Also, automobile movements do not make a puppy feel secure. Keep the puppy close by you in a small crate or serpa bag placed firmly on the front passenger's seat if you are driving alone or on a passenger's lap. Security builds confidence in puppy nerve. The problem usually resolves itself by the time the puppy reaches a year of age. Until she was past a year of age, my Naughty dreaded traveling, even short distances. The moment I reached for my car keys she hid. If she had to travel far, I dared not feed her until we reached our destination. A 5 mg tablet called "Ace," given one-half hour before traveling, prescribed by my veterinarian, allowed her to ride in comfort no matter how great the distance until she outgrew the problem.

Cataracts

Cataracts are a common eye disorder in dogs. Most of them are inherited, thus the annual CERF (Canine Eye Registry Foundation) examination by a veterinary opthamologist is desired for breedable purebreds. Cataracts develop as a small white area in the eye and is not often discernable. They may involve one or both eyes, completely or partially. Sometimes a cataract is the result of trauma, inflammation or nutritional deficiences. Usually it is inherited. Refer to the HCA website for more information.

Coprophagy

Stool eating! According to Webster's Dictionary, coprophagy is the practice of feeding on or eating of dung or excrement. It is normal behavior among many insects, birds, and other animals but in man is a symptom of some forms of insanity. It's a common practice in dogs.

Dogs are basically scavengers. All practice some form of coprophagy. Without exception, if allowed to run free in woods or fields, dogs sample dung of other species of animals and birds. Many also eat their or other dogs' droppings. History tells us that because of the canine habit of scavenging, villagers did not have to move too frequently. Dogs kept the garbage as well as dung of humans cleaned up. For centuries small dogs were used to help clean up slums in cities as well as performing this job on the farms.

There are complaints from Havanese owners regarding their pets' stool eating. The dog intent on stool eating is difficult to correct. He receives his reward each time he indulges in the practice. Dogs that practice coprophagy avoid stools in summertime because swarms of insects feed on the nutrients and leave only bulk. They also avoid old stools because they no longer contain nutrients.

Several remedies: Avoid over supplementation. Nutritionists claim supplements over twenty percent of a dog's diet may cause deficiencies and/or non-digestion of all foods eaten. Another suggestion comes from a retired zoo veterinarian. He says coprophagy is common among zoo animals. He recommends the following solution for many dogs. Feed one daily meal consisting of one-half cottage cheese and one-half tomato juice. Tomato juice, one of

the two ingredients used in this remedy, is high in vitamin C. It is also acidic. Perhaps dogs with this habit require more of this vitamin and more acid in their diets.

Diarrhea

Intestinal upsets have many causes. They could be infectious, parasitic or toxic, even an allergic reaction to an innoculation. Certainly bad food and rubbish intolerance (including retained grass, twigs, rocks, etc.) is a huge cause. Vomiting usually accompanies an acute case of diarrhea.

An immediate remedy is withholding of food for 24 hours since resting of the intestinal tract is important. A half teaspoonful of Pepto-Bismol, if tolerated, may relieve the symptoms. If the attack persists more than 24 hours, a more serious cause - bacteria, worms, poisoning, disease - must be treated by a veterinarian. Any loose stool in a puppy weakens and dehydrates that puppy. Get a puppy with loose stools to a veterinarian for treatment.

Dietary

Not all foods are easily digested by dogs, particularly puppies. In one of my litters, one puppy continually vomited food that contained well-mixed egg yolks. Eggs were too rich for her developing stomach. Chicken and rice, lamb and rice, fish and rice, cottage cheese and rice are common protein and carbohydrate dietary determinators. (Tapioca can be substituted for the rice.) The puppy or dog is taken off of its regular diet, placed on one of the above combinations, with other foods gradually added one at a time to fnd which foods the dog can tolerate. A veterinarian check is important.

Elbow Dysplasia

Elbow dysplasia causes lameness and an awkward gait. If a dog is so afflicted, lameness can occur at an early age, unlike hip dysplasia which often is never recognized by owners unless a hip X-ray is taken.

Epilepsy

This is a nervous system disorder. It is common in many breeds. It is caused by nerves in the brain which become uncoordinated for a few or more minutes. The dog goes into a convulsion, displaying rapid and jerky body movements. When the seizure is over, he may wobble about for a few minutes, then revive and appear perfectly normal. Drugs are readily available from your veterinarian to help most afflicted dogs live long and comparatively normal lives.

Foxtails

Foxtails are barbed grass awns. They can grab onto humans and animals and easily find their way inside ears and noses and pads of feet. They then penetrate the skin and work their way into organs and joints. They are very dangerous. A friend had a foxtail work into her dog's foot. The veterinarian had to operate to remove it. A dozen foxtails were found in the ears of a returned Portuguese Water Dog of mine with one of them working its way behind his eye. The ophthalmologist who had to treat the dog with medicine for months before the awn dissolved, told me if I had delayed in getting the dog to him, the dog would have gone blind.

Foxtails are prevelant in most parts of the country from late spring through late fall. Be sure to thoroughly examine your Havanese feet, ears, and nose after it is exposed to grass awns. If you find one, there are more hidden from view.

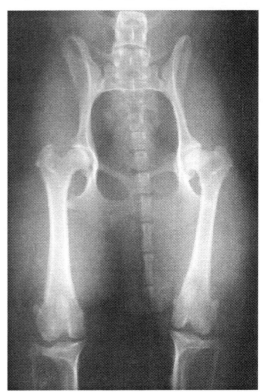

Hip dysplasia was found in one of the author's bitches. The dysplasia is seen in the right hip. The photo is deliberately large so the deformity can be seen.

Grief

The loss of an owner, a dog companion, a change in ownership, any traumatic event can cause crippling grief in dogs. They become despondent, lose their appetite, have intermittant periods of vomiting or diarrhea, with their immune systems suffering. A dog's grief can be quite profound, although many times unnoticed since some are very stoic. Grief usually is overcome within three to five months. TLC is important.

Hip Dysplasia

Dysplasia means abnormality. The abnormality in this case is "the failure of the head of the femur to fit into the acetabulum snugly" ("Genetics for Dog Breeders"). Some dogs never show a sign of affliction; others with severe cases must be treated and/or operated on for comfort. Hip dysplasia is hereditary. Havanese used for breeding should have an OFA hip X-ray taken by their veterinarian before breeding, at the age of two years. The OFA evaluates hip joint conformation as Fair, Good or Excellent. Dogs that are affected vary from mild to severe. Hip dysplasia is of paramount concern to responsible dog breeders. Many eliminate breedings if evaluation given by OFA is Fair, finding it helpful in reducing affected offspring.

The author's Tawney resting in a large crate set up in the living room after her patella operation.

Hypothyroidism

A common disease in many breeds, the hair thins and dries and dogs are constantly cold. If your Havanese continually hugs a heater or fireplace or seeks the sun on a warm day, have it examined by your veterinarian for thyroid deficiency. Thyroid deficiency can be easily treated by medication given for life.

Luxating Patellas

The patella is the kneecap in dogs. It lies in a shallow groove at the bottom of the femur. If the groove is too shallow, it slips to one side or the other. It is painful. It is a common affliction in toy dogs and in the Havanese. Predisposition to it is inherited. Breeders should not use parents of dogs so afflicted for further breeding. Breeders can have their veterinarian check puppies for "slipping patellas" each time they are brought in for vaccination. I was not aware my Tawney had luxating patellas until she was over a year of age and began to limp in pain. Both of her patellas had to be operated on. She is now comfortable and only exhibits a slight limp.

Poisoning by Pesticides

Pesticide poisoning of pet animals is common. The chemicals used in lawn sprays, insecticide sprays, fertilizers, etc. can affect the immune system if the animals walk on or are near the treated areas. Many are carcinogens. Symptoms may be nonexistant but insidious. Many affect fertility. It is claimed that after treatment of lawns, weeds, etc., and keeping pet animals away from the treated areas until the area is dry makes the products harmless. There is no proof this is so! Owners of pet animals should hand pick weeds, mow grass frequently and leave the pesticides on the store shelves. When moving always inquire as to what, if any, pesticides have been used on the property you are moving to. After one of our moves, my dogs began ailing. The veterinarian who examined and treated my dogs could find no cause for their loss of weight and bouts of nausea and diarrhea. I found the cause when I learned the former owners had treated both front and back yards with pesticides before vacating the premises. It took several months and expensive veterinary treatments before my dogs regained their health.

164

Reverse Sneezing *(spasm of epiglottis)*

The first time Punxsy began wheezing as if he was having some sort of throat or breathing difficulty, I rushed him to my veterinarian. "That snorting sound," my veterinarian told me, "is because he is trying to clear the back of his nasal passages. Nothing to worry about. He might be allergic to something. If it is persistent, you might give him a quarter of a teaspoon of cough medicine." Punxsy intermittently suffers a bout of reverse sneezing and I have noted it usually occurs after he has come inside after one of his outside adventures.

Worms

There are many different kinds of worms that infect dogs. Roundworms, whipworms, tapeworms, hookworms and heartworms are the most common. Most puppies are infected with roundworms when they are born because the larvae can live inside the mother and come to life with newborns. Roundworm eggs can also survive in the ground for many years. When we moved to Washington, the ground we moved on to was completely saturated with roundworm eggs. Each litter my dogs had there became infested with roundworms. A heavy infestation can kill puppies.

Always follow your veterinarian's advice on worming. Every puppy needs to be wormed at four or six weeks, depending on the area in which you live with a follow-up worming two weeks later. And do not worm puppies or dogs with worm medicine available at stores. Each worm requires different medication to kill it. Hookworms are more prevalent in clay and wet soils. Worms find it difficult to survive in Montana where I live.

Common problems with eye staining, ears, teeth and yeast infections are discussed in the grooming chapter. The briefs above require further delineation by your veterinarian. I have discussed only a few health problems. There are excellent books referencing canine medical problems. One is the *UC Davis School of Veterinary Medicine Book of Dogs* (1995), published by Harper Collins. Others are available at your local book store and/or library.

Chapter 13

Performance Events

The Havanese, used for centuries as performance dogs entertaining people at fairs, in circuses, on shipboard, and community gatherings, are ideal workers in the present day performance sports sponsored by kennel clubs such as Obedience, Agility, Tracking and Flyball.

The Havanese has great focus abilities as well as an instinctive willingness to please. They are therefore quick studies. They exhibit such joy in dog sports activities that they enthrall onlookers.

OBEDIENCE

Dog Obedience is a natural for Havanese. I believe every Havanese should be entered in a positive obedience class and be taught the basic Novice exercises: heel (walking calmly at the owner's left side), sit, down, stand, stay and come. Positive taught classes are fun activities for the dogs as well as learning tools in canine behavior for their owners. One of the greatest rewards in class participation is building confidence in the dog when learning the ins and outs of companion animal living in this complex human world. It is rewarding for the owner in that the dog's behavior improves (as if one could ever scold a joyous Havanese)!

Advanced obedience classes, called Open and Utility, help you teach your Havanese to retrieve, jump over obstacles, scent discriminate and respond to signals as well as to voice commands.

We have introduced you to a few training suggestions in Chapter 10. We add a few more for obedience training here.

Supplies Needed

Choose either a rolled leather collar or harness with a slim, nylon leash attached or a thin nylon show lead which consists of a slip collar and leash. Treats: use nickel sized pieces of roast chicken or hot dogs or other tasty real meat treats. Small biscuit treats take too long for the dog to ingest, consequently attention span disappears.

LESSON ONE

The Sit

Sit your dog by your side on leash, with the leash held in your left hand, raising your right hand with a treat in it until he sits. Be sure to raise your hand above the dog's head. Treat him when he sits, saying "Sit, good boy" **as** he sits. The first several days do not worry if he sits crooked. We want him to hear the word "SIT" as he sees and follows the treat.

After several days, walk straight forward two or three steps while guiding your dog to your left side with both of you facing forward, his shoulders even in line with your hips. Your leash should be in your left hand only six or so inches away from your dog's neck. Not taut, loose yet close to you. Stand up straight as you walk forward. Stop. Command "Sit" *as* you stop, transferring the leash to your right hand and bending your knees (do not turn to face the dog as you do so). As you bend your knees (straight forward, please, don't turn sideways), slide your left hand down his back and push on his rear as you pull up on the leash with your right hand. Pull the leash up and *forward*, not to either side. Do not yank the leash. The dog will follow through in his sit in the direction the leash is held. As soon as he sits, allow slack in the leash. Make certain the dog is sitting in the basic position, both of you facing dead front, his shoulders in line with your hip. If all is okay, give him a break and praise. Let him jump up to you or you bend down to play with him. Praise him highly *as* you give him a treat. If either of you are not facing dead front, if your feet or his are facing sideways, start over. Be exact. Your dog will be imprinted with the right or wrong way.

Remember Rule: Timing is the essence in good training. Always praise and treat your dog **AS** he is doing what you want, not after.

Bad example: "Sit." Second or two wait. "Good boy." Fumble for treat. Treat.

Good example: Dog begins to sit. Instantaneously, "Sitgoodboy" and treat.

Question: Why instantaneously?

Answer: Dog attention span is so short, behavior needs to be rewarded or corrected *at* the instant or an instant *before* behavior to be effective. Dogs think about an action just before they do it. That is the moment to praise.

Remember Rule: Never correct a dog while he is learning an exercise. Praise for what he is trying to do to please you, even though it may not be up to your expectations. It is only when he has thoroughly learned an exercise and/or a behavior, that you can correct for slop-

pyness, inattentiveness or laziness. Refusal to do an exercise means the dog has temporarily forgotten how or is confused. If confused, it is your fault in teaching, never the dog's. Be patient. Motivate him by playing with him for a few minutes before starting over.

Sit and Stay

Within a week's time, your dog should be attentive when your actions and voice tell him you are commanding "sit."

LESSON TWO

Sit and Stay

Now that your dog is sitting with your hand gently guiding his rump down after moving the two or three steps forward, it is time to teach him how to sit and "stay."

Place your dog on a sit at your left side facing front as you are. The tab of your leash is held in your right hand at about the center of your tummy. Move your left hand, full palm, fingers closed and hand facing the dog, right in front of his mouth or just above his muzzle.

Command "Stay" as you give the hand signal. Move out in front of your dog, starting out on your right foot. Only move one step in front of him. NO further.

Turn and face your dog. Hold the leash taut, straight up. Keep him on a sit-stay for 30 seconds, return to his side and after a few more silent seconds, praise and release him.

Repeat the exercise twice; keeping him on a sit-stay the second time for 45 seconds, the third time for 20 seconds.

Question: Why should I vary the time he is kept on a sit-stay.

Answer: You vary the time before you return to heel position and praise the dog on a stay command because dogs quickly learn time and will anticipate release if you do not do so. Therefore, by varying stay times and praise times you keep him guessing and attentive.

Within a week, your dog should be sitting and staying on both voice and hand command without your nudging him into a sit. He is learning the "automatic sit." When he can do this, begin returning to your heel position by walking to the left around in back of him. Always remember to return to your dog to your exact heel position stopping when his shoulders are even with your hip and both of you facing dead front.

If he breaks at any time on these sit and stay exercises, nudge the leash upward slightly, at the same time commanding "sit." Repeat the exercise.

After a few days, when you leave your dog stop two or more feet away from him. Increase the stay time up to one and then two minutes.

Remember rule: If your dog keeps breaking a stay, you must go back to square one, standing only a foot away. He needs more confidence. Without it, he cannot learn. Increase your distance, a foot at a time, gradually. Easy does it.

Alternating Sit and Stay with Heel and Sit

Remember Rule: When you step forward to heel start out on your left foot. Step forward on your right foot only when you leave the dog in a static position. Your dog will respond to these body movement commands quickly. Left foot he moves with you; right foot he remains where he is.

We will now commence walking more than three or four steps with our dog before stopping. Please walk in a straight line. Walk with clean, bold steps, not short, slow ones. When you want to stop, shorten your step, walk slowly for a step or two, command "sit" and stop.

Remember Rule: You must always let the dog know what you are going to do.

Automatic Sit

Within a matter of days, your dog will automatically sit when you stop. Wonderful! He is learning. You are both having fun.

In heeling and stopping vary the time you wait before starting out again. If your dog lags behind you, pat your left leg as you keep on walking. And walk faster. When he catches up, praise highly, continuing to heel. Give him a break and try again.

If he is not paying attention to you or is forging (pulling away to the side or front), quickly and without saying a word, turn around and go the other way. When he catches up with you, praise and heel.

Practice the heeling and sitting exercise in a hallway or close to a curb, with the dog always closest to the wall or curb. This helps keep him close to you and prevents his bottom swinging out away from you.

Remember Rule: Your dog will have both good and bad days, just like you do. Gradual improvement turns into success.

The sit and stay and heel exercises are the first basic exercises usually taught in obedience classes. I urge you to enjoy a session in a positive taught class with your Havanese.

When the down, stand and come exercises are added and learned, you can enjoy earning two titles from the American Kennel Club: A Canine Good Citizenship (CGC) title and a Companion Dog obedience (CD) title. Do it.

The Canine Good Citizenship title is an easy one consisting of 10 items, each exercise performed on leash. They are: 1) Accepting a friendly stranger; 2) Sitting politely for Petting; 3) Appearance and Grooming; (4) Out for a Walk on a Loose Leash; 5) Walking through a Crowd; 6) Sit and down on command and staying in place; 7) Coming when called; 8) Reaction to another Dog; 9) Reaction to distractions; and 10) Supervised Separation.

The Novice Obedience exercises are:1) Heel on Leash with sits and turns; 2) Heeling around two posts, called the Figure Eight; 3) Stand for Examination; 4) Heel Free; 5) Come on Recall; 6) Sit and Stay for one minute; 7) Down for three minutes.

These are performance titles you will be proud your dog has earned.

RALLY OBEDIENCE

A new class has been added to obedience in 2005. It is called Rally Obedience. The class

sits between CGC and Novice. It's a fun class in that the handler can talk, coax and praise his dog as they perform exercises between signs which tell them what to do. Write to AKC for your free copy of the rules.

AGILITY

Agility, which began in England in 1980, is an obstacle-course for dogs with tunnels to run through, ramps to climb up and down on, jumps to leap over and weave poles to wind through all the while being directed by their owners against a time clock.

These two photos are of Jerry Tate's Lucy, Waltron's I Love Lucy AX AXJ. She is a Canadian Agility performer, bred by Ron Walters.

Agility is a sport dogs thrill to. Watching dogs perform in Agility is watching happiness on bodies with four legs.

Many dog owners (including this author) have built agility play courses in their own back yards because it is a great confidence builder as well as a muscle exerciser. I deem it absolutely necessary when one wants to build confidence in a puppy or adult dog. Dogs are mentally stimulated and come away from classes with confidence in themselves.

Agility clubs abound throughout all countries,

here and abroad. Millions watch agility competitions on television. It is currently the most popular dog performance sport. The waiting lists for classes are long and some clubs insist dogs first go through a basic obedience class before enjoying agility.

We cannot leave this section without having Susan Nelson tell you why she loves her Havanese. We wish to enthuse you into joining a performance sport for your dog.

Ch Tapscott's Mufasa MX MXJ is a top performing Havanese in Canada. Rico is owned by Jerry Tate. Rico 's breeder is Pamm Tapscott.

WHY I LOVE MY HAVANESE *by Susan Nelson*

The thing I love best about Havanese is that they are ready, able and willing to do anything you ask of them. When my first Havanese, Sparky, came to live with us in early 1992, he joined a household that included two Old English Sheepdogs who were exceptional obedience/agility dogs. Sparky quickly learned everything there was to know about agility and obedience from them. In fact, he was doing obedience scent discrimination work at the age of 12 weeks. He taught himself!

Sparky's life was a whirlwind of adventures. Agility had just started in the U.S. and our club was traveling up and down the coast of California introducing Agility to other clubs. My Old English Sheepdogs were West Coast members of the IAMS Super Dogs for many years prior to Sparky coming to live with them. Sparky soon became a regular on the team. Because of his delightful personality and looks, Sparky also made it to both stage and screen. He was a quick learner and able to perform what anyone wanted him to do. When AKC added Agility as a titling event, Sparky became the first Havanese to earn Agility titles. Tippy, my second Havanese, followed by becoming the second Havanese to earn Agility titles. Both are still running Agility at the ripe ages of 11 and 13 years old.

TV was another adventure for Sparky. He played a key role in an episode of the Power Rangers. And Tippy appeared in a TV Special called The Miss Dog Beauty Pageant. She, along with 50 other dogs, competed for top K-9 in the country, a show based on beauty and talent. She was selected as one of the top K-9 finalists. A few months later she filmed an episode of Animal Kidding on Animal Planet.

Tippy started her show career in January 1999 and immediately jumped to No. 1 Havanese All Breed. She was the first Havanese at the Palm Springs, CA show to take a Group 3. She was the second Havanese in the country to earn AKC Agility titles. She returned to the ring five years after retiring and at the age of 10-1/2 years, she won BOB and a Group 3 going over three top-ranking Havanese.

Susan Nelson and Tippy performing in Agility. Tippy is AKC/ARBA/HCA Ch Shaggyluv's Golden Girl ROM OA OAJ CGC TDI.

Showing that the quality of the line is long lasting, she then entered the Rally Obedience ring and took High Scoring Rally Dog.

AKC/UKC/INT Ch Shaggyluv's Blockbuster NA NAJ CGC enjoying his skateboard. Owner, of course, is Susan Nelson.

Dancing was one of the special talents that evolved over time. In 2003 both Sparky and Tippy were one of a handful of dogs that were invited to perform for the Executives of the Super Bowl at their pre-game events. Both continue to dance at events in California.

Whether it is dancing, agility, conformation, obedience, tricks or just sitting on your lap, your Havanese is always ready, able and willing to do whatever makes you happy. What more can you ask from a dog?

Thank you again, Susan, for your contributions to the Havanese.

TRACKING

Tracking, an extension of obedience since dogs must be under the control of their handler at all times, uses the dog's scenting ability to search for objects.

Susan Nelson dancing with Tippy.

This is a natural sport for the Havanese.

To learn more about performance sports from the American Kennel Club, write to the American Kennel Club, 5580 Centerview Drive, Suite 200, Raleigh, NC 27006-3390. Ask for the booklets on Obedience Regulations, Agility Regulations, Tracking Regulations. Single copies are free.

SHOWING YOUR DOG

If you own a potential show Havanese or a potential breedable Havanese, you'll want to show it to its championship in the confirmation ring before you breed. The conformation ring is for intact dogs who have excellent temperaments and structures adhering to the standard of the breed. Of course, since no dog is perfect in every regard, each dog being shown will have a fault or two. Some faults will disqualify a dog from being shown, however, and a thorough understanding of the standard is an unspoken responsibility of every owner who wishes to show their dog.

A good handler makes showing a dog look effortless. Here, Sheryl Roach is handling puppy Selena at a fun match. Note the loose leash and the attention of the dog on her owner.
Selena's registered name is Ch Tapscott Tickled Pink. Her breeders are Pamm and Jeanne Tapscott.

Judging is a subjective art. Each judge interprets the standard of a breed differently. A dog who wins one day may not win the next. That's one reason dog showing is such an exciting sport, why it keeps attracting exhibitors and infecting them with such fever they become lifetime enthusiasts.

The training of a potential show dog requires practice and more practice. When ready to compete the trained dog makes gaiting around the ring and standing in a beautiful stacked position in front of the judge look easy. It is not. Neither is the pre-ring and ongoing presentation of the dog which includes intense conditioning and grooming. Any dog show enthusiast will tell you that a potential show dog's career begins in the whelping box, abetted by quality diet, socialization and conditioning of body and coat long before it enters its

first dog show.

The American Kennel Club (AKC) has booklets explaining Dog Show Regulations. Write to their address in Raleigh if you have a potential champion Havanese in your family. On the web, the AKC address is www.americankennelclub.org

These four photos are examples of excellent ring handling. The top photo is of handler Beverly Wilson baiting Naughty so the judge can observe her stacked on the table. In the second photo he is examining her.

The two bottom photos show Ted Zalec moving his bitch, Maddy, Ch Los Companero's Golden Sunrise, for the judge, the third step in the conformation ring procedure. In the bottom photo Ted Zalec has stopped Maddy and keeps her at attention so the judge can examine her again. Maddy's breeders are Heather Warnock and Paula Martell-Lavallie.

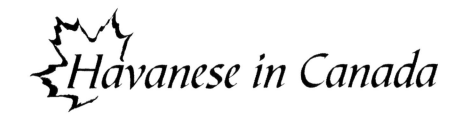

Chapter Fourteen

The Havanese in Canada

by

Suzanne McKay

HISTORY IN CANADA - 1985 TO 1993

In Canada, in the 1980s, references to Havanese were few and far between; perhaps our first awareness was a brief mention in a rare breed book or a note and photo here or there in other publications; just enough to pique the interest of fanciers looking for that elusive something. Once the bug bites, knowing that this is what you have been looking for makes you forever "Hooked on Havanese." Elusive as the references were, finding one of these delightful charmers proved to be even more difficult. Determination persevered and the first Havanese arrived in Canada. While a few fanciers started with plans to breed future generations, the majority were delighted simply to have found their ultimate canine companion. Acquiring a Havanese took happenstance, luck and perseverance. The first Havanese owners in Canada have some interesting stories to tell.

Kennedy's Patches (Feb 25, 1988-Apr 5, 2003). Bred by Dorothy Goodale, Havana Doll House, and owned by Gail and Bob Kennedy.

Patches

"In 1988, we moved into our new home in Winnipeg and decided to get a dog. In Joan Palmer's book 'How to Choose and Care for Your Dog,' I came across the Havanese and fell instantly in love. We called almost every kennel club, but at that time no one had heard of the breed. After dozens of phone calls and going around in circles for weeks, as a last resort we contacted the publisher of the book who gave us the author's phone number who then gave us the name of Dorothy Goodale in Colorado. As luck would have it, the Goodales had just had a litter of puppies. After many phone calls and questions, we were approved for a precious puppy from the Havana Doll House. Kennedy's Patches became my little shadow from day one. He followed me everywhere. He loved to cuddle, play hide and seek, chew Kleenex or toilet paper and had many other cute little quirks. Patches was a wonderful pet. He died on April 5, 2003 at 15 years of age."

Gail Kennedy, Winnipeg, Manitoba

BJ and Misty

Patches, accompanied by his brother BJ, flew from Colorado to Fargo where they were picked up by the Kennedys. BJ's new family drove from Regina to Winnipeg to pick him up. Unlike the Kennedys, who got their first Havanese without ever having met one in person, Jean and Ron Pekush had already been introduced to the breed by Sylvia Diko who lived nearby and had a young pair. From their first encounter,

Beau James (Feb 25, 1988-June 29, 1999) and Majestic's Morning Mist (Apr 14, 1989-Feb 2001). BJ and Misty bred by Dorothy Goodale, Havana Doll House, owned by Jean and Ron Pekush.

176

Jean and Ron were entranced with the breed and anxious to have one of their own. Sylvia got them in touch with Dorothy Goodale and their first precious puppy "Beau James," "BJ," soon arrived. "Majestic's Morning Mist," "Misty," another Havanese from the Goodale's Havana Doll House followed a year later.

Sylvia Diko was one of the first to own and breed Havanese in Canada. She came across mention of the Havanese while researching breeds to choose a family companion that was non-shedding and good with children. The Havanese sounded exactly right. Additional research led Sylvia to Colorado and Dorothy Goodale. Two endearing Havanese soon joined her family from the Havana Doll House in 1983, a champagne male named "Toby" and an unrelated golden apricot female named "Tsuki." In November 1984, Toby and Tsuki produced their first litter of four puppies and went on to have three more litters. Toby and Tsuki lived out their lives as beloved companions; Toby to the ripe old age of 16-1/2 years and Tsuki to 17-1/2 years.

Similar stories were repeated as arriving Havanese started to dot the country. Among the first to acquire and breed Havanese in Canada were Sylvia Diko, Verna Backus (Belvern), Cathy Enns (Jonaran), Connie Jacobson (Millpond) and Anne Dixon-Zborowski (Sineade).

Here is how Anne got started. Anne has been in purebred dogs for over 30 years, first with Irish Terriers, then with Bichons. Anne met her first Havanese in 1988 when she was still breeding Bichons and was instantly in love. They stole her heart and soon found their way into her home and kennel with a few older dogs as well as young pups arriving from Setacane and Hadassah kennels. With her extensive breeding experience and years of knowledge, Anne is a wonderful mentor and resource for the rest of us involved in Havanese.

CHANGING TIMES - 1994 TO 1999

In the mid 1990s, Havanese were still scarce in Canada. A look back at the early years shows that fanciers imported the first Havanese in Canada from the United States, where the breed was somewhat established and already had a two-decade history. These initial dogs in Canada were registered either with the Havanese Club of America (HCA) and/or with the United Kennel Club (UKC). Neither groups' registries were recognized by the Canadian Kennel Club (CKC), meaning ultimately that early breeders in Canada were not able to offer CKC registration for their dogs. During this period, the Havanese was often referred to as a "Rare Breed," which led to the widely mistaken assumption that the breed could never be registered with the CKC because of this "rareness." Movement towards official recognition for the Havanese in Canada, however, was only temporarily at a standstill. In the USA,

Hadassah's Bubba (Dec 3, 1993-Sep 2003). Bubba was bred by Jean Ford, Hadassah, and owned by Pat Dixon-Zborowski, Sineade.

after years of diligent effort, the Havanese Club of America (HCA) sought official recognition with the American Kennel Club and turned over their breeding records and registrations to the AKC in late 1995. This development meant that HCA registered dogs which had been imported into Canada as foundation dogs were eligible for assignment of AKC registration numbers from 1996. This in turn enabled Canadian breeders and breed fanciers to start the process for registry and legitimization of the Havanese breed in Canada.

Through the hard work and dedication of a few Canadian breeders, the Havanese, known then as *"Bichon Havanais,"* was approved for Canadian Kennel Club Miscellaneous Class listing in 1996. Havanese with newly acquired AKC numbers began the lengthy process for registration in Canada. Special credit goes to Verna Backus, who was instrumental in initiating this recognition. Only dogs registered with the AKC or other approved registry were eligible for Miscellaneous listing. The first Havanese to be given CKC miscellaneous numbers were: "Jomaran's Fidel Of Belvern" owned by Verna Backus. "Hadassah's Bubba" owned by Anne Dixon-Zborowski and Connie Jacobson and "Hadassah's Champ" owned by Cynthia Brown. Unfortunately, not all Havanese in Canada were eligible for entry to the Miscellaneous Class listing, either from lack of ancestry into the HCA registry which disallowed them from getting AKC registrations and/or from missed registration deadlines. These dogs were lost to the registered gene pool.

A year later the Havanese, along with a handful of other Miscellaneous Class breeds were put forward to be voted on for official CKC recognition. There were not enough votes at this first referendum for approval. A second referendum in 1999 granted the Havanese full accreditation for the following year.

Around this time, Wanda Backus-Kelly and other dedicated individuals banded together to form Canada's first Havanese breed club. The "Havanese Fanciers of Canada" (HFC), a non-event club, was formed in November of 1998 as a way of bringing breeders together and begin working towards full recognition for the breed. The goals of the club were to 1) Responsibly promote the Havanese breed, 2) Educate the general public about the Havanese,

3) Provide a breed rescue service, 4) Hold seminars to educate and ensure responsible ownership, 5) Offer a health registry for breeders and 6) Serve as a resource to Canadian Havanese breeders.

Along with the first president, Wanda Backus Kelly, founding members of the Havanese Fanciers of Canada were Sandra Addison, Lynda Altman, Cynthia Brown, Anne Dixon-Zborowski, Stan and Pat Parkhouse, Sylvia Redl, Grace Westerson, Margaret Wettlaufer and Penny Will.

By the time full recognition was achieved, some Havanese in Canada had gone through the registration process five or more times - UKC, HCFA, AKC, MISC and finally CKC.

*Havanese head sketch
by artist Ron Volk.*

The first publication of the HFC was an informational brochure. An excerpt reads: "These little charmers are part of the Bichon family. Rare today, they are being revived by fanciers in the United States, Canada and Europe. The Havanese is an intelligent, robust and affectionate little dog. As natural show-offs, they are often the center of attention. They thrive on human companionship and do not fare well if left alone for long periods of time. Excellent with children, they are very playful, yet gentle. The Havanese can be a good watch dog because of their alert demeanor and their close relationship with their family. They will bark at strange noises but they are not constant barkers. The Havanese is a small dog that is equally at home actively playing or snuggling on a lap.

Am/Can Ch Couture's Oreo Cooky Tapscott. Oreo was bred by Betty Couture and is owned by Penny Will, Havana Canada.

"One owner summed it up very well: 'The Havanese is extremely affectionate, very devoted and always entertaining.' This very special little dog can bring years of love and loyalty when treated with love and kindness in return. The beauty of the breed is enhanced by a profuse coat from wavy to curly which comes in a great variety of colours. This rainbow of colours is one aspect that distinguishes the Havanese from others in the Bichon family and adds to the beauty and charm of the breed. All colours are equal and no preference is given to one colour over the other. Havanese are non-shedding and odourless. Their coat requires moderate/high maintenance including minimum twice weekly brushing along with periodic bathing. Even though the Havanese is small and is considered a Toy breed, they are not meant to be a tiny, fragile dog. They may be small in stature but they are muscular, and very lively, with great stamina."

CKC RECOGNITION - YEAR 2000

For us to have been part of a new millennium was truly exciting, but there was more to come. Not only did we celebrate a new year, a new century and a new millennium, we also celebrated our new status with the Canadian Kennel Club. January 1st, 2000, as the new millennium dawned, the Havanese breed was fully recognized by the CKC and accepted as the newest member of the Toy Group.

CHAMPIONS - FIRST CKC CHAMPIONS

2000 was a hallmark year for the Havanese. Throughout the year, Havanese across Canada made their mark in the show ring, obedience ring and agility arena.

U.S. bred and owned "Starkette Pride of Wincroft" became the first Havanese to earn a Canadian Championship, at 16 months of age. It was awarded at the Prince Albert Kennel

Am/Can Ch Starkette Pride of Wincroft, Buster. Owned by Barb and Michele Johannes. Wincroft.

Club show March 3, 2000 with a Group 1st placement under Judge Virginia Lyne, handled by Dave Scheiris. "Buster" is bred by Jan Stark (Starkette) and owned by Barb and Michele Johannes (Wincroft).

"Sineade's Peppe at Hugabrew" became the very first Canadian-bred Havanese to earn his CKC championship. Three year old "Peppe" earned this honour on March 24th, 2000 at the Oceanside Kennel Club show in Aldergrove, B.C. under Judge Leslie Rogers. Bred by Anne Dixon-Zborowski (Sineade) and proudly

Ch Sineade's Peppe at Hugabrew.

owned by Stan and Pat Parkhouse (Hugabrew). Peppe's achievements were all exclusively owner-handled by Stan; the two of them make quite a team. Peppe also has his National and International titles. Peppe is a gorgeous white and champagne Havanese who loves giving kisses, being groomed and going for rides in the truck with Dad. He is the king of the castle at his house, even lording over the Newfies he shares his home with. Peppe is a typical happy, outgoing, itnelligent and mischievous Havanese who charms all who meet him.

"Pocopayosos Q-bin Star Candi" became Canada's first female Havanese CKC champion in June 2000 at the Sault St. Marie dog show. At the tender young age of only seven months, "Candi" made quite a splash in the ring. She finished in style with four group placings. Canadian-bred by and owned by Paula Martel-Lavallie (Pocopayasos), Candi has been breeder/owner handled to the majority of her successes in the show ring. Candi is a sweet-tempermented, loyal and affectionate little dog. Nine pounds loving, beautifully wrapped up in a striking black and white Irish Pied coat, Candi is also training in other disciplines and hopes in the future to strut her stuff in obedience and agility as well.

In the year 2000, the first official year with the CKC, club members were very

Ch Pocopayasos Q-bin Star Candi. Candi is owned and bred by Paula Martel-Lavallie, Pocopayasos.

busy in and out of the ring, with a number of new show champions owned and bred by HFC club members. The majority of these accomplishments were owner-handled.

Ch Sineade's Peppe at Hugabrew, bred by Anne Dixon-Zborowski, owned by Stan and Pat Parkhouse. Peppe finished his championship on March 24, 2000 at three years of age.

Ch Sineade's IB. Trouble O'Havana, bred by Anne Dixon-Zborowski, owned by Penny Will. Slick finished his championship on May 28, 2000 with a multitude of Best of Breed wins as well as the first Group placement for a Canadian-bred Havanese.

Ch Qbin Star Candi, bred and owned by Paula Martel-Lavallie. Candi finished her championship on June 24, 2000 at seven months of age.

Ch Poco Tesoro's Pancho Villa, bred by and owned by Sylvia Redl. Pancho finished his championship on July 2, 2000.

Ch Poco Tezaro, bred by Cathy Enns, owned by Sylvia Redl. Taz finished his championship July 4, 2000.

Ch CrossOver Millpond's Carlos, bred by Lynda Altman, owned by Margaret Wettlaufer and Connie Jacobson. Carlos finished his championship on August 10, 2000 at three years of age.

Ch Estoy Morena at Cross Over, bred by Connie Jacobsen and Anne Zborowski, owned by Margaret Wettlaufer. Rena finished her championship on August 26, 2000.

Ch Setacane's Zoey O'Havana, bred by Eugene Malcolm and Anne Dixon-Zborowski, owned by Penny Will. Zoey finished her championship September 17, 2000 at 11 months.

Ch Hugabrew's Pequena Zarzamora, bred by and owned by Stan and Pat Parkhouse. Chloe finished her championship on September 23, 2000 at 16 months of age.

Am/Can Ch Havana's Touched By An Angel ROM.

Since that great start in the year 2000, there are several other little champions in the making as well as a number of Havanese competing in obedience, agility and other pursuits.

Another Special "first" was achieved in 2001 by Ch Havana's Touched By An Angel, bred by and owned by Penny Will (Havana Canada). Angel, a delightful black Irish Pied, received her Canadian championship May 21, 2001 under Judge

Charles Hunt at the young age of seven months. Angel then moved to the United States to join Tapscott Havanese. Her American championship soon followed on September 9, 2001, just shy of her first birthday, making Angel the first Havanese female as well as the first Canadian-bred Havanese to become dual championed CKC/AKC.

And yet another very exciting first was accomplished by Am/Can Ch Sunberry's 911 in Manhattan and Am/Can Ch Sunberry's Pandora's Box, both bred by and owned by Grace Westerson (Sunberry). Manny and Dora were the first Canadian Havanese to attend the prestigious Westminster show in New York. Manny did us proud by winning the Best of Opposite Sex award at the Westminster Show 2003 under Judge Dr. Edward N.K. Patterson.

Am/Can Ch Sunberry's 911 in Manhattan.

CLUB ACCREDITATION

The Havanese, although still uncommon, were popping up in conformation and performance rings all around the country since their full recognition into the CKC Toy Group in 2000.

Starting a breed club sounds so simple, however doing it takes quite a bit of effort. In the late 1990s, a dedicated group of people got things started for the Havanese in Canada, but the newly formed *Havanese Fanciers of Canada* was only the beginning. In order to become a CKC recognized national Breed Club, many stringent requirements had to be met. You might think there is little difference between being an unofficial non-event club and an accredited one but there are a number of significant changes. The status of being a National Breed Club would mean that the Havanese Fanciers of Canada club is recognized by the CKC as the official guardian of the breed. Only a recognized club can host sanctioned events such as matches, boosters and breed specialties, something which the club was looking forward to with great anticipation. It also would mean that the Club would finally be able to address the Havanese breed standard.

When the Havanese was recognized by the CKC, an existing FCI standard was put into place as the breed standard. The current standard has a lot of room for improvement and is quite vague on many points. However, the CKC has many safeguards in place so that breed standards are not changed on a whim. One of those is that national breed clubs can-

not present any standard changes for a period of five years after being granted official club status. Members eagerly looked forward to the accredited Club status and the many new opportunities it would afford to serve the Havanese community to promote and protect their special breed.

In April 2003, the Havanese Fanciers of Canada proudly received CKC accreditation as the sole Official National Breed Club for the Havanese in Canada.

Wanda Backus Kelly, founding president of the Havanese Fanciers of Canada tells us, "...Lines of fully registered CKC Havanese will now meet one another in the conformation ring where further refinement toward the ultimate representation of the breed standard can begin. Such attention to the correct interpretation of the standard will also help to define the strengths of this amazing little creature, including other pursuits such as Agility, Flyball, Obedience and Therapy work. Besides helping to fully recognize the breed, Club membership benefits breeder members most by serving as a resource and information base to consult with other breeders nationwide.

"Given the fact that the Havanese are a small companion breed ideally suited as pets and therefore facing enormous potential for exploitation, the main focus of the Havanese Fanciers is to educate the buying public about the breed in general and to help breeder members responsibly promote them. A quarterly newsletter links subscribing members from coast to coast offering opportunities for pet owners to brag about their Havanese and gain insight into the world of this special little breed. The club is also working to establish a health data base, a rescue network and to provide a breeder referral service for would-be pet buyers."

For more information, visit our website at www.havanesefanciers.com.

HFC BREEDERS - WHO ARE THEY?

What's in a name? A name identifies us. It's who we are. Parents-to-be spend countless hours searching for the perfect name to bestow upon their baby. When we get to kennel names a whole new game begins! A kennel name needs even greater creativity. While there may be five Suzies at the playground and a dozen dogs named Max in the neighbourhood, kennel names are unique in that no two can be the same. The search is on to find a name that is a unique reflection of ourselves. It is fascinating to see the myriad of ways to go about this. Here is a sampling from our Canadian Havanese Fanciers community.

Initials, anagrams and derivatives are all possibilities. Like the short and snappy "LA" chosen from the breeder's initials. Or "SYRYN," a name invented by using the last letter of each of the family's first names. "BELVERN" is a second generation kennel name started

Mimosa's Champagne Trio. Ten week old Jasmine, Jewel and Piper, bred by Suzanne McKay, Mimosa.

by Verna Bell, a derivative of her first name and her maiden name.

Name combinations and creative spellings are other choices like "JABIRE-US," a melodious blend of "Jabirs and Us" which honors the Danish kennel Jabirs from whence came their foundation dogs. Another blended name "HUGABREW" came from breeding Newfoundland dogs many years ago. A first Newfie named "Summer's Brew" was bred to "Hug" and the combination created the name. Other options are names tied to a location. One such is "SUNBERRY," a tranquil acreage on a ridge running between a town called Sundre and a little hamlet called Bearberry in an area called Sunberry Ridge. "ROCKHURST," gaelic for "spine of the rock" is another such location name, a street on a hill carved into the rock, built as it were, on the hill's spine.

Touches of nostalgia, fantasy or whimsy are other good starting spots for names. Still others choose memorable places, people or events for their names. "CROSS-OVER" is another second-generation kennel name. The name came from having to cross over the road or the river to hunt with their Beagles. After retiring from breeding, the kennel name crossed over to a

Four month old Carlos, bred by Anne Dixon-Zborowski, Sineade, owned by Nova Hutt.

daughter and hopefully one day it will cross over again to a grand-daughter.

A name may also be tribute to a beloved person or pet, such as "SINEADE" in loving memory of a special dog. Descriptive names are often used as are names taken from other languages.

Many Havanese breeders have found inspiration in the Spanish language. Because Havanese amuse and delight with their silly clownish antics, this led to the kennel name "POCOPAYASOS" (Little Clowns). "SONRISAS" means smiles in Spanish and of course this also describes our smiley, happy Havanese and how they affect the people around them. "LOS COMPANEROS" (the Companions), again an apt reflection of the Havanese whose prime form and function is as a companion, a role it fills admirably. Or "HAVANA," not only the capital of Cuba, where the Havanese breed developed, but also a tribute to foundation bitch "Savannah" as well as the name of a popular Latin night club. And finally, my own "MIMOSA," a Spanish adjective meaning pampered, cosseted, frolicsome, endearing, beguiling - in short, one word that encompasses all that a Havanese is.

HAVANESE IN ACTION

The Havanese is much more than a pretty face and a cuddly lap warmer. Once people have a Havanese and realize how intelligent they are, they start to think of activities that they might like to pursue with their dog. Havanese are highly responsive, intelligent, eager to learn and are highly motivated to please you which makes them perfect to be trained in many capacities. Owners are beginning to realize just how versatile these little dogs truly are. Many Havanese are multi-disciplined. Of course, showing is the first thing that comes to mind; but, not only are Havanese making a splash in the Canadian show ring, they are also making their presence known in obedience, agility and other performance events.

OBEDIENCE

All dogs should have acceptable social manners; puppies will benefit from basic obedience training so they can mature into the confident, reliable, well-behaved companions we all dream of. If you really enjoy training and find your Havanese to be especially responsive, then you may wish to pursue Obedience at a competitive level. Obedience is not for everyone nor is it for every Havanese. This does not mean that Havanese are incapable of doing it: they can!

"I am delighted, doubly so, to be able to present to you one such special Havanese OTCh Jomaran's Little Miss Muffet. This clever little beauty is not only the first Havanese listed in the CKC Obedience standings but she also happens to be my own wonderful girl. Mitzi's obedience career started in 1997 with her Companion Dog (CD) title earned from the Miscellaneous class.

"In the summer of 2003, Mitzi reached a milestone for the Havanese, becoming the very first Havanese Obedience Trial Champion (OTCh). Mitzi can be very creative in her responses; that clownish Havanese

OTCH Jomaran's Little Miss Muffet CD CDX UD CDC CGN AGN NGC NAC NJC PSI SJATD. Bred by Cathy Enns, Jomaran, and owned by Suzanne McKay, Mimosa.

personality surfaces at the most inopportune times, but she always has fun. Mitzi is currently the most titled Havanese in Canada, multi-disciplined in conformation, obedience, agility and pet therapy. At nine years of age, she has 12 assorted titles to her name and six more in the works." Suzanne McKay, Winnipeg, Manitoba.

While Mitzi was the first to lead the way, she is followed by some outstanding youngsters and we know there will be many more obedience titles in Canada in years to come. Coming up fast with flash is Ch Sunberry's 911 Was Chaos CD CDX AGN AGI NAC. Chaos, bred by Grace Westerson, owned by Chris Gibson, was the number 1 Obedience Havanese in Canada for 2003. Rain or shine, you can also find Chaos flying high in the Agility ring.

Ch Sunberry's 911 Was Chaos CDX AGN AGI NAC.

AGILITY

A lively exercise featuring focus, speed and accuracy. Agility is basically a timed

obstacle course for dogs including A-frames, board walks, jumps, teeter-totters, open and collapsed tunnels, weave poles, pause table, etc. Havanese are perfectly suited to this activity as they are very nimble and quick. Agility can be a just-for-fun activity for you and your dog or an exciting competitive sport. Agility is an up-and-coming dog sport in Canada. There are a number of different agility organizations. Agility became a titled performance event with the CKC in the year 2001.

Many of these are "firsts" for the breed but they certainly won't be the last. There is more to come. And that brings us to 2004. In October 2004, history was made again. Havanese fanciers across the country rejoiced at the exciting announcement of Canada's first Best in Show Havanese, Canadian bred and owned by one of our very own HFC members, Rita Thomas (Sonrisas). Her extra special boy BIS Ch Sonrisas Tiny Thomas, handled by Drobel Rojas, earned the award on October 31, 2004 at the Club Canin Chomday dog show in Montreal under Judge Max Madger. He was the first Havanese in Canada and only the

Canada's First Havanese Best In Show

third in North America so far to achieve this high honor. As of the end of 2004, Tiny tops the charts as the all-time top winner for any Havanese in Canada.

THE YOUNGER GENERATION

Havanese puppies are clowns of the first degree, pure 100 percent fun. Their silly antics in the show ring always draw an appreciative audience. Not to be outdone by the more experienced dogs, there are many youngsters who have started their show careers in style, earning Toy Group placements and Puppy Groups. A few of these have gone on to higher honors and can proudly claim CKC "Best Puppy in Show" awards.

The first few to win Best Puppy awards were BPIS Am/Can Ch Sunberry's Pandora's Box (Dora), bred by and owned by Grace Westerson (Sunberry); BPIS Ch Havana's June Storm Rockhurst (Libby), bred by Penny Will (Havana Canada), owned by Elizabeth Obrecht (Rockhurst); BPIS Am/Can Ch Pocopayasos I'm Too Sexy (Mogawy), bred by and owned by Paula Martel-Lavallie (Pocopaya-

BPIS Ch Los Companero's Fred The Man, proudly handled by 10 year old Jr. Handler Sara Szauerzopf.

sos); BPIS Am/Can Ch Sineade's Marcella At Tuscany, bred by Anne Dixon Zborowski (Sineade) and owned by Brenda Kainberger (Tuscany); BPIS Am/Can Ch Mia V.T.Leurse Hoefpad (Mia), Dutch import bred by M. Hoefnagels, owned by David and Cheryl Drake (Ashstone); BPIS Ch Misty Trails Katreeya by Emmy, bred by and owned by Bev Dorma (Misty Trails); BPIS Ch Los Companero's Fred The Man, proudly handled by 10 year old Jr. Handler Sara Szauerzopf, winning top puppy grades under Judge Martin Doherty at the Burlington Kennel Club show. Fred is bred by Heather Warnock (Los Companeros), owned by Joanna Swayze (Everspring).

One year old Mia and eight year old Rags shown here with their young handlers in the Junior Novice class.

JUNIOR HANDLING

A number of Havanese in Canada are finding their way into the ring with Junior Handlers as they are an excellent size and disposition for even the youngest peewee handlers. For the most part, the dogs love children and are just happy to have a new game to play with their best friends. Mimosa's Midnite in Havana, bred by Suzanne McKay, owned by Susan Bel and Jomaran's Ragamuffin CGC CGN AGN SJATD, bred by Cathy Evens and owned by Suzanne McKay are shown here.

WHAT'S NOT TO LOVE?

Adorable, cuddly, fuzzy teddy-bear looks and an incredibly luxurious super-soft coat, combined with a gentle, sweet disposition and a bright, lively personality endear the Havanese to everyone it meets. It all adds up to a fasicanting little dog that's hard to resist.

A number of Canadian Havanese are active members of therapy dog programs to provide cheerful visits to the sick, elderly and disabled. A good therapy dog needs to be calm, gentle and friendly. Many of these important traits come naturally to the Havanese.

Dogs don't care about things like age, appearance or infirmity, but accept people as they are. Havanese are especially well-suited to visits in seniors facilities and nursing homes. Their small size is ideal for curling up on a lap or cuddling on a bed. The super soft fur is irresistible and just begs to be stroked. Shown here is Bailey, a typically outgoing Havanese who freely shares kisses and cuddles, started volunteering as a pet visitor in nursing homes in 2003 when he was one year old with the volunteer organization "BC Pets and Friends."

Hugabrew's Bailey, bred by Pat and Stan Parkhouse, Hugabrew, and owned by Ethel Adachi.

190

FUTURE IN CANADA - 2005

As another page turns on the calendar, Havanese in Canada are on to more special events. Summer 2005 will see the first Canadian National Havanese Breed Speciality in Winnipeg, Manitoba. It is hoped this special event will draw Havanese from Atlantic to Pacific and everywhere in between.

We look forward to the future of the Havanese in Canada and anticipate great things to come. And yet, special though all these events, activities and accomplishments are, we hope to never lose sight that it is the little dog at our feet, the one we live with every day, who sleeps by the pillow at night - they are the ones who are our pride and joy.

The fulfillment of Havanese ownership is not the awards in the ring; it's the everyday moments that make up our everyday life.

Ch Havana's Mimosa Midnite Medley CGN. Cricket was bred by Penny Will, Havana Canada, and is owned by Suzanne McKay, Mimosa.

Appendix

Resources

Books on the Breed

Bichon Havanese by Zoila Portuondo Guerra (translated by Jane McManus). Distributed by Pet Love, Vincent Lane, Dorking, Surrey RH4 3YX England. Excellent book.

Havanese, A Complete and Reliable Handbook by Dorothy Goodale. T.F.H. Publications, Inc., 1 TFH Plaza, Neptune City, NJ 07753; also on the internet at tfh.com. *Havanese* can also be obtained at the internet book stores such as Barnes and Noble and Amazon.com. This is a must-have book for the Havanese enthusiast.

American Havanese Champions is a yearbook published by Natalie Armitage, 10999 East Bushnell Road, Floral City, FL 34436. Phone 352-341-5188; e-mail NRarmitage@aol.com. This spiral bound book contains photos and pedigrees of the champions of the year. It's a must-have yearbook for Havanese fanciers.

The Havanese, An Illustrated Study of the AKC Breed Standard, Illustrations by Diane Klumb. Published by The Havanese Club of America, 2002.

Kennel Clubs and Registries

American Kennel Club (AKC), 5580 Centerview Drive, Raleigh, NC 27606. Phone: 919-233-9767, e-mail: info@akc.org, web site: www.akc.org. The AKC is the United States principal registry for purebred dogs, including the Havanese breed. All pedigrees are compiled from its official Stud Book records. Single copies of booklets on all Performance Events are free; you may write for them. Many can also be downloaded from the AKC web site

www.akc.org

Inside the AKC site you will want to go to

www.akc.org/classified.

This is a new AKC service designed to bring breeders and potential pet buyers together. Also, the AKC Library, which contains the largest dog library in the U.S. is at

www.akc.org/insideAKC/depts/library.cfm

Canadian Kennel Club (CKC), Commerce Park, 89 Skyway Avenue, Suite 100, Etobicoke, Ontario M9W 6R4, Canada. Phone 416-675-6506, fax 416-675-6506,

wwwckc.ca.

Havanese Fanciers of Canada (HFC). Do visit this club's web site for information and the activities of Havanese in Canada.

www.havanesefanciers.com

Havanese Club of America (HCA), AKC Parent Club for the Havanese Breed. Web site: www.havanese.org. Addresses and telephone numbers of HCA officers and Board Members change yearly, therefore addressing officers or committee members is best done via its internet website. HCA's current president, through 2005, is Cherie Belcher.

Current HCA committees total 17. Information about these committees is also available at the HCA website - www.havanese.org.

Havanese Rescue is a must-see committee on this site.

The Havanese website contains a wealth of education information for new owners at www.havanese.org/newOwnerEd.utm

Clicking the above leads you to a Havanese wearing glasses, looking at a book entitled, "My First Book of Pets." Also of particular interest on the HCA website will be the health concerns.

If you own a Havanese, your HCA member breeder will be able to assist you in locating addresses of officers, current board members and/or committee chairs.

The local Havanese clubs recognized by the HCA are listed below. These e-mail address are subject to change on a yearly basis. They are correct as of January 1, 2005.

Blue Ridge Havanese Club. Contact Mary Lou Novak

mlak@att.net.

www.brhavclub.org.

Capitol Havanese Club of Northern California. Contact Kathy Patrick

Aweseomehavanese@aol.com.

http.www.capitalhavaneseclub.com/

Cascade Havanese Club WA OR & BC. Contact Leslie Hunt

hunt@express56.com

Delaware Valley Havanese Club. Contact Alison Brackman

sparkyboy1@earthlink.net.

Gateway Havanese Club. Contact Michele Johannes

Myhavs@sbcglobal.net.

www.gatewayhavanese.com.

Grand Canyon Havanese Club AZ, NM, CO, NV, UT. Contact Charlene Cain

jcain1cableaz.com.

http://gchc.homestead.com/home.html.

Havanese Club of Southern CA. Contact Linda Strike

lestrike@adelphia.net.

www.socalhavs.org.

Lake Erie Havanese Club. Contact Sue Bing

jsbing@accesstoledo.com.

Lone Star Havanese Club TX & surrounding states. Contact Eileen Santman

esantman@earthlink.net.

www.she.org

North Star Havanese Club MBN, Twin Cities area. Contact Susan Zenk

zenksrus@yahoo.com

Tropical Havanese Club FL. Contact Judith Jones

namaskar@mindspring.com

Windy City Havanese Club IL & surrounding states. Contact Laura Pfab

pfabulus@dwx.com.

www.windycityhavs.org

The HCA publishes a breed magazine four times a year. It is called *Havanese Hotline.* Its editor is Margie Staniszeski. Subscriptions are available. Contact the editor for further information. Margie Staniszeski's e-mail address is

erashavanese@comcast.net

As you have read in this book, OFA, CERF and BAER health certifications are important. The addresses of two organizations, the Orthopedic Foundation for Animals (OFA) and Canine Eye Registry Foundation (CERF) should be in your Havanese Health book. They are listed as follows:

Orthopedic Foundation for Animals

2300 E Nifong Blvd., Columbia, MO 65201

phone: 573-442-0418; web-site: www.offa.org

Canine Eye Registration Foundation

SCC-A Purdue University, West Lafayette, IN 47907

phone: 317-494-8179; web-site: www.prodogs.com/chn/cerf

Your general care veterinarian is your contact for OFA x-rays and will give you the name of the nearest opthamologist who examines eyes for the CERF certificate.

OFA and CERF employees, at the above telephone numbers, can also help answer questions. The OFA web site also offers results of screening tests for genetic and orthopedic diseases. You can research the testing history of either sire or dam of a dog you have or want to have on the link to the Canine Health Information Center (CHIC). CHIC is a database sponsored by both the AKC Canine Health Foundation and OFA. To quality for a CHIC certificate, a breeder must submit the animal for the required health screenings of the breed's parent club. For the HCA the screenings are for hips, elbows, eyes and ears.

Miscellaneous: Books, Training, Supplies

There are excellent dog books pertaining to behavior, care, diet, genetics, grooming, health, showing, structure, training, travel - books that cover all facets of the dog world. There are also excellent dog magazines. Browse through some of them at your public library, your local book store and your magazine specialty stores. Your public library will have a research resource available for you which will list many books not available at that particular library but are available to order from another library for loan.

Go onto the internet in search of information on any canine subject. You will find hundreds of sites with valuable information.

Dog supply catalogs are available on the internet also. Pick and choose.

Modern technology has made available wonderful informational and educational material. You'll find the subject you are interested in right on the internet. The Havanese you want or have will be glad you did. So will all responsible dog lovers. We know that although genetics plays a critical role in the Havanese you choose to become a member of your family, learning about his species and his individuality will make your adventures together all the more wonderful.

Again - the Havanese breed is truly a reflection of all of God's goodness - love, joy, exuberance, and zest of life in this wonderful world of ours. His sweetness and love of life will lift the soul of even the saddest person. So take the Havanese to your heart.

Enjoy responsibly!!

Books by Kathryn Braund

The Uncommon Dog Breeds, 1972 (Arco)

Dog Obedience Training Manual, The First Ten Weeks, 1982 (Denlingers)

Dog Obedience Training Manual, The Second Ten Weeks, 1984 (Denlingers)

The Complete Portuguese Water Dog, 1986 (Howell Book House)

The New Complete Portuguese Water Dog, 1997 (Howell Book House)

Rosa and the Prince, A Historical Novel, 2000 (X-Libris)

Devoted to Dogs, 2002, 2004 (Roughrider - Kathryn Braund Publications)

The Joyous Havanese, 2005 (Roughrider - Kathryn Braund Publications)

Kathryn Braund books are available on the Internet at BarnesandNoble.com; Amazon.com; Borders.com or at your favorite book store.

You may also call the publisher, Kathryn Braund at 406-454-0537 or for extra copies call 1-800-431-1579.

The first chapters of several of Kathryn's books can be read on her websites:
www.kathrynbraund.com
www. joyoushavanese.com